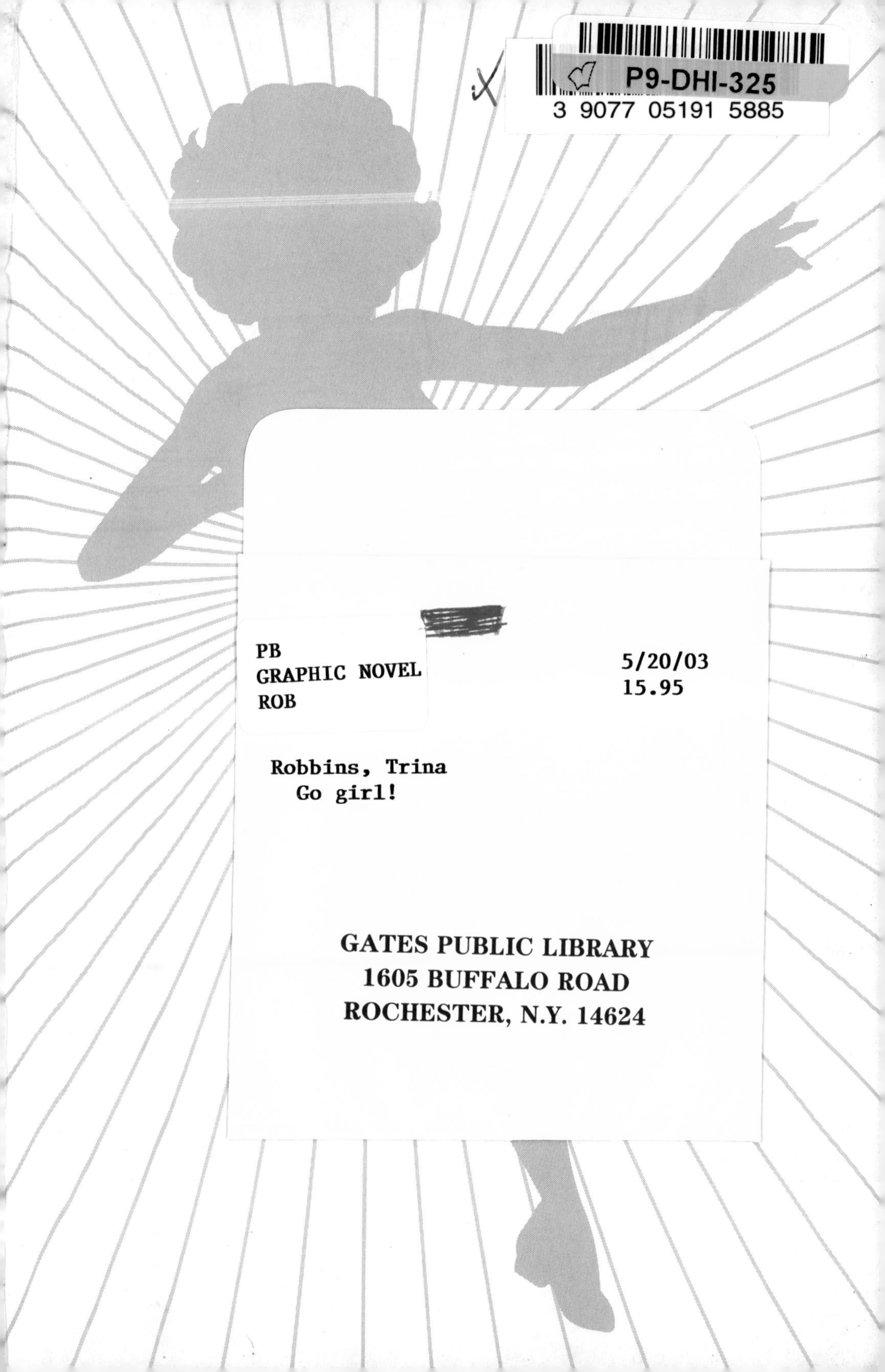

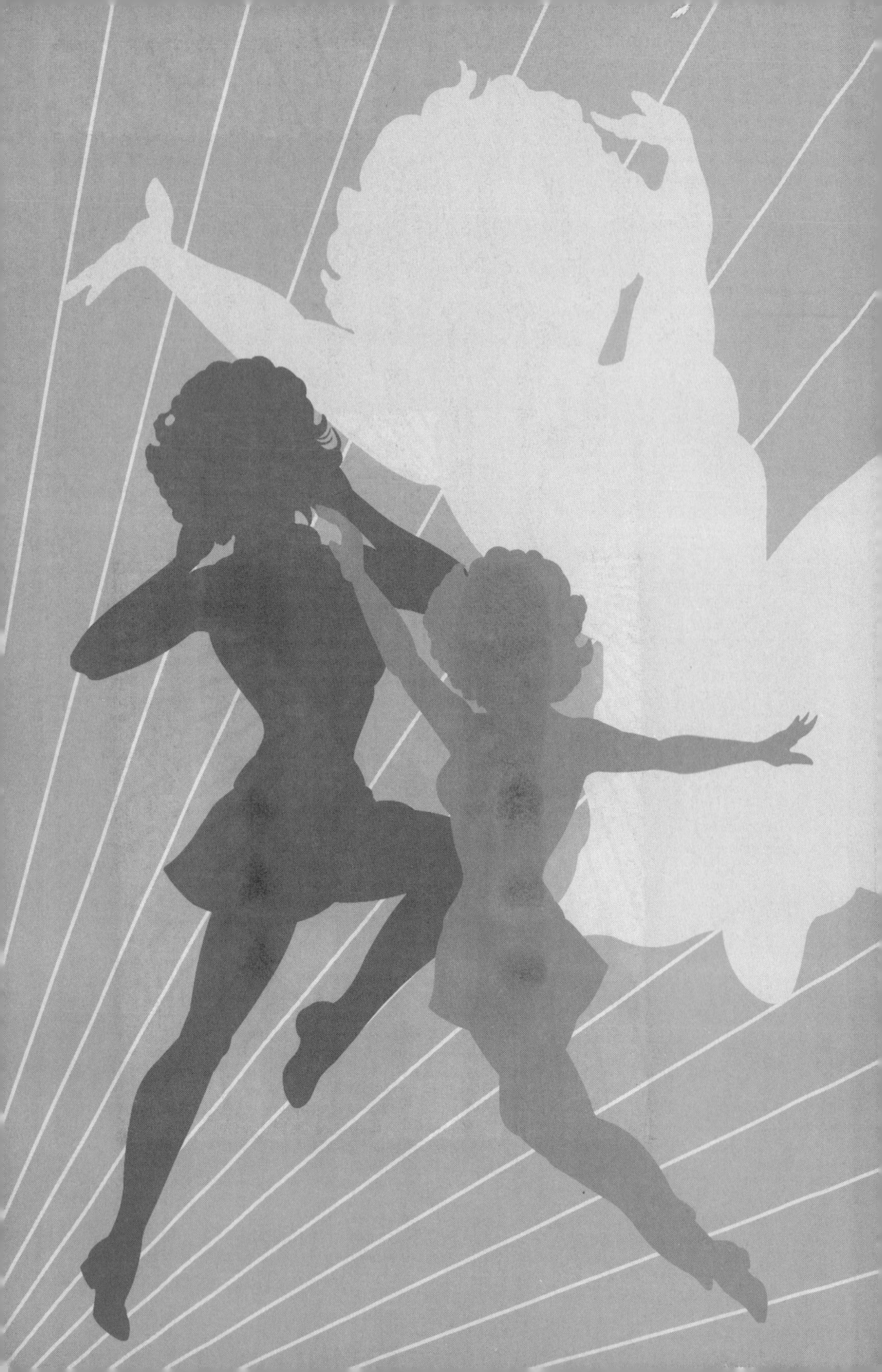

GO GIRL!™

story **TRINA ROBBINS**

art **ANNE TIMMONS**

lettering **TOM ORZECHOWSKI** & **SEAN GLUMACE**

cover colors **CHRISTOPHER BUTCHER**

DARK HORSE COMICS, INC®

publisher **MIKE RICHARDSON**

collection editor **CHRIS WARNER**

collection designer **LIA RIBACCHI**

art director **MARK COX**

GOGIRL!™

This volume collects issues one through five of the Image comic-book series *GoGirl!*, the story "GoGirl!" from *Friends of Lulu Presents Storytime*, and the previously unpublished *GoGirl!* story, "Blast From the Past."

Published by
Dark Horse Comics, Inc.
10956 SE Main Street
Milwaukie, OR 97222

www.darkhorse.com

To find a comics shop in your area, call the Comic Shop Locator Service toll-free at 1-888-266-4226

First edition: October 2002
ISBN: 1-56971-798-2

10 9 8 7 6 5 4 3 2 1

PRINTED IN CANADA

WHAT'S GO GIRL!™

For me — writer Trina Robbins — and Anne Timmons (artist), *GoGirl!* (yes, she spells it with an exclamation point) is a dream come true and our chance to prove that girls — and the boys who like them — will read comics, when there are comics for them to read. In fact, *GoGirl!* is a dream that almost didn't come true.

When we first decided to produce a series of comics about the flying teenager, we had hoped to produce them in luscious full color, but the advance orders were too low to afford color, and for a heartbreaking moment it looked like *GoGirl!* would be grounded before her maiden flight.

Ta da! The internet came to our rescue! We had sent out advance copies to comics websites and reviewers all through cyberspace, and they loved what they saw. Furthermore, their howls of indignation when they thought *GoGirl!* was kaput resounded all the way to the editorial offices of our publisher, Image comics, where publisher Jim Valentino took a second look and said, "Hmmm... we can publish this in black and white..."

The rest is herstory. Anne and I have been in hog heaven doing what we love best, working on the adventures of our favorite flying teen. We want to thank all the great reviewers (and all their great reviews), and the wonderful readers whose letters have spurred us on. (In case you've ever wondered, yes, we read, pay attention to, and are encouraged by all letters.) We especially want to thank Larry Marder and Jim Valentino of Image Comics, for believing in us, and Chris Warner of Dark Horse Comics, for knowing that, even if people think girls don't read comics, they DO read books. Chris knows, as we do, that when you, the reader, find this collection in your libraries and bookstores, you'll enjoy reading it as much as we've enjoyed creating it.

— Trina Robbins

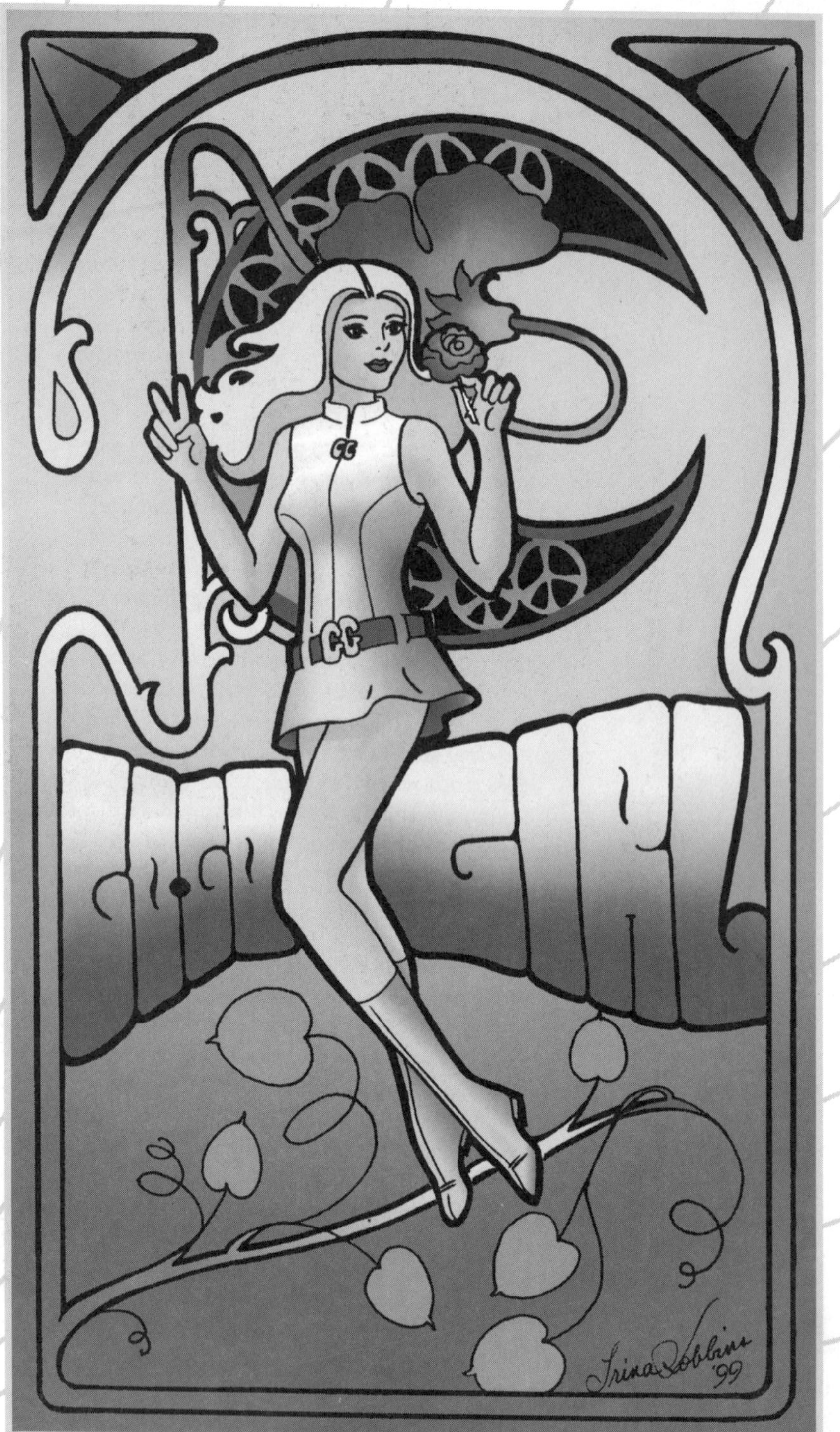
GIRL
Trina Robbins
'99

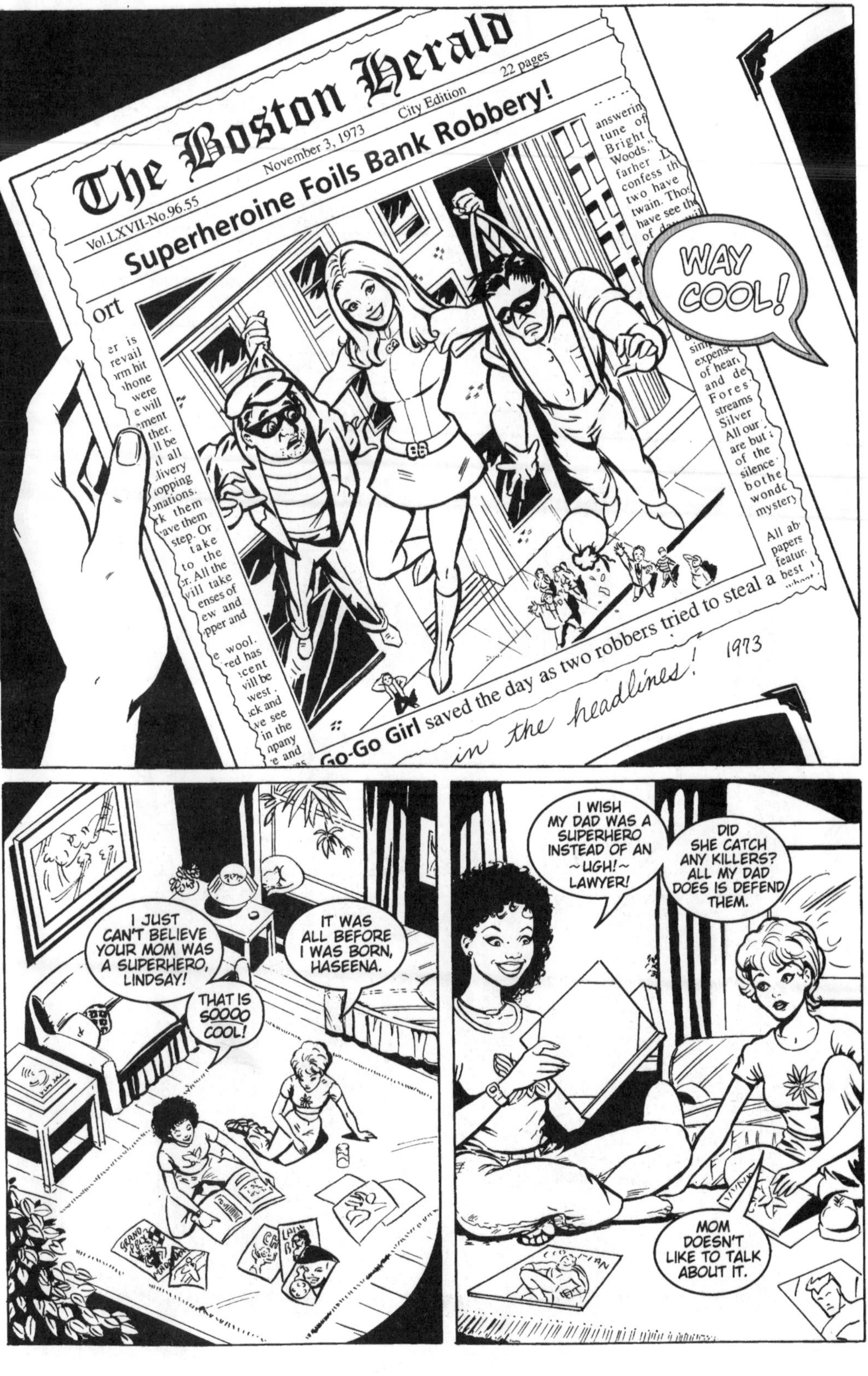
The Boston Herald
Vol.LXVII-No.96.55
November 3, 1973
City Edition
22 pages
Superheroine Foils Bank Robbery!
Go-Go Girl saved the day as two robbers tried to steal a
in the headlines! 1973
WAY COOL!
I JUST CAN'T BELIEVE YOUR MOM WAS A SUPERHERO, LINDSAY!
THAT IS SOOOO COOL!
IT WAS ALL BEFORE I WAS BORN, HASEENA.
I WISH MY DAD WAS A SUPERHERO INSTEAD OF AN ~UGH!~ LAWYER!
DID SHE CATCH ANY KILLERS? ALL MY DAD DOES IS DEFEND THEM.
MOM DOESN'T LIKE TO TALK ABOUT IT.

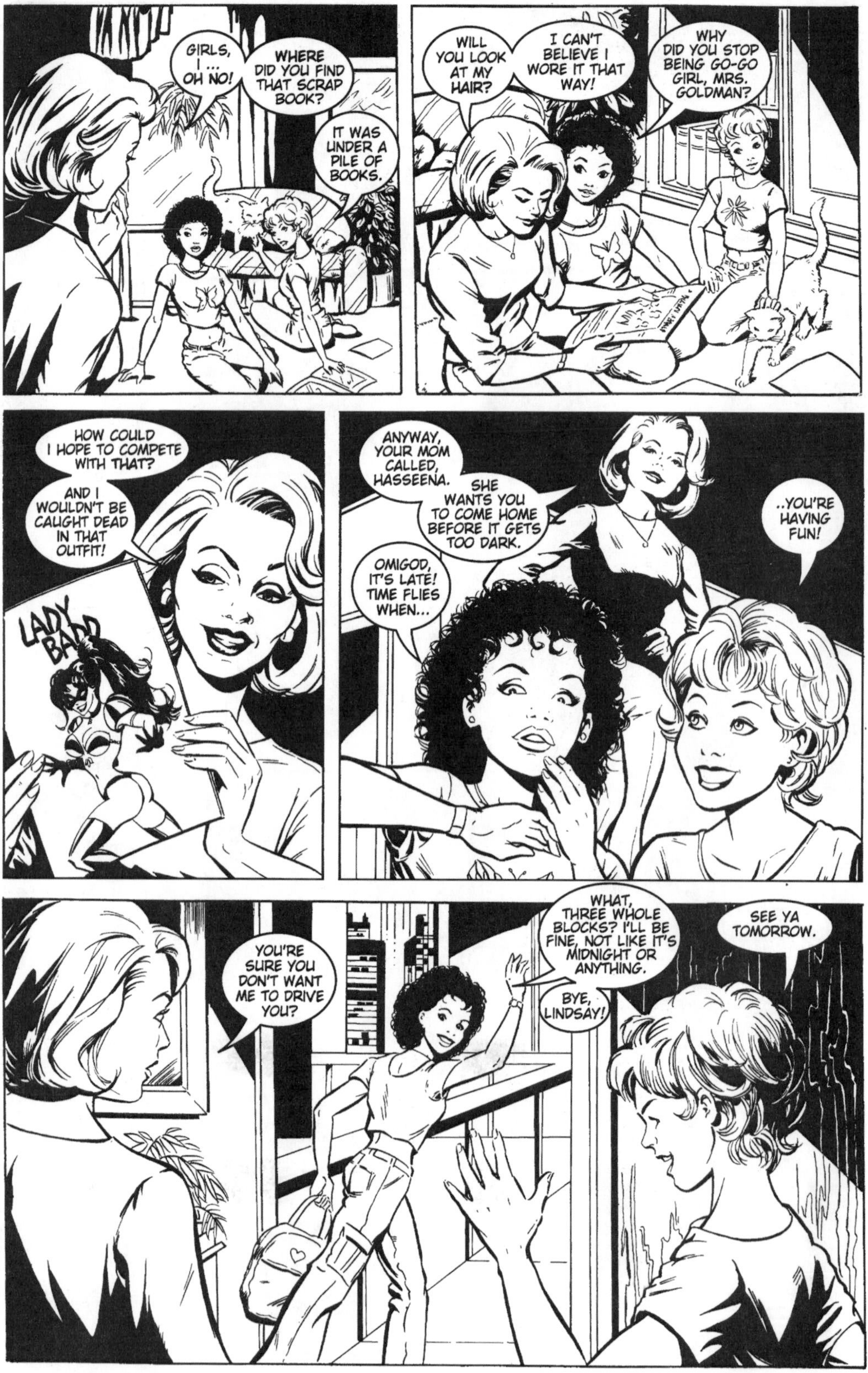
GIRLS, I ... OH NO!
WHERE DID YOU FIND THAT SCRAP BOOK?
IT WAS UNDER A PILE OF BOOKS.
WILL YOU LOOK AT MY HAIR?
I CAN'T BELIEVE I WORE IT THAT WAY!
WHY DID YOU STOP BEING GO-GO GIRL, MRS. GOLDMAN?
HOW COULD I HOPE TO COMPETE WITH THAT?
AND I WOULDN'T BE CAUGHT DEAD IN THAT OUTFIT!
LADY BADD
ANYWAY, YOUR MOM CALLED, HASSEENA.
SHE WANTS YOU TO COME HOME BEFORE IT GETS TOO DARK.
OMIGOD, IT'S LATE! TIME FLIES WHEN...
..YOU'RE HAVING FUN!
YOU'RE SURE YOU DON'T WANT ME TO DRIVE YOU?
WHAT, THREE WHOLE BLOCKS? I'LL BE FINE, NOT LIKE IT'S MIDNIGHT OR ANYTHING.
BYE, LINDSAY!
SEE YA TOMORROW.

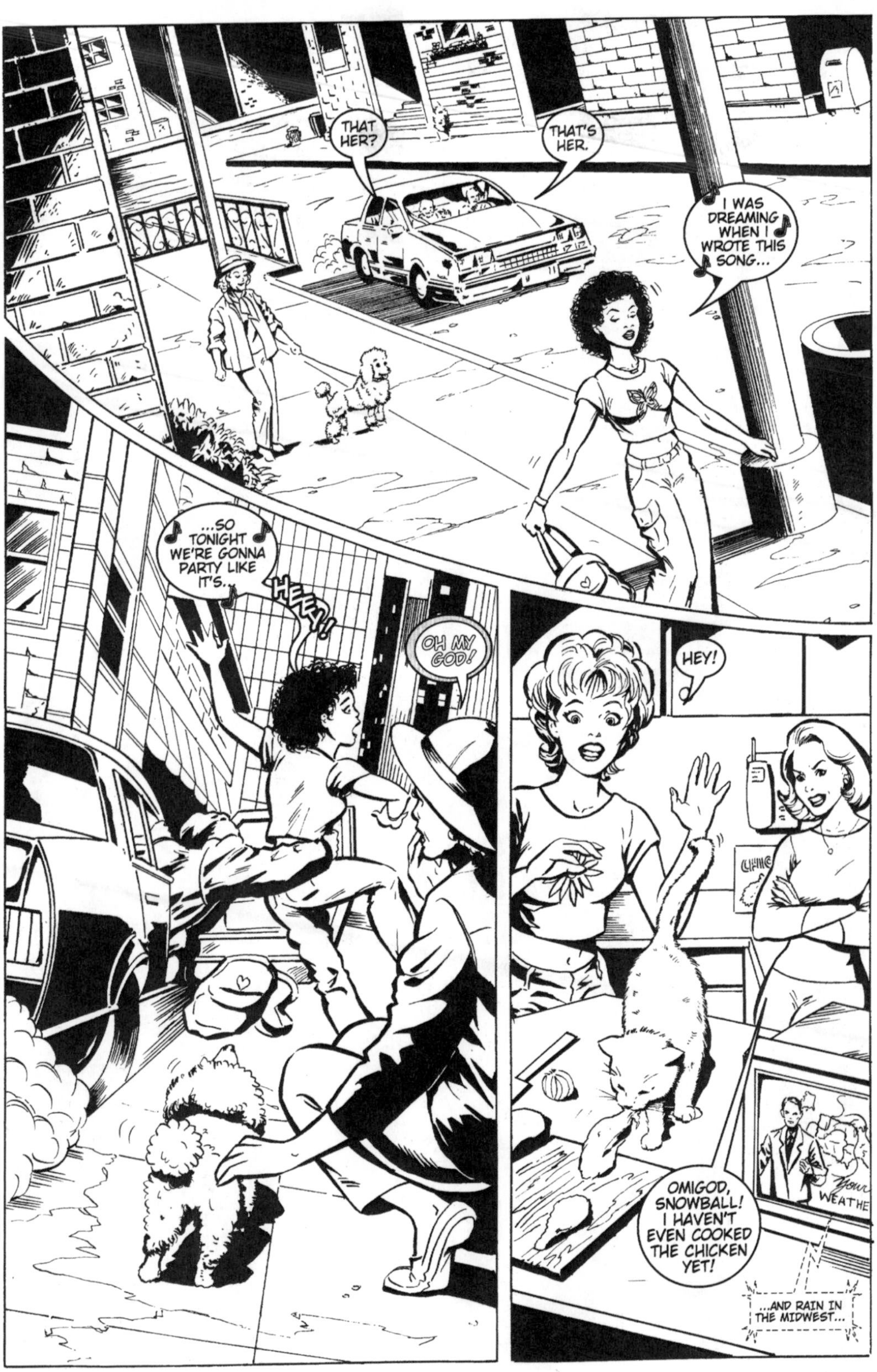
THAT HER?
THAT'S HER.
I WAS DREAMING WHEN I WROTE THIS SONG...
...SO TONIGHT WE'RE GONNA PARTY LIKE IT'S...
HEEY!
OH MY GOD!
HEY!
OMIGOD, SNOWBALL! I HAVEN'T EVEN COOKED THE CHICKEN YET!
...AND RAIN IN THE MIDWEST...

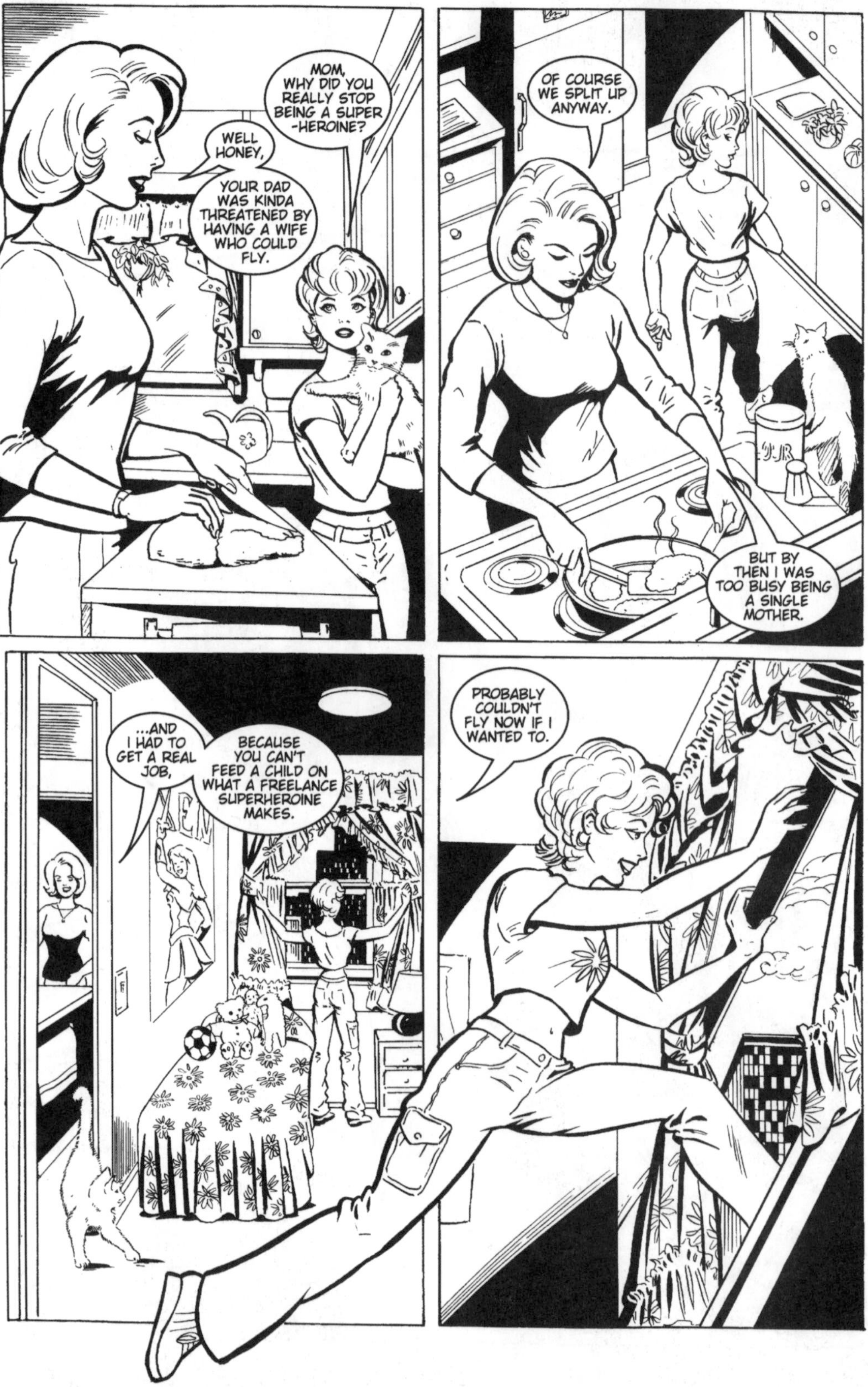
MOM, WHY DID YOU REALLY STOP BEING A SUPER-HEROINE?
WELL HONEY,
YOUR DAD WAS KINDA THREATENED BY HAVING A WIFE WHO COULD FLY.
OF COURSE WE SPLIT UP ANYWAY.
BUT BY THEN I WAS TOO BUSY BEING A SINGLE MOTHER.
...AND I HAD TO GET A REAL JOB,
BECAUSE YOU CAN'T FEED A CHILD ON WHAT A FREELANCE SUPERHEROINE MAKES.
PROBABLY COULDN'T FLY NOW IF I WANTED TO.

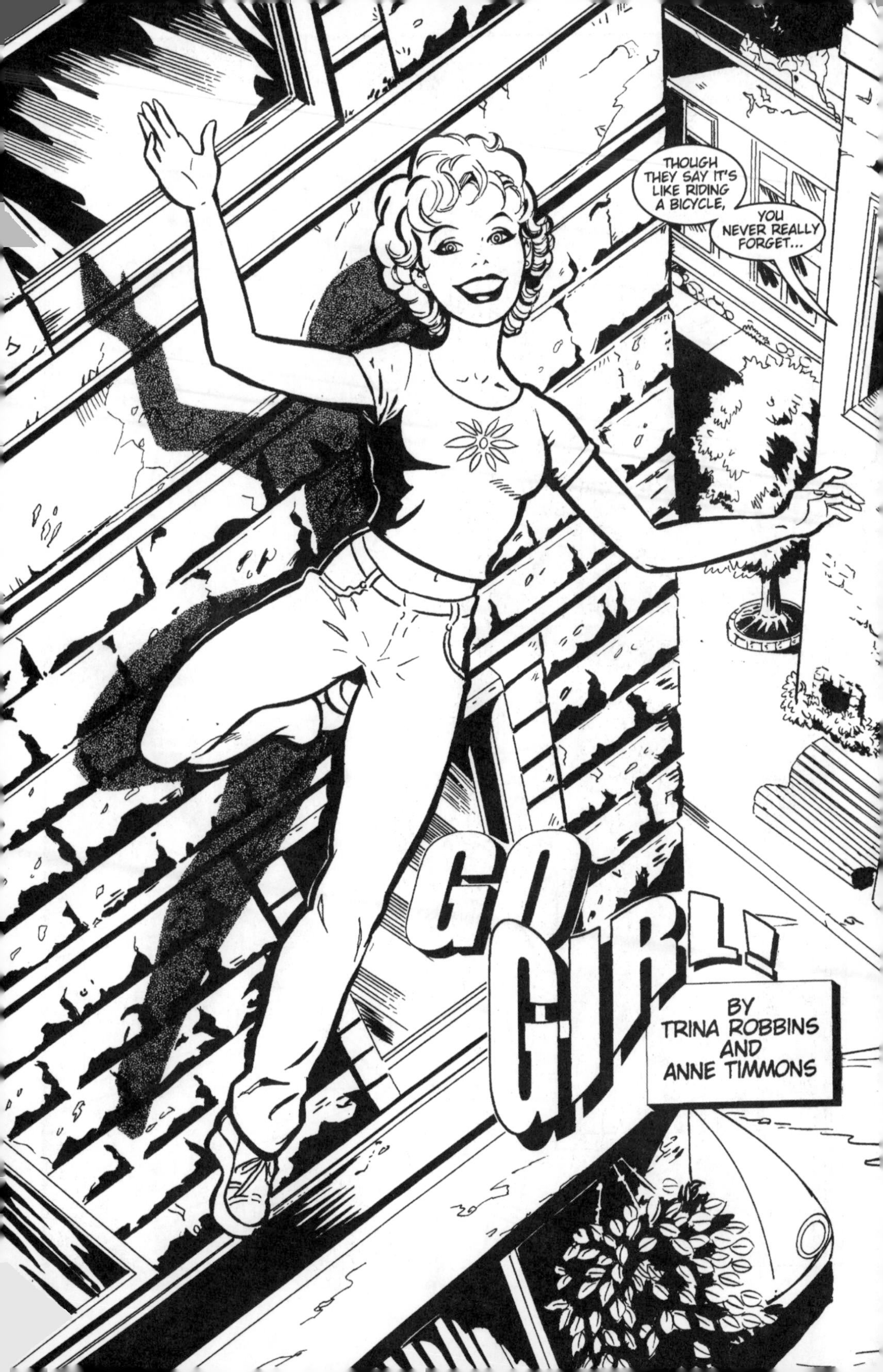
THOUGH THEY SAY IT'S LIKE RIDING A BICYCLE,
YOU NEVER REALLY FORGET...
GO GIRL!
BY TRINA ROBBINS AND ANNE TIMMONS

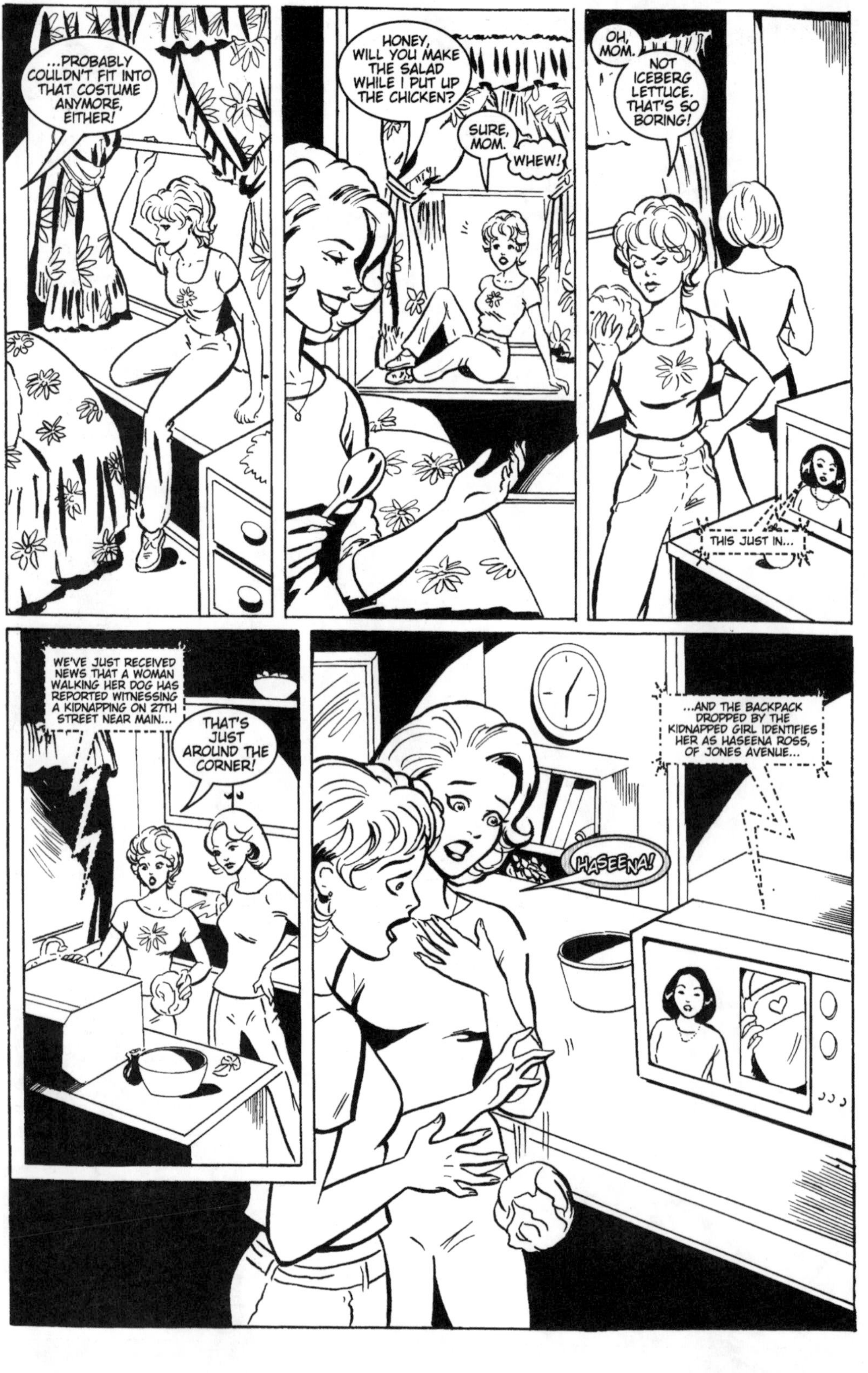
...PROBABLY COULDN'T FIT INTO THAT COSTUME ANYMORE, EITHER!
HONEY, WILL YOU MAKE THE SALAD WHILE I PUT UP THE CHICKEN?
SURE, MOM.
WHEW!
OH, MOM.
NOT ICEBERG LETTUCE. THAT'S SO BORING!
THIS JUST IN...
WE'VE JUST RECEIVED NEWS THAT A WOMAN WALKING HER DOG HAS REPORTED WITNESSING A KIDNAPPING ON 27TH STREET NEAR MAIN...
THAT'S JUST AROUND THE CORNER!
...AND THE BACKPACK DROPPED BY THE KIDNAPPED GIRL IDENTIFIES HER AS HASEENA ROSS, OF JONES AVENUE...
HASEENA!

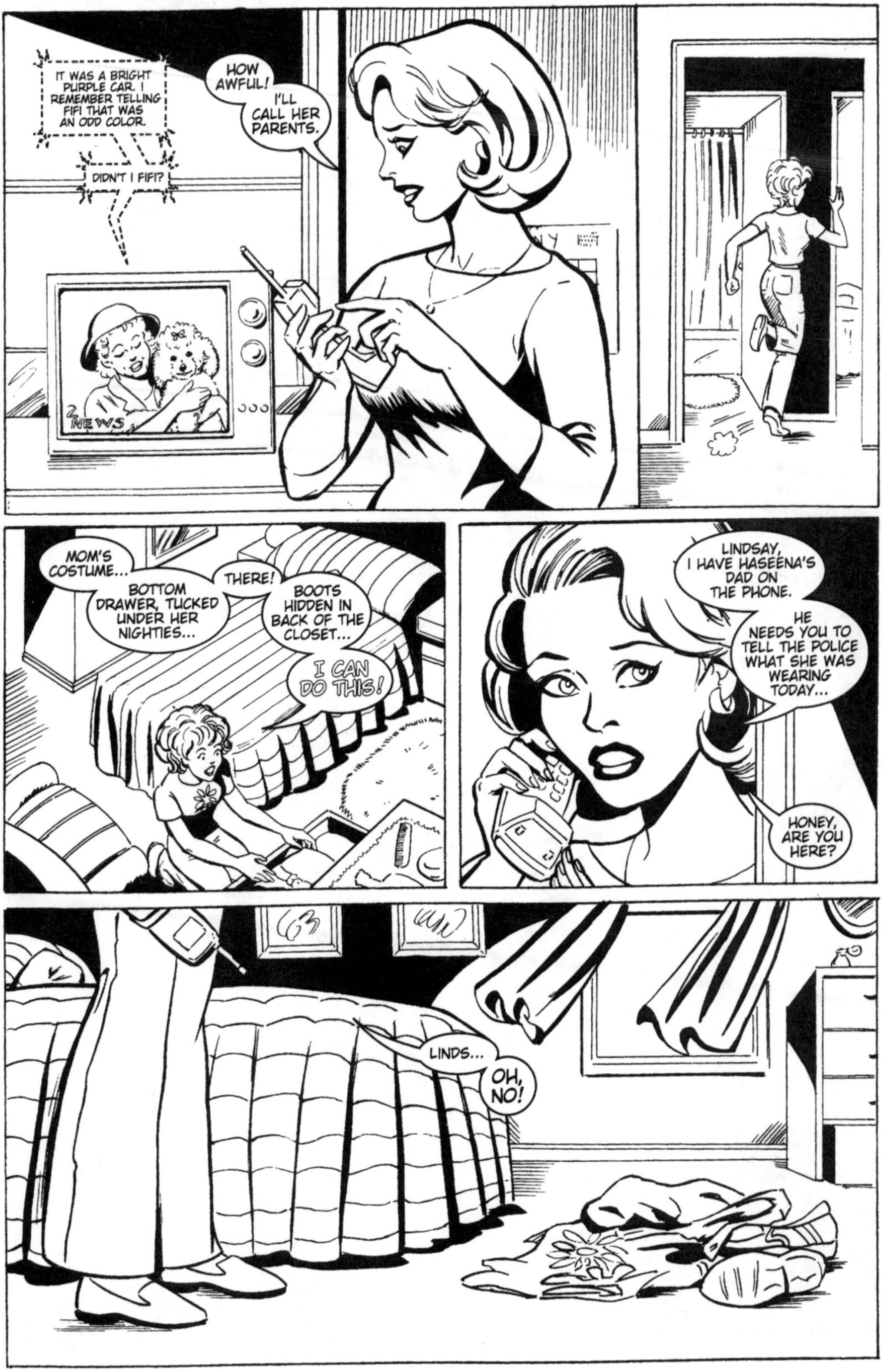
IT WAS A BRIGHT PURPLE CAR. I REMEMBER TELLING FIFI THAT WAS AN ODD COLOR.
DIDN'T I FIFI?
HOW AWFUL!
I'LL CALL HER PARENTS.
2 NEWS
MOM'S COSTUME...
BOTTOM DRAWER, TUCKED UNDER HER NIGHTIES...
THERE!
BOOTS HIDDEN IN BACK OF THE CLOSET...
I CAN DO THIS!
LINDSAY, I HAVE HASEENA'S DAD ON THE PHONE.
HE NEEDS YOU TO TELL THE POLICE WHAT SHE WAS WEARING TODAY...
HONEY, ARE YOU HERE?
LINDS...
OH, NO!

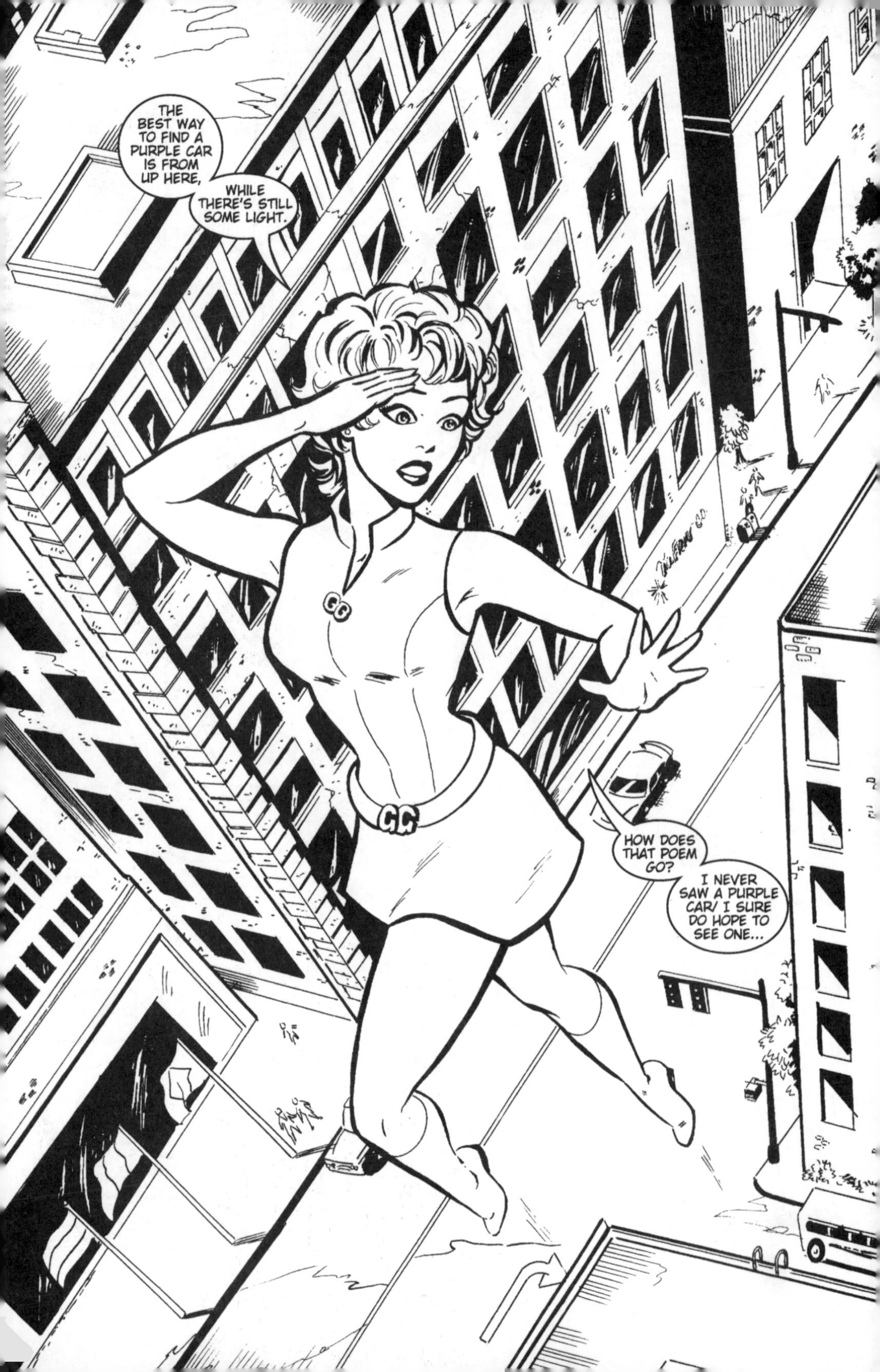
THE BEST WAY TO FIND A PURPLE CAR IS FROM UP HERE,
WHILE THERE'S STILL SOME LIGHT.
HOW DOES THAT POEM GO?
I NEVER SAW A PURPLE CAR/ I SURE DO HOPE TO SEE ONE...

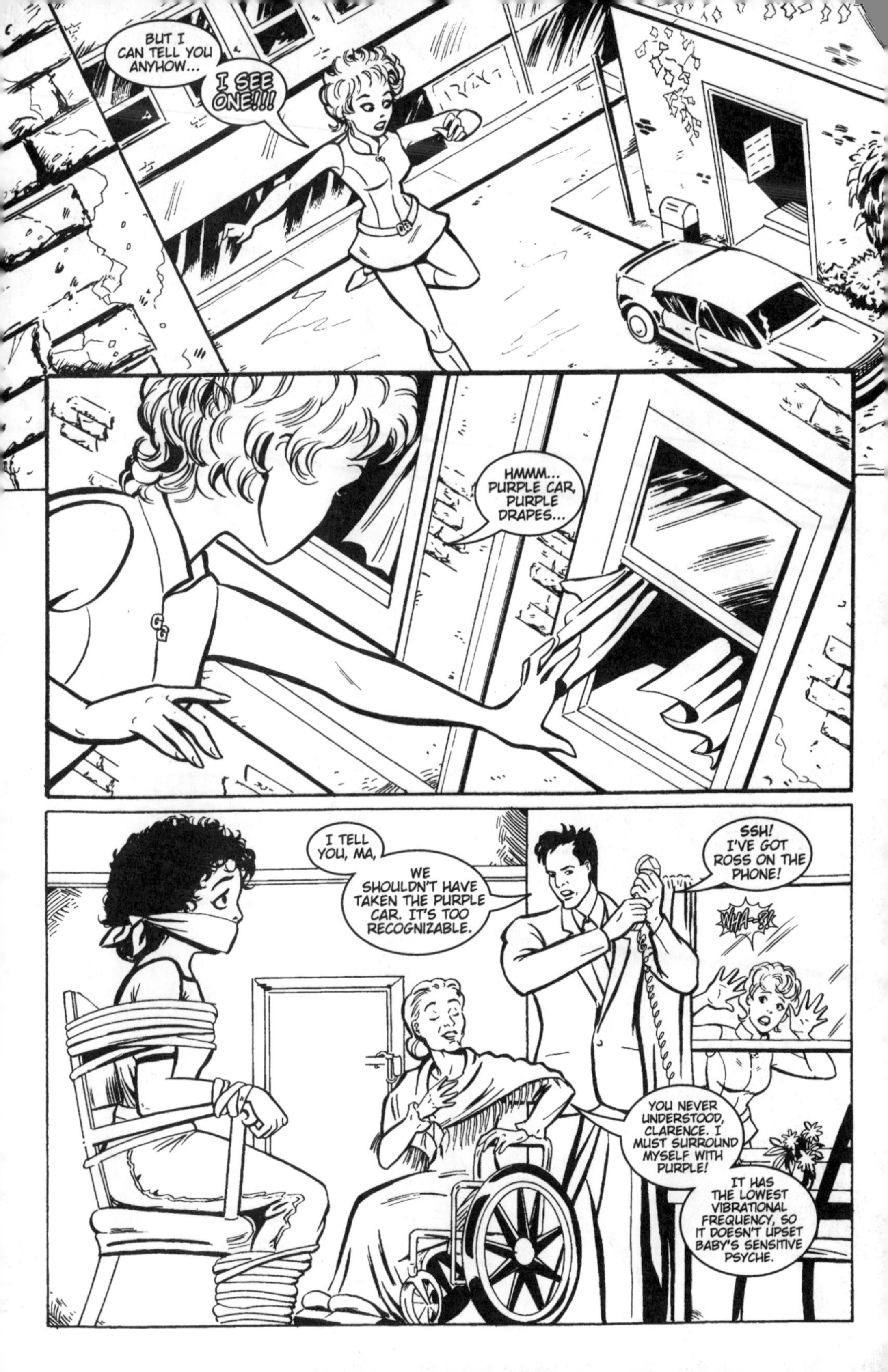
BUT I CAN TELL YOU ANYHOW...
I SEE ONE!!!
HMMM... PURPLE CAR, PURPLE DRAPES...
I TELL YOU, MA,
WE SHOULDN'T HAVE TAKEN THE PURPLE CAR. IT'S TOO RECOGNIZABLE.
SSH! I'VE GOT ROSS ON THE PHONE!
WHA-?!
YOU NEVER UNDERSTOOD, CLARENCE. I MUST SURROUND MYSELF WITH PURPLE!
IT HAS THE LOWEST VIBRATIONAL FREQUENCY, SO IT DOESN'T UPSET BABY'S SENSITIVE PSYCHE.

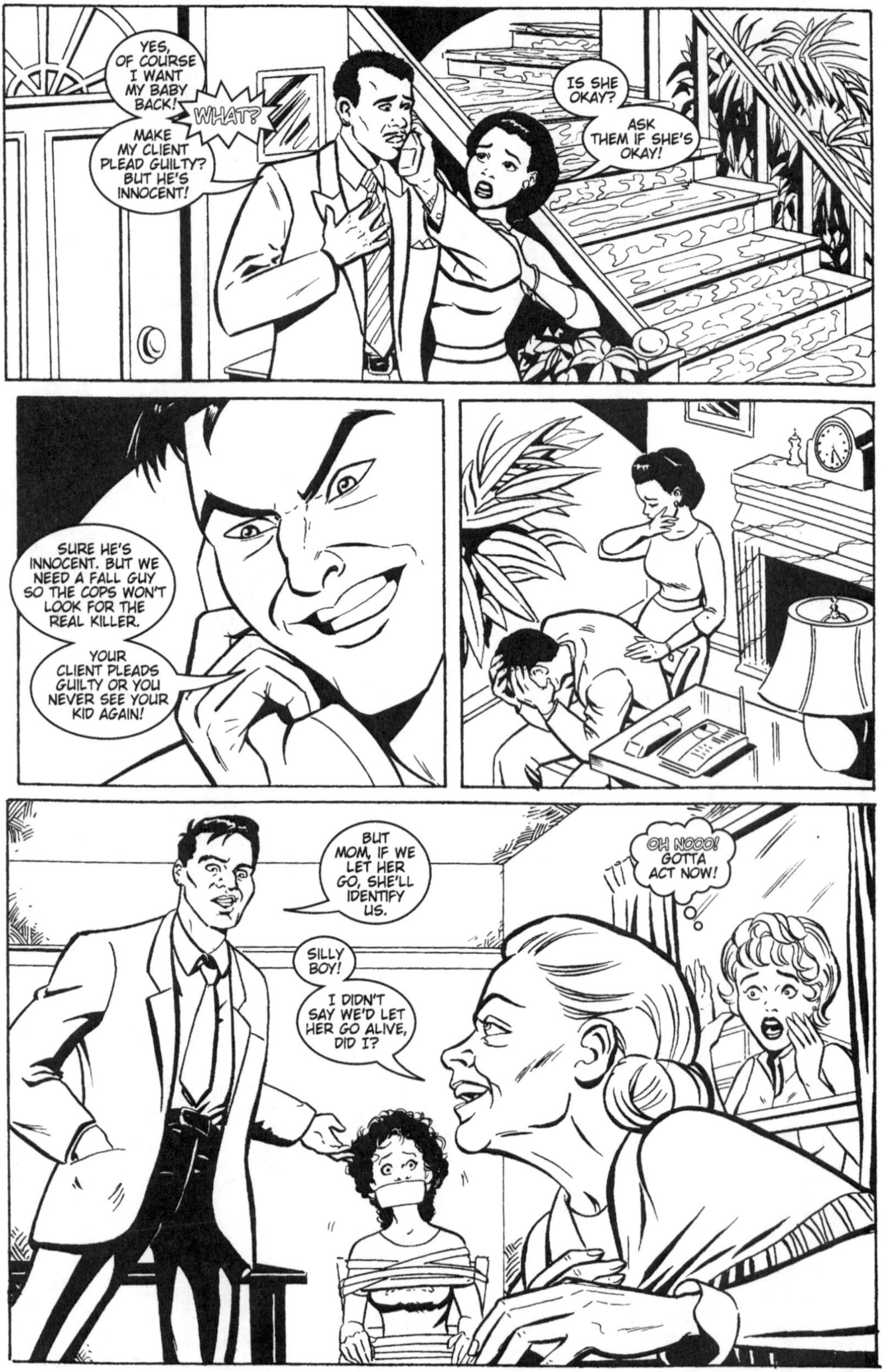
YES, OF COURSE I WANT MY BABY BACK!
WHAT?
MAKE MY CLIENT PLEAD GUILTY? BUT HE'S INNOCENT!
IS SHE OKAY?
ASK THEM IF SHE'S OKAY!
SURE HE'S INNOCENT. BUT WE NEED A FALL GUY SO THE COPS WON'T LOOK FOR THE REAL KILLER.
YOUR CLIENT PLEADS GUILTY OR YOU NEVER SEE YOUR KID AGAIN!
BUT MOM, IF WE LET HER GO, SHE'LL IDENTIFY US.
SILLY BOY!
I DIDN'T SAY WE'D LET HER GO ALIVE, DID I?
OH NOOO! GOTTA ACT NOW!

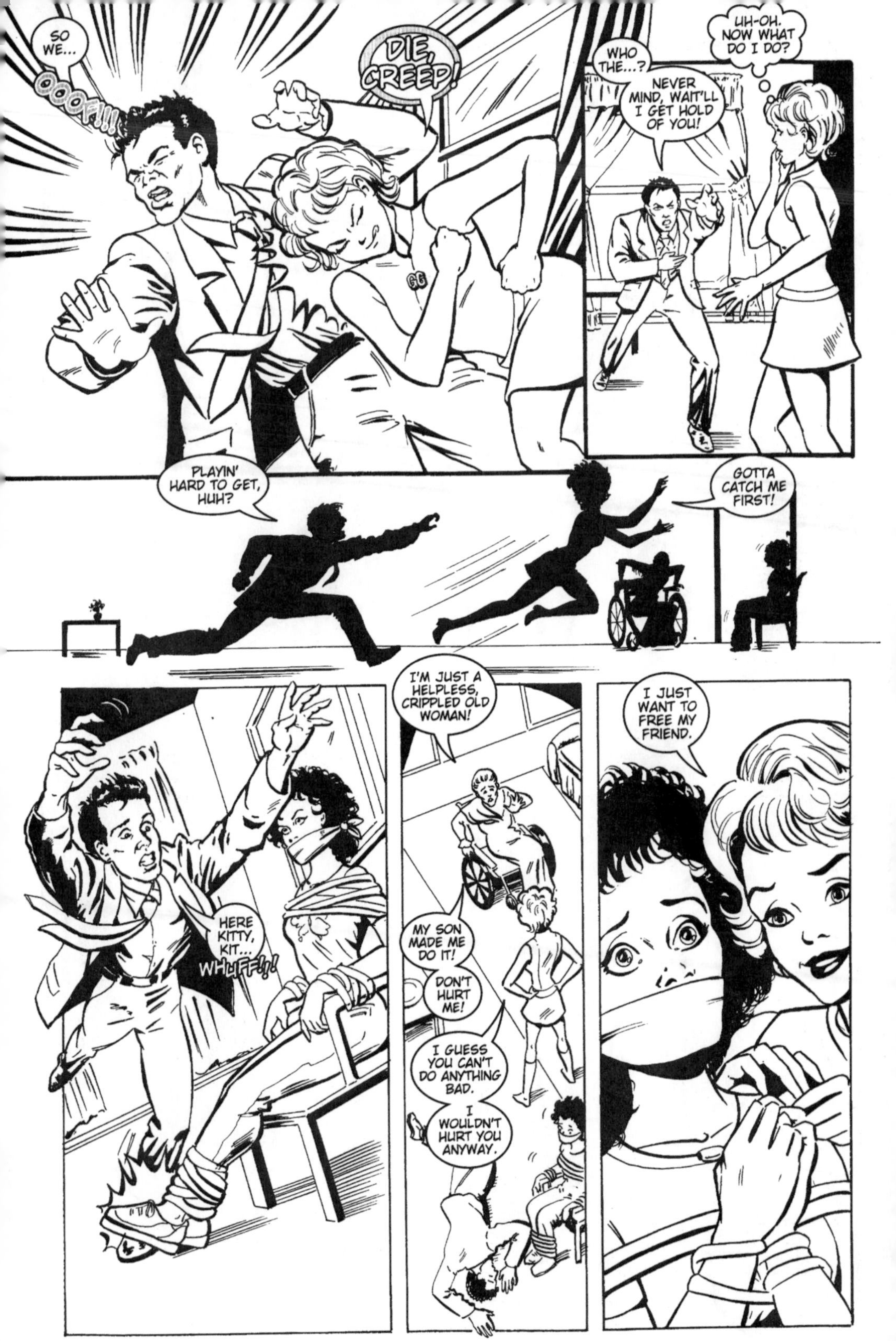

SO WE...
OOOF!!!
DIE, CREEP!
WHO THE...?
NEVER MIND, WAIT'LL I GET HOLD OF YOU!
UH-OH. NOW WHAT DO I DO?
PLAYIN' HARD TO GET, HUH?
GOTTA CATCH ME FIRST!
HERE KITTY, KIT...
WHUFF!!
I'M JUST A HELPLESS, CRIPPLED OLD WOMAN!
MY SON MADE ME DO IT!
DON'T HURT ME!
I GUESS YOU CAN'T DO ANYTHING BAD.
I WOULDN'T HURT YOU ANYWAY.
I JUST WANT TO FREE MY FRIEND.

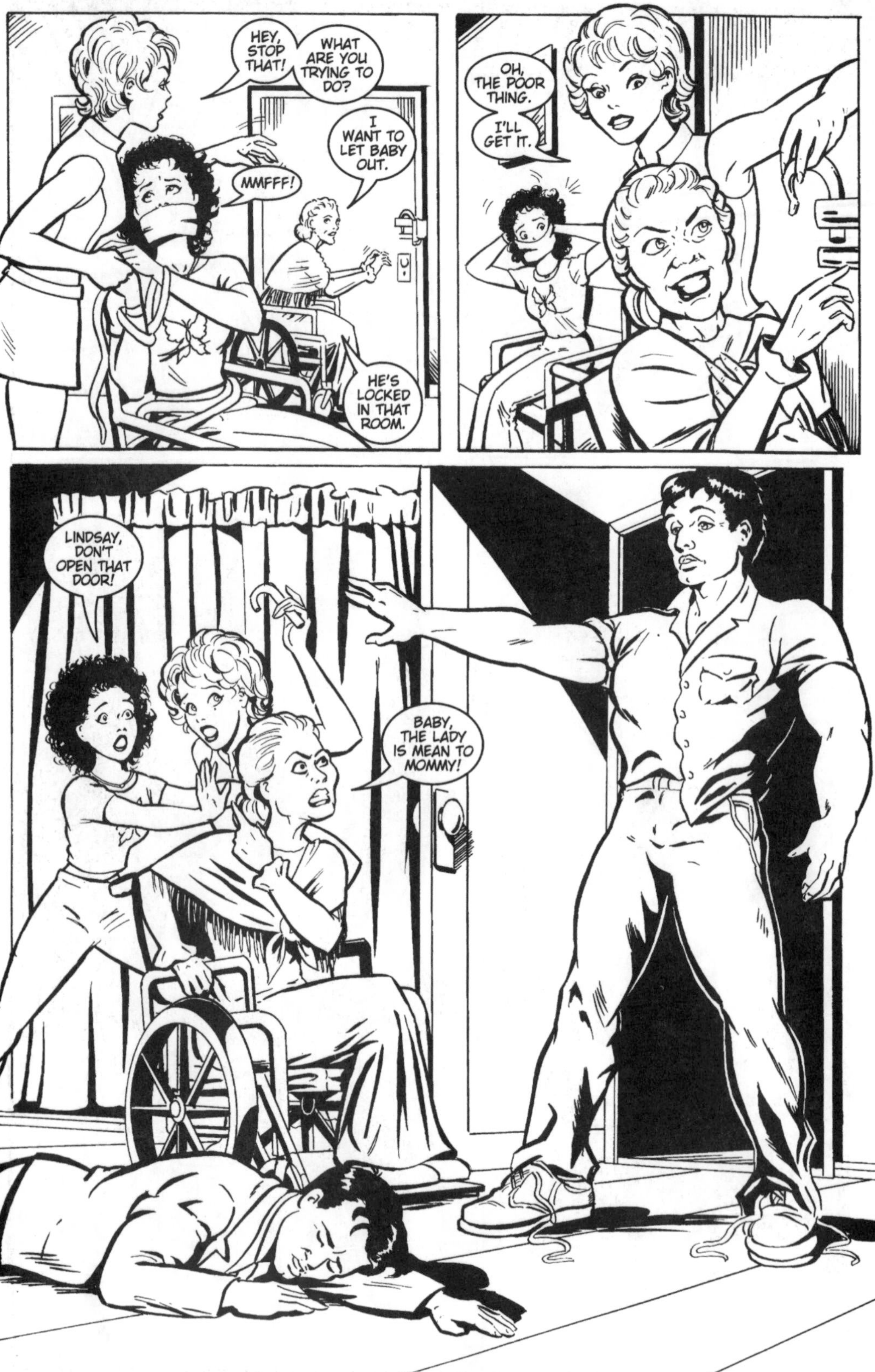

HEY, STOP THAT!
WHAT ARE YOU TRYING TO DO?
MMFFF!
I WANT TO LET BABY OUT.
HE'S LOCKED IN THAT ROOM.
OH, THE POOR THING.
I'LL GET IT.
LINDSAY, DON'T OPEN THAT DOOR!
BABY, THE LADY IS MEAN TO MOMMY!

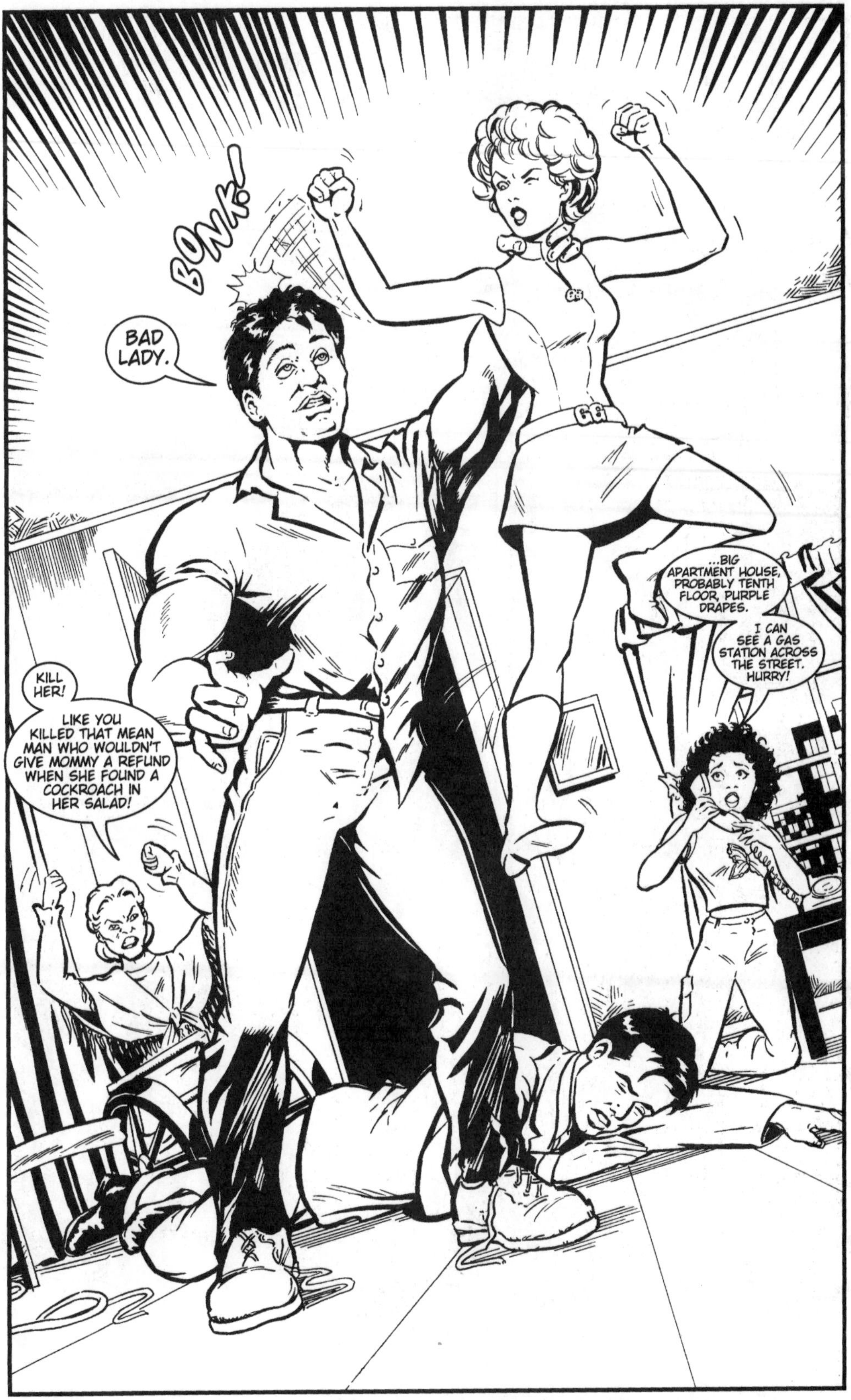
BONK!
BAD LADY.
...BIG APARTMENT HOUSE, PROBABLY TENTH FLOOR, PURPLE DRAPES.
I CAN SEE A GAS STATION ACROSS THE STREET. HURRY!
KILL HER!
LIKE YOU KILLED THAT MEAN MAN WHO WOULDN'T GIVE MOMMY A REFUND WHEN SHE FOUND A COCKROACH IN HER SALAD!

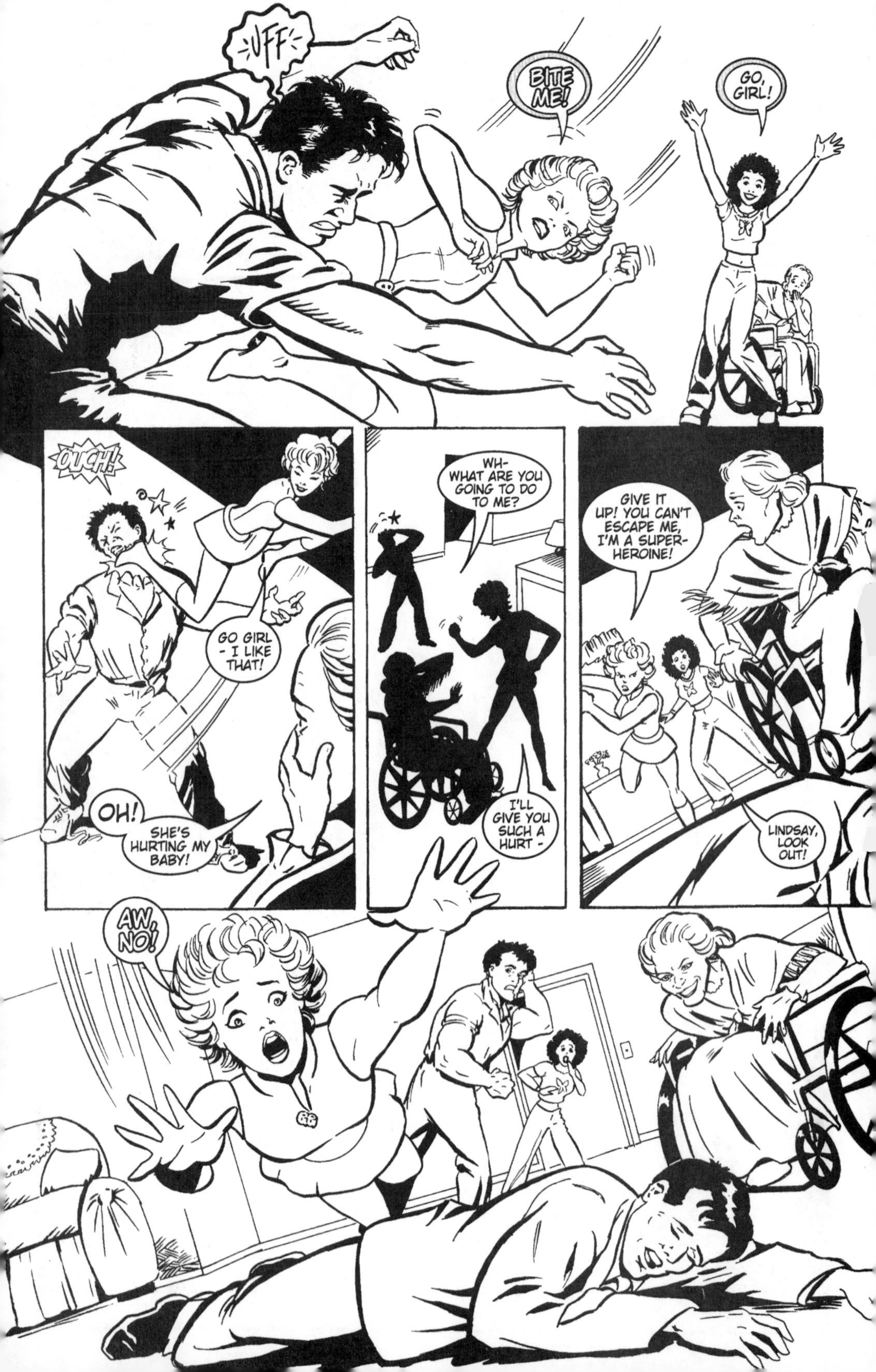
UFF
BITE ME!
GO, GIRL!
OUCH!
GO GIRL - I LIKE THAT!
OH!
SHE'S HURTING MY BABY!
WH- WHAT ARE YOU GOING TO DO TO ME?
I'LL GIVE YOU SUCH A HURT -
GIVE IT UP! YOU CAN'T ESCAPE ME, I'M A SUPER-HEROINE!
LINDSAY, LOOK OUT!
AW, NO!

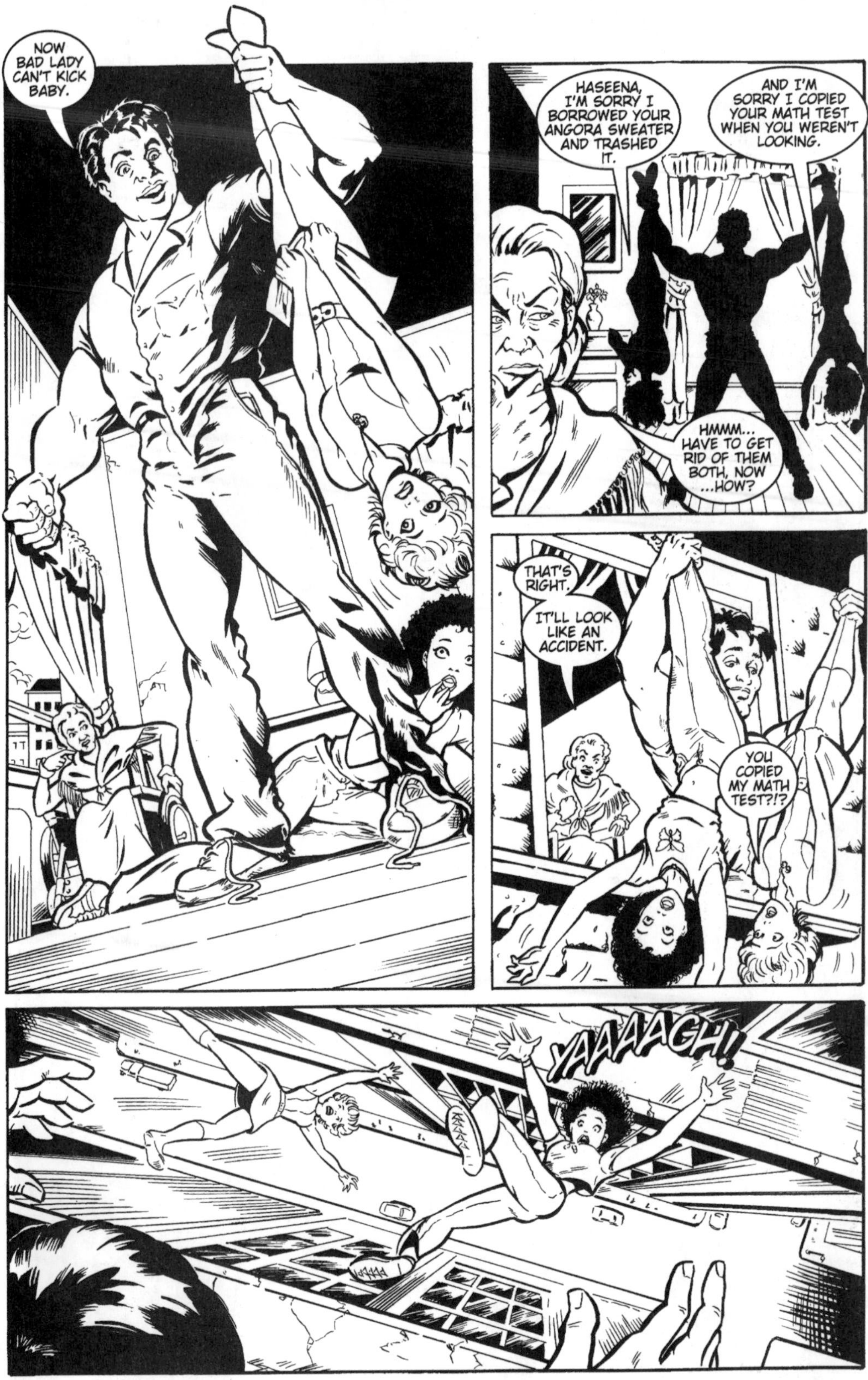
NOW BAD LADY CAN'T KICK BABY.
HASEENA, I'M SORRY I BORROWED YOUR ANGORA SWEATER AND TRASHED IT.
AND I'M SORRY I COPIED YOUR MATH TEST WHEN YOU WEREN'T LOOKING.
HMMM... HAVE TO GET RID OF THEM BOTH, NOW ...HOW?
THAT'S RIGHT.
IT'LL LOOK LIKE AN ACCIDENT.
YOU COPIED MY MATH TEST?!?
YAAAAGH!

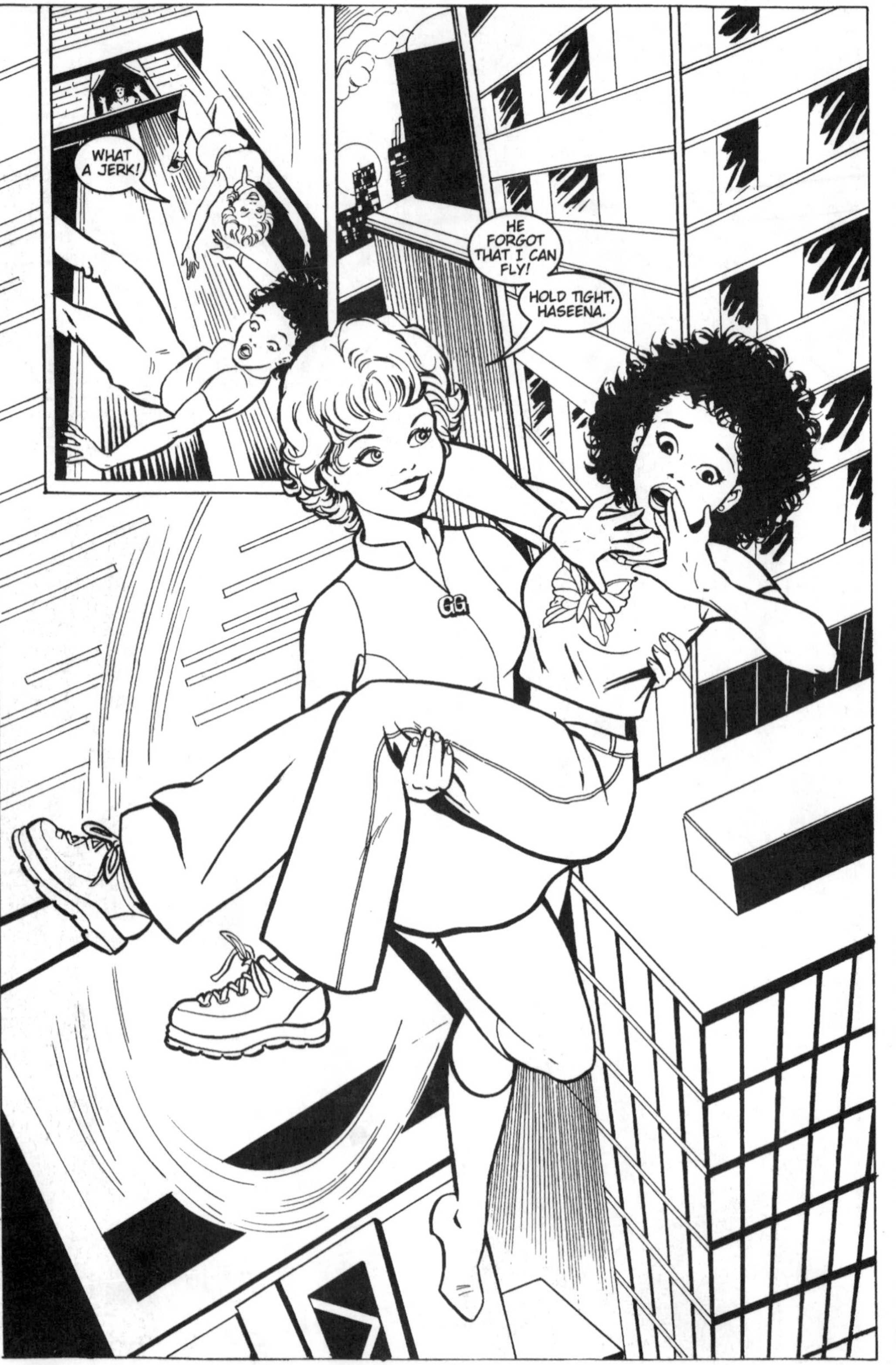
WHAT A JERK!
HE FORGOT THAT I CAN FLY!
HOLD TIGHT, HASEENA.
GG

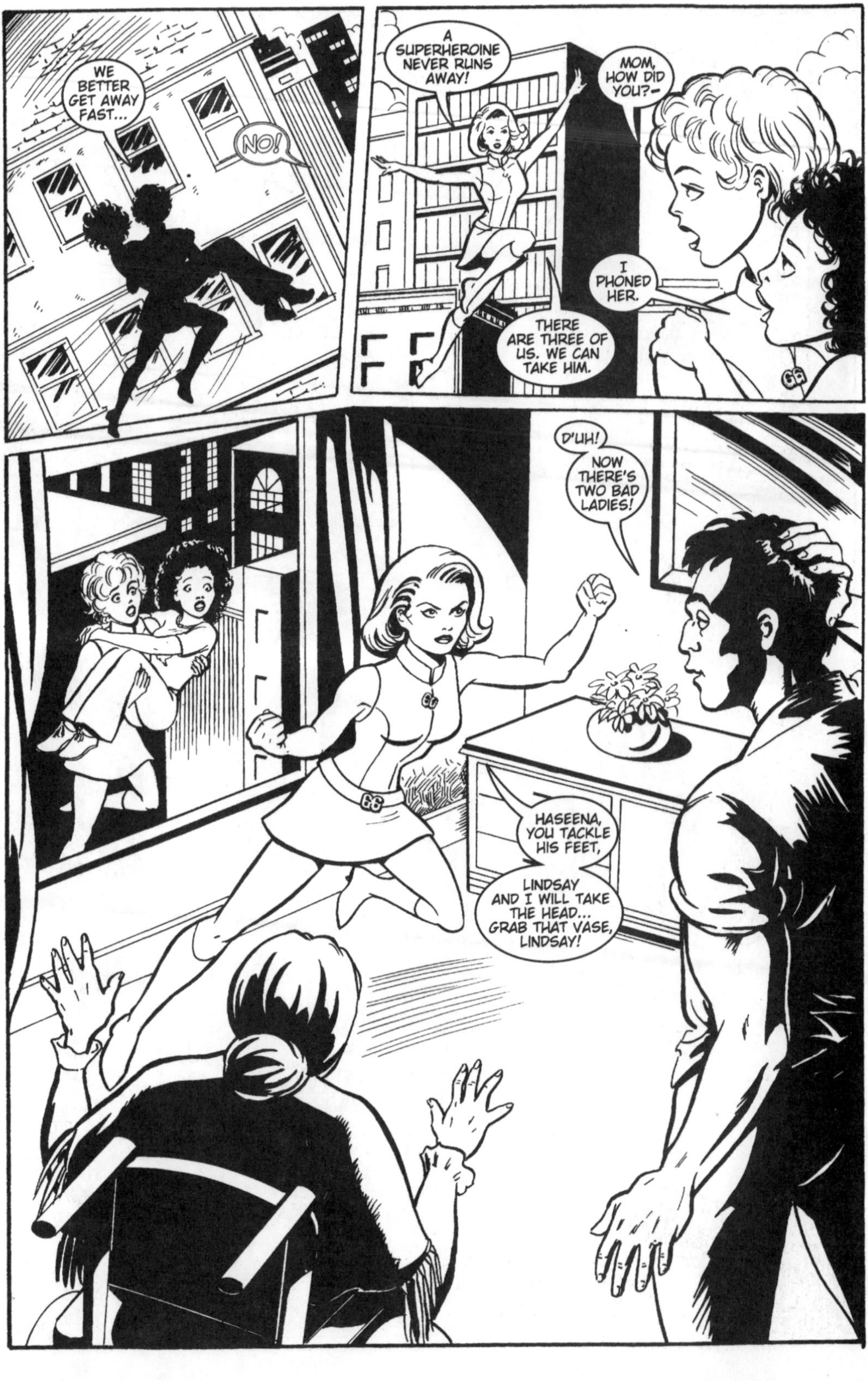
WE BETTER GET AWAY FAST...
NO!
A SUPERHEROINE NEVER RUNS AWAY!
MOM, HOW DID YOU?-
I PHONED HER.
THERE ARE THREE OF US. WE CAN TAKE HIM.
D'UH!
NOW THERE'S TWO BAD LADIES!
HASEENA, YOU TACKLE HIS FEET,
LINDSAY AND I WILL TAKE THE HEAD... GRAB THAT VASE, LINDSAY!

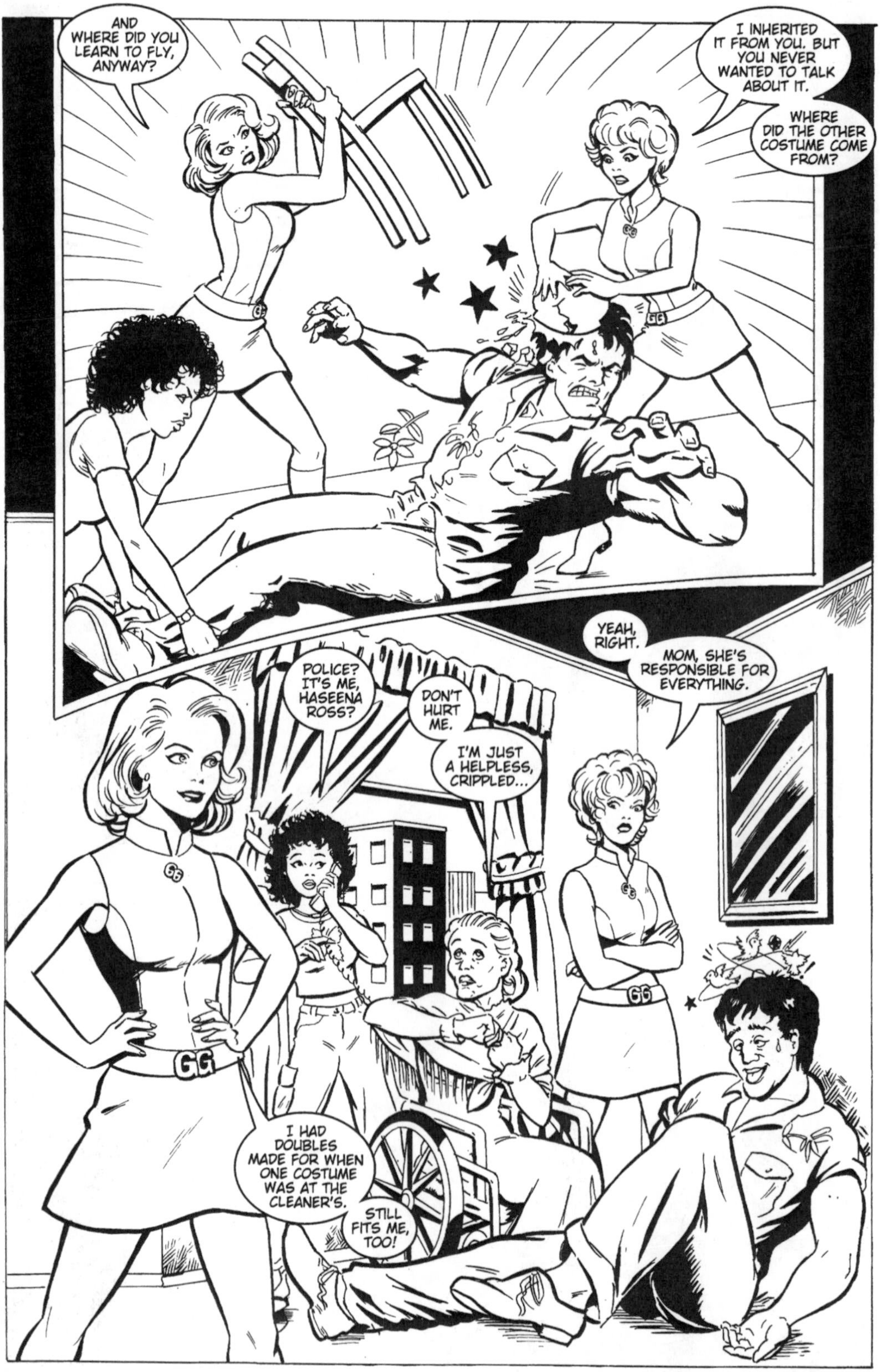
AND WHERE DID YOU LEARN TO FLY, ANYWAY?
I INHERITED IT FROM YOU. BUT YOU NEVER WANTED TO TALK ABOUT IT.
WHERE DID THE OTHER COSTUME COME FROM?
POLICE? IT'S ME, HASEENA ROSS?
DON'T HURT ME.
I'M JUST A HELPLESS, CRIPPLED...
YEAH, RIGHT.
MOM, SHE'S RESPONSIBLE FOR EVERYTHING.
I HAD DOUBLES MADE FOR WHEN ONE COSTUME WAS AT THE CLEANER'S.
STILL FITS ME, TOO!

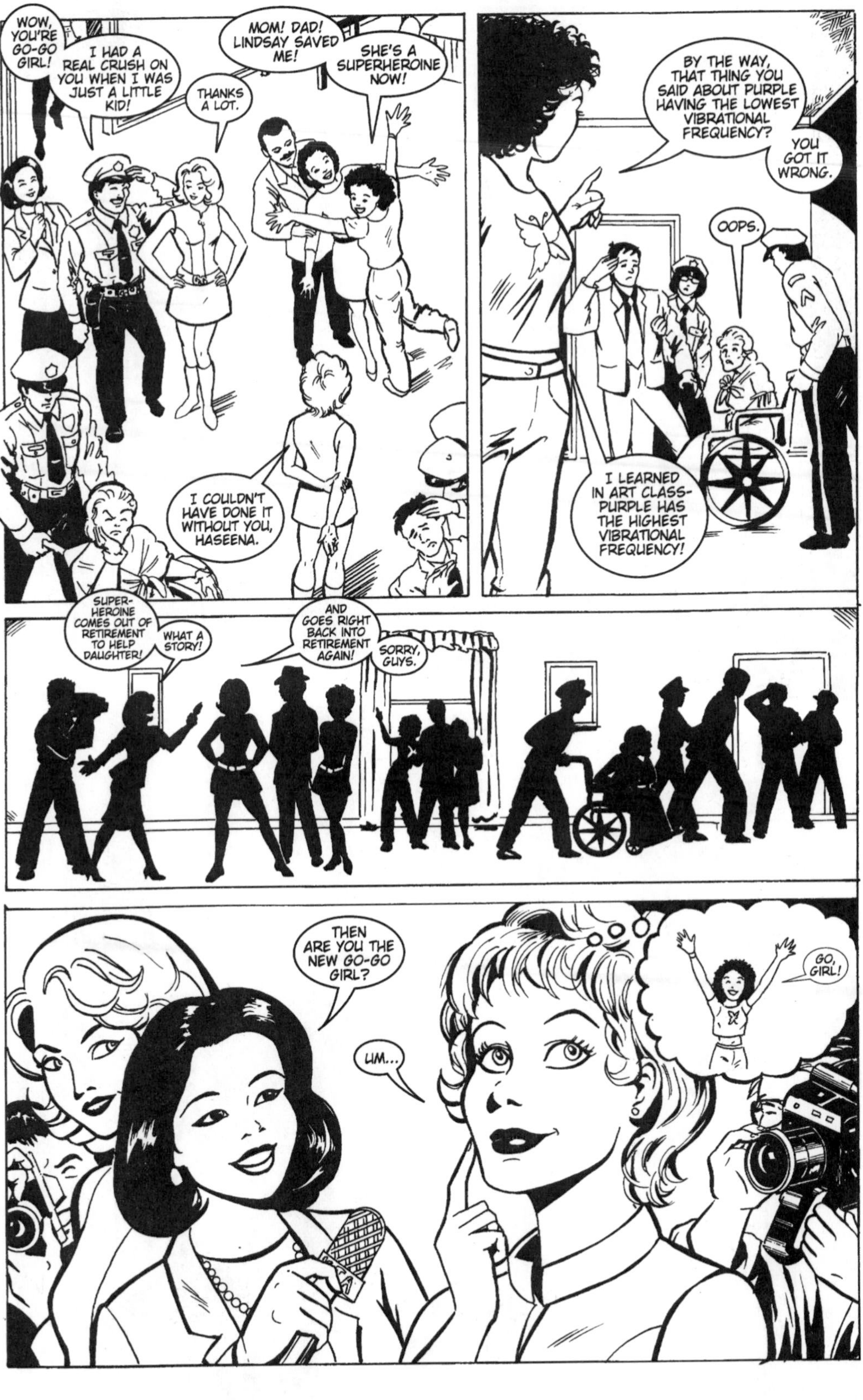
WOW, YOU'RE GO-GO GIRL!
I HAD A REAL CRUSH ON YOU WHEN I WAS JUST A LITTLE KID!
THANKS A LOT.
MOM! DAD! LINDSAY SAVED ME!
SHE'S A SUPERHEROINE NOW!
I COULDN'T HAVE DONE IT WITHOUT YOU, HASEENA.
BY THE WAY, THAT THING YOU SAID ABOUT PURPLE HAVING THE LOWEST VIBRATIONAL FREQUENCY?
YOU GOT IT WRONG.
OOPS.
I LEARNED IN ART CLASS-PURPLE HAS THE HIGHEST VIBRATIONAL FREQUENCY!
SUPER-HEROINE COMES OUT OF RETIREMENT TO HELP DAUGHTER!
WHAT A STORY!
AND GOES RIGHT BACK INTO RETIREMENT AGAIN!
SORRY, GUYS.
THEN ARE YOU THE NEW GO-GO GIRL?
UM...
GO, GIRL!

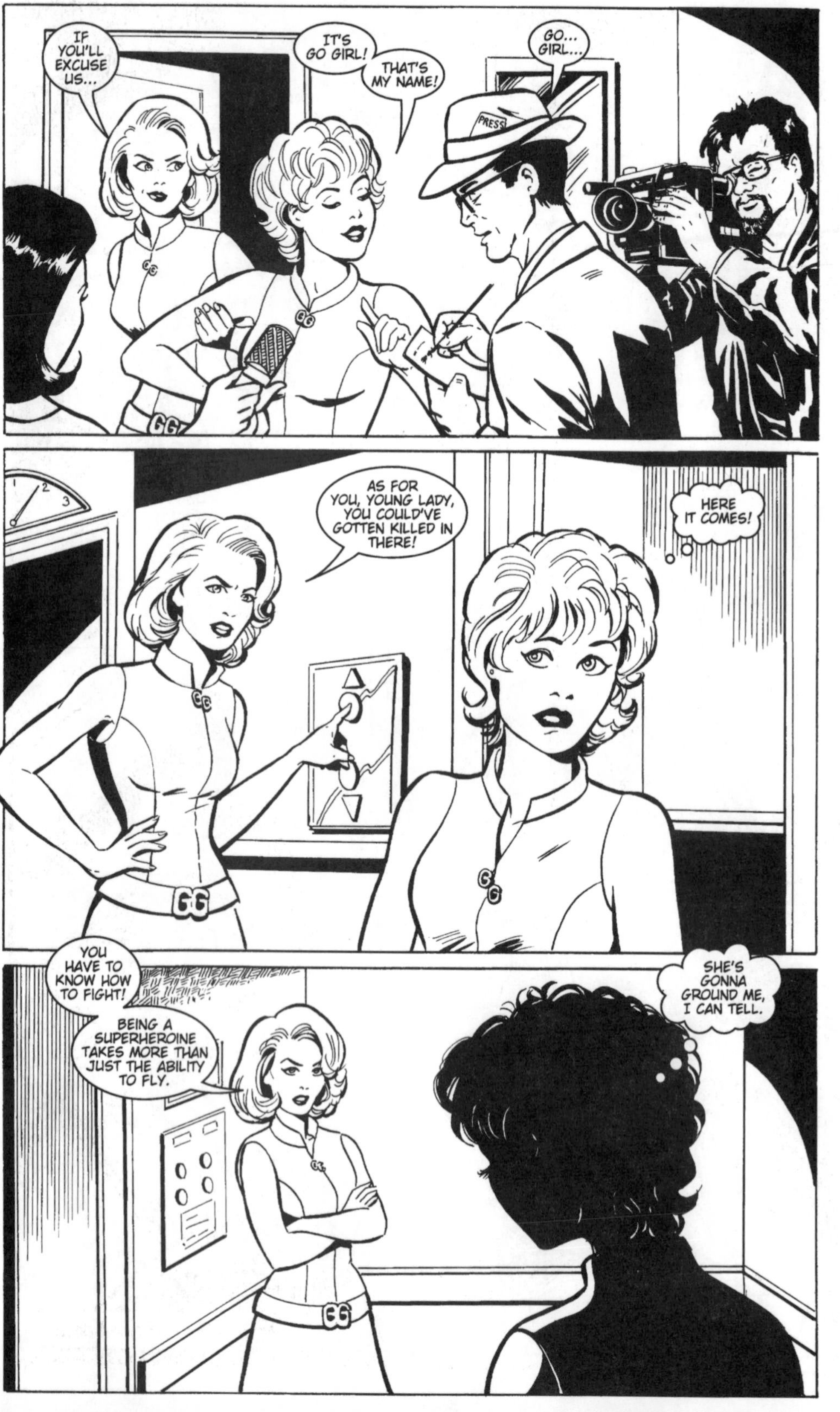

IF YOU'LL EXCUSE US...
IT'S GO GIRL!
THAT'S MY NAME!
GO... GIRL...
PRESS
AS FOR YOU, YOUNG LADY, YOU COULD'VE GOTTEN KILLED IN THERE!
HERE IT COMES!
YOU HAVE TO KNOW HOW TO FIGHT!
BEING A SUPERHEROINE TAKES MORE THAN JUST THE ABILITY TO FLY.
SHE'S GONNA GROUND ME, I CAN TELL.

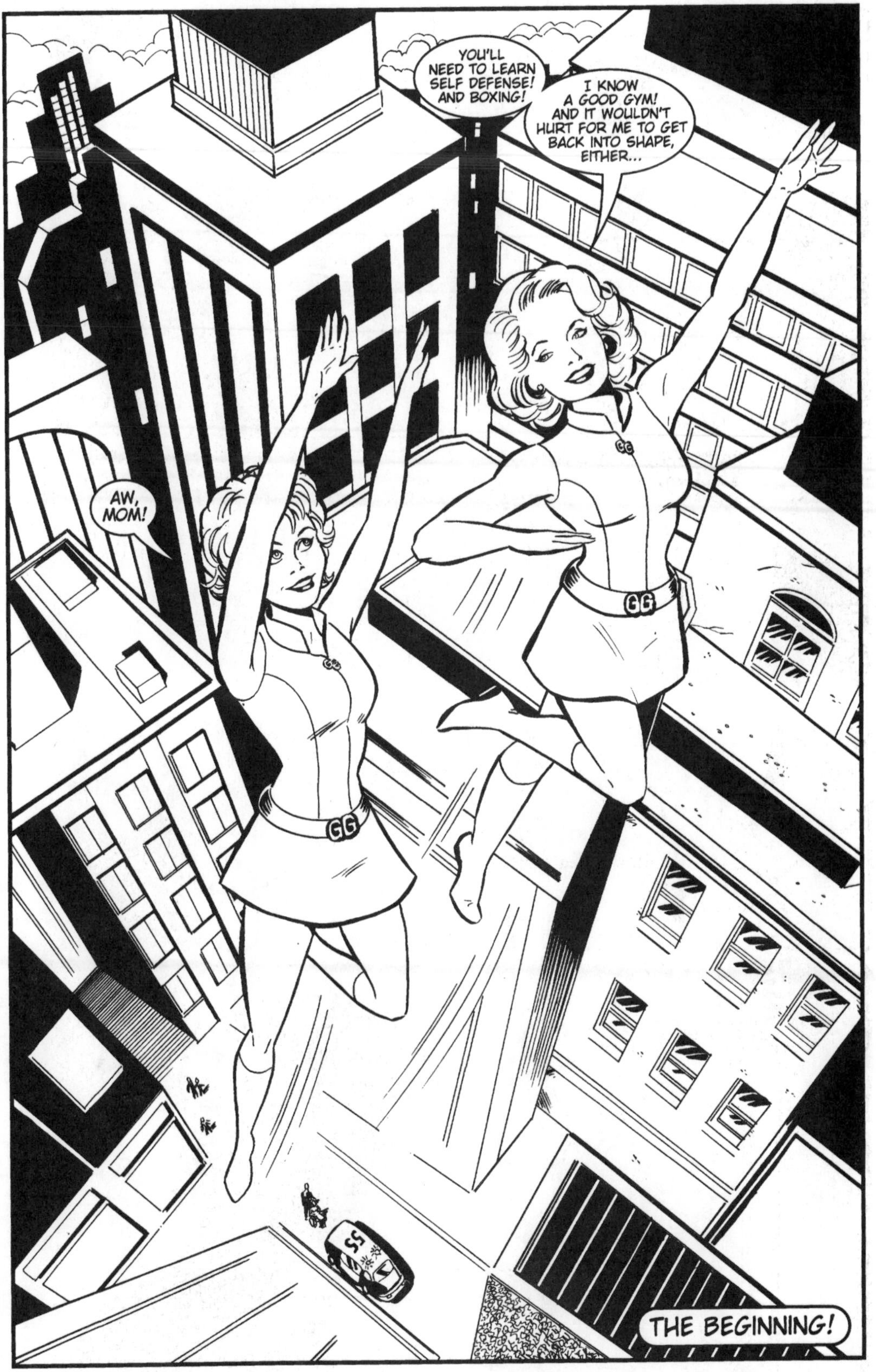
YOU'LL NEED TO LEARN SELF DEFENSE! AND BOXING!
I KNOW A GOOD GYM! AND IT WOULDN'T HURT FOR ME TO GET BACK INTO SHAPE, EITHER...
AW, MOM!
THE BEGINNING!

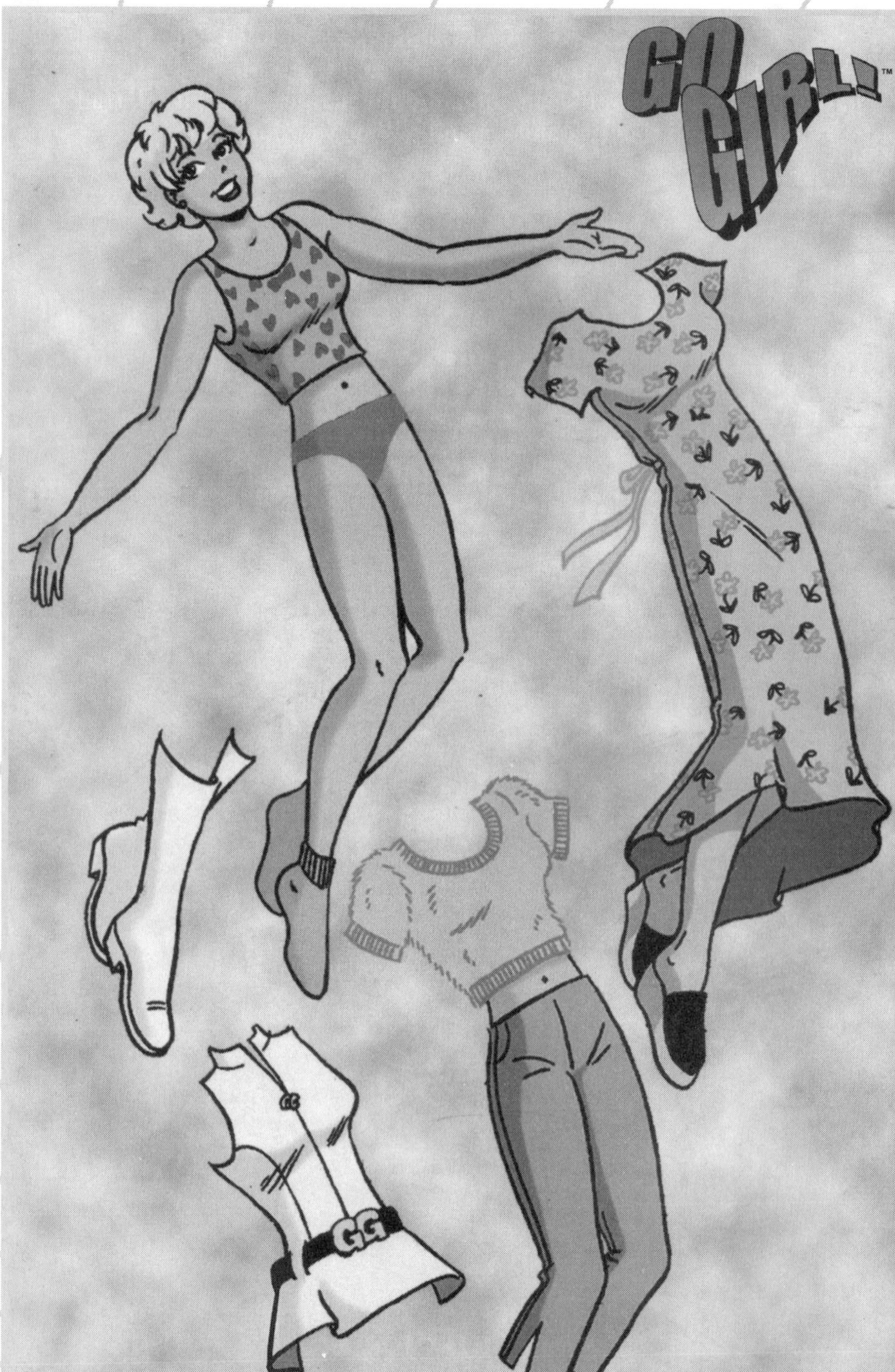
GO GIRL!™
GG

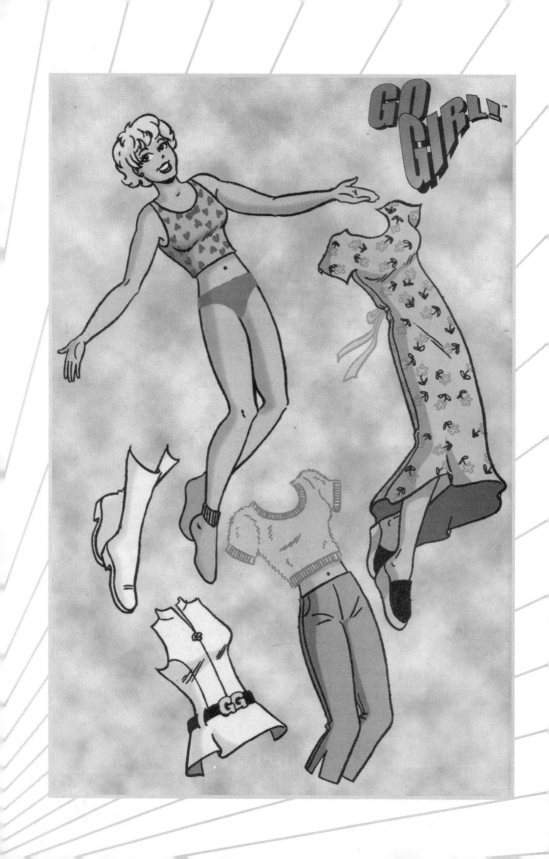

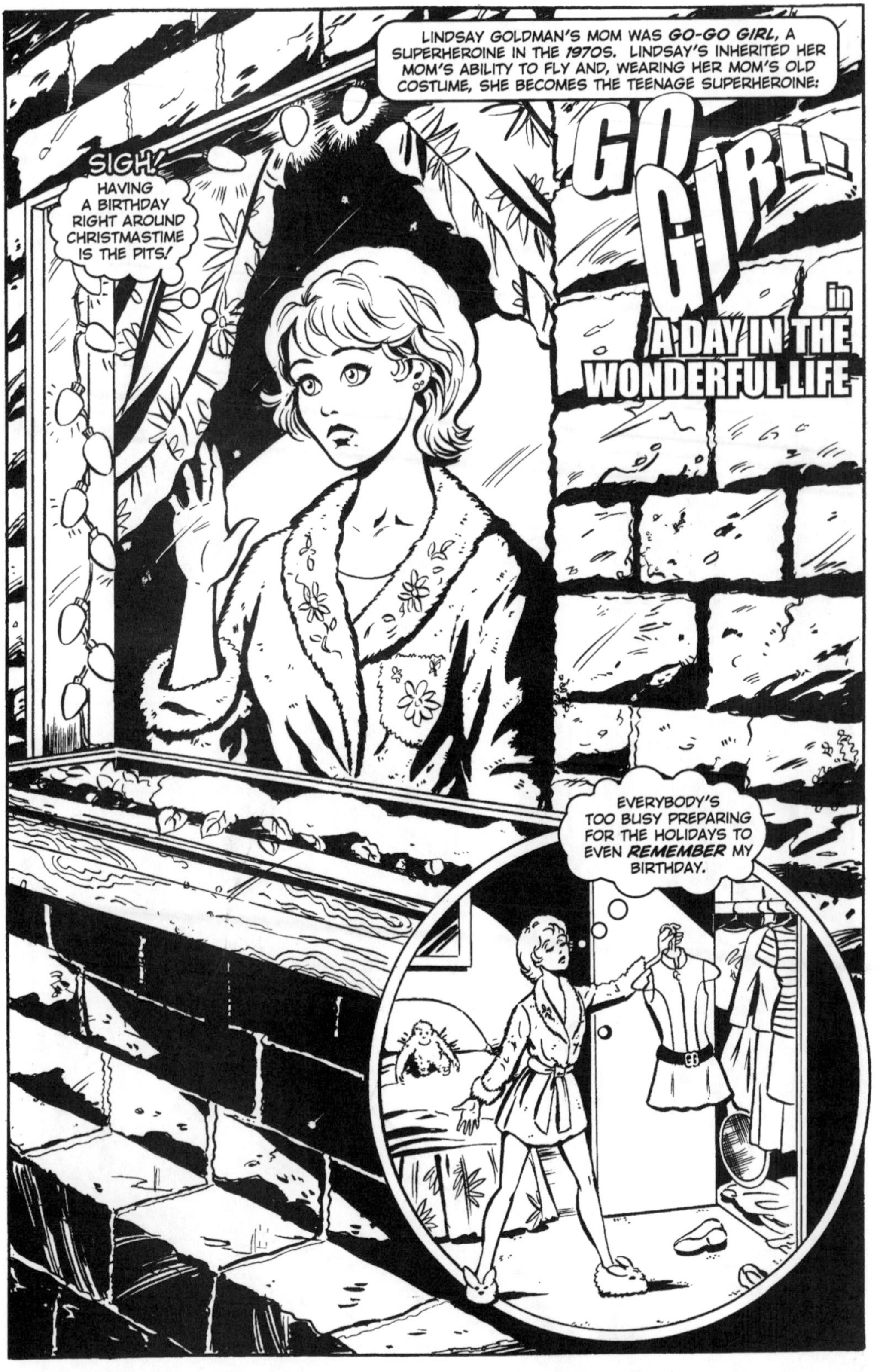
LINDSAY GOLDMAN'S MOM WAS GO-GO GIRL, A SUPERHEROINE IN THE 1970S. LINDSAY'S INHERITED HER MOM'S ABILITY TO FLY AND, WEARING HER MOM'S OLD COSTUME, SHE BECOMES THE TEENAGE SUPERHEROINE:
GO GIRL!
in
A DAY IN THE WONDERFUL LIFE
SIGH! HAVING A BIRTHDAY RIGHT AROUND CHRISTMASTIME IS THE PITS!
EVERYBODY'S TOO BUSY PREPARING FOR THE HOLIDAYS TO EVEN REMEMBER MY BIRTHDAY.

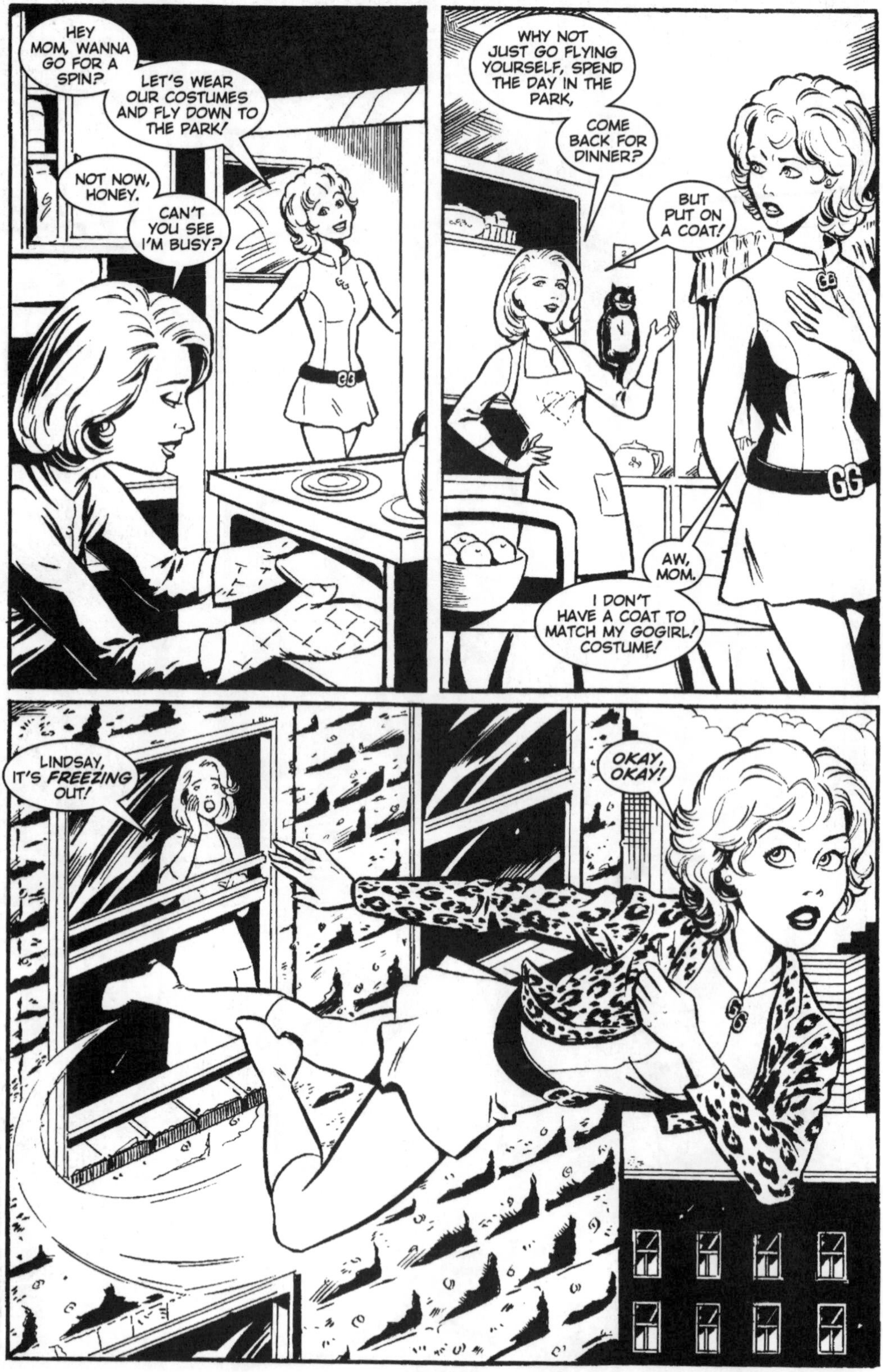
HEY MOM, WANNA GO FOR A SPIN?
LET'S WEAR OUR COSTUMES AND FLY DOWN TO THE PARK!
NOT NOW, HONEY.
CAN'T YOU SEE I'M BUSY?
WHY NOT JUST GO FLYING YOURSELF, SPEND THE DAY IN THE PARK,
COME BACK FOR DINNER?
BUT PUT ON A COAT!
AW, MOM.
I DON'T HAVE A COAT TO MATCH MY GOGIRL! COSTUME!
LINDSAY, IT'S *FREEZING* OUT!
OKAY, OKAY!

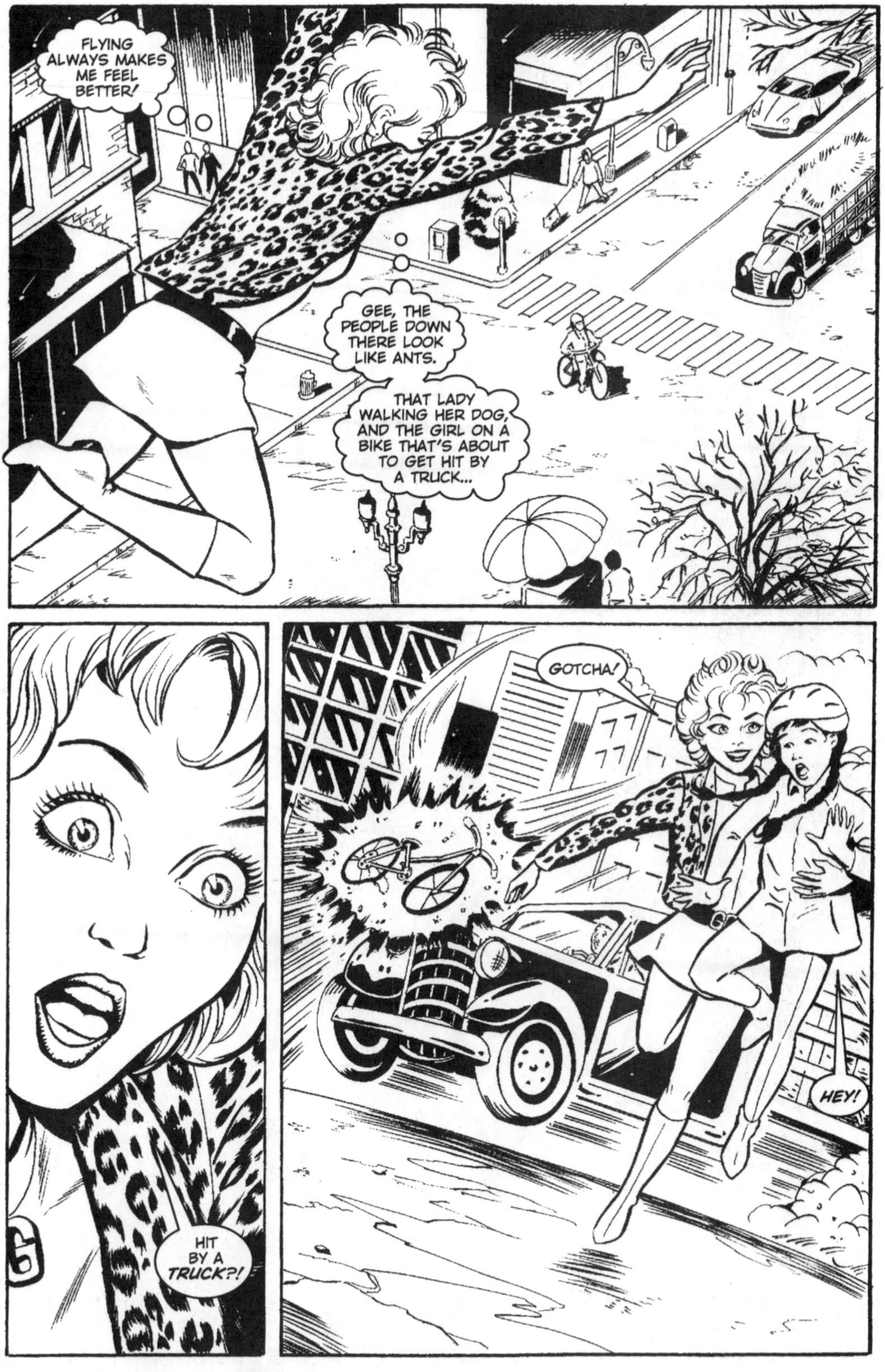
FLYING ALWAYS MAKES ME FEEL BETTER!
GEE, THE PEOPLE DOWN THERE LOOK LIKE ANTS.
THAT LADY WALKING HER DOG, AND THE GIRL ON A BIKE THAT'S ABOUT TO GET HIT BY A TRUCK...
HIT BY A TRUCK?!
GOTCHA!
HEY!

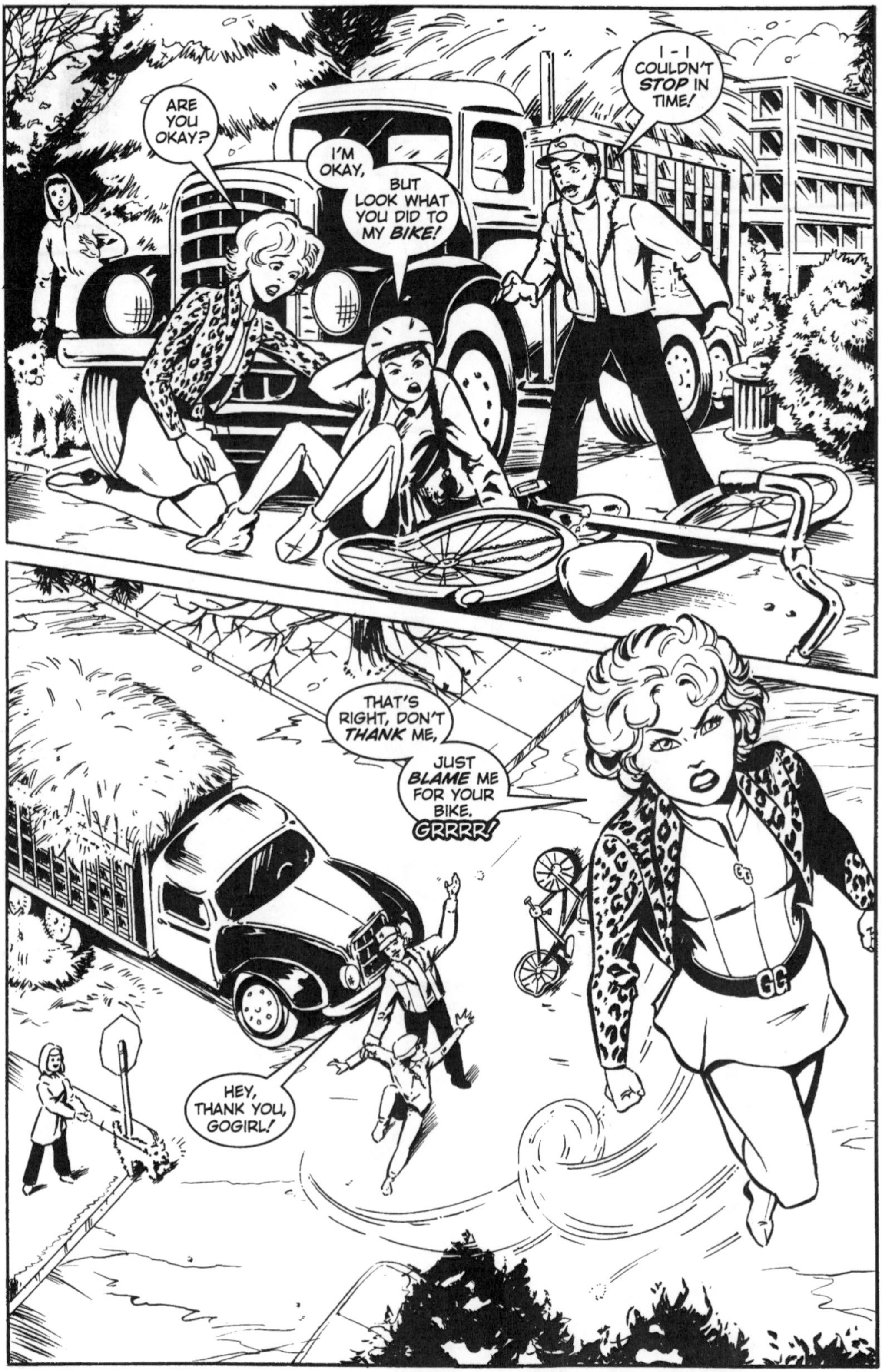
ARE YOU OKAY?
I'M OKAY,
BUT LOOK WHAT YOU DID TO MY BIKE!
I - I COULDN'T STOP IN TIME!
HEY, THANK YOU, GOGIRL!
THAT'S RIGHT, DON'T THANK ME,
JUST BLAME ME FOR YOUR BIKE.
GRRRR!

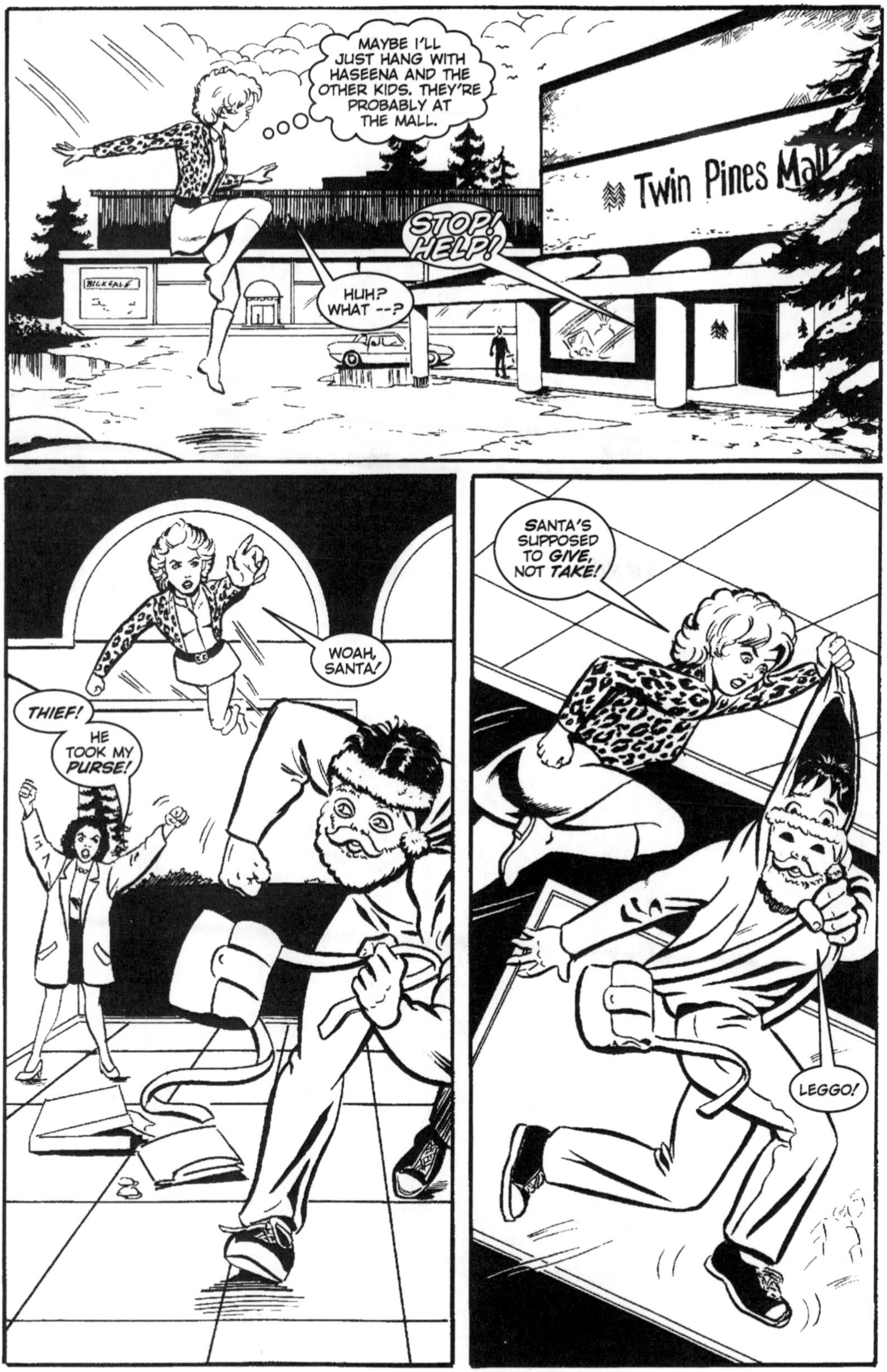

MAYBE I'LL JUST HANG WITH HASEENA AND THE OTHER KIDS. THEY'RE PROBABLY AT THE MALL.
Twin Pines Mall
STOP! HELP!
HUH? WHAT --?
WOAH, SANTA!
THIEF!
HE TOOK MY PURSE!
SANTA'S SUPPOSED TO GIVE, NOT TAKE!
LEGGO!

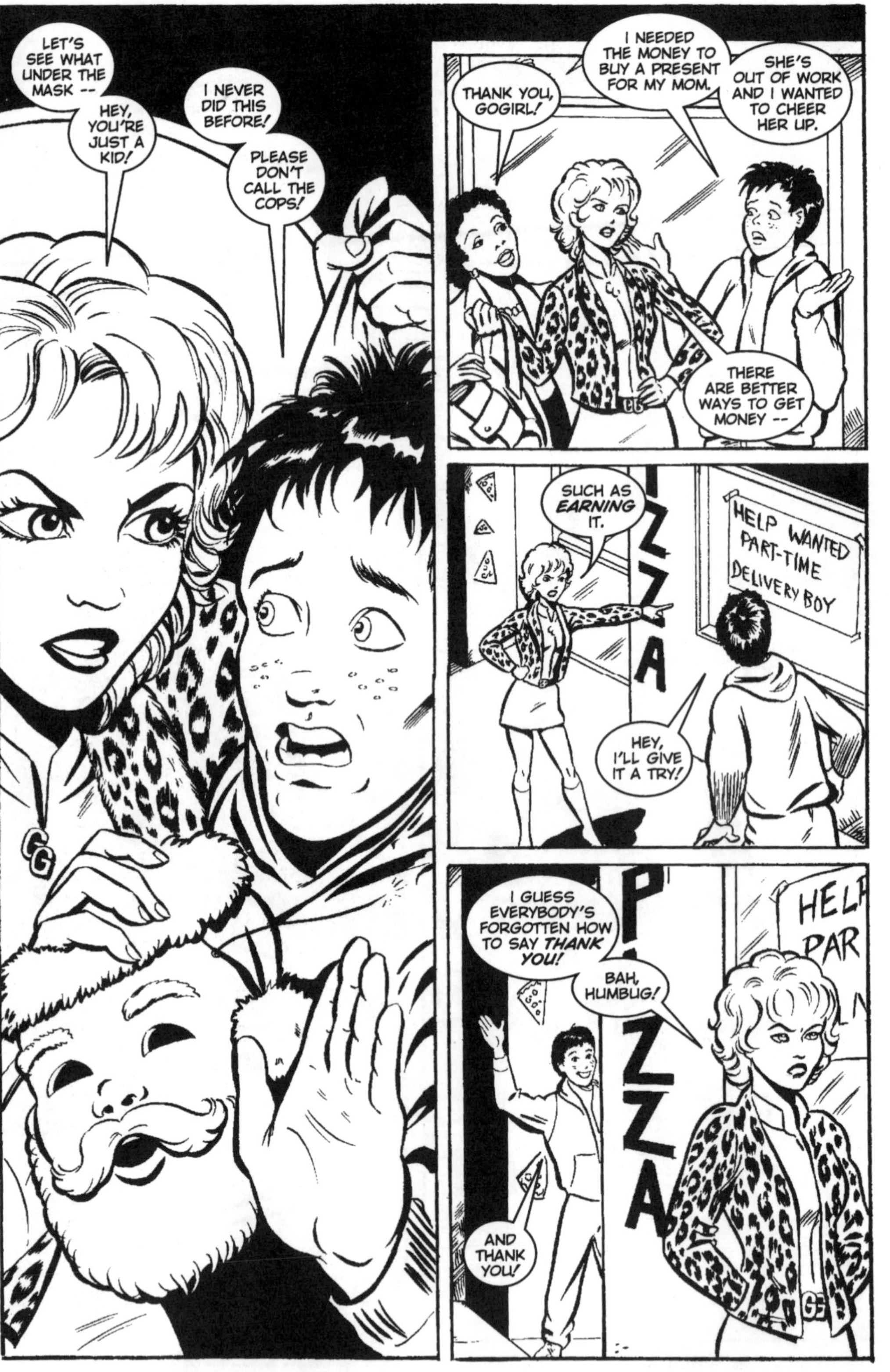
LET'S SEE WHAT UNDER THE MASK --
HEY, YOU'RE JUST A KID!
I NEVER DID THIS BEFORE!
PLEASE DON'T CALL THE COPS!
THANK YOU, GOGIRL!
I NEEDED THE MONEY TO BUY A PRESENT FOR MY MOM.
SHE'S OUT OF WORK AND I WANTED TO CHEER HER UP.
THERE ARE BETTER WAYS TO GET MONEY --
SUCH AS EARNING IT.
HELP WANTED PART-TIME DELIVERY BOY
HEY, I'LL GIVE IT A TRY!
I GUESS EVERYBODY'S FORGOTTEN HOW TO SAY THANK YOU!
BAH, HUMBUG!
AND THANK YOU!

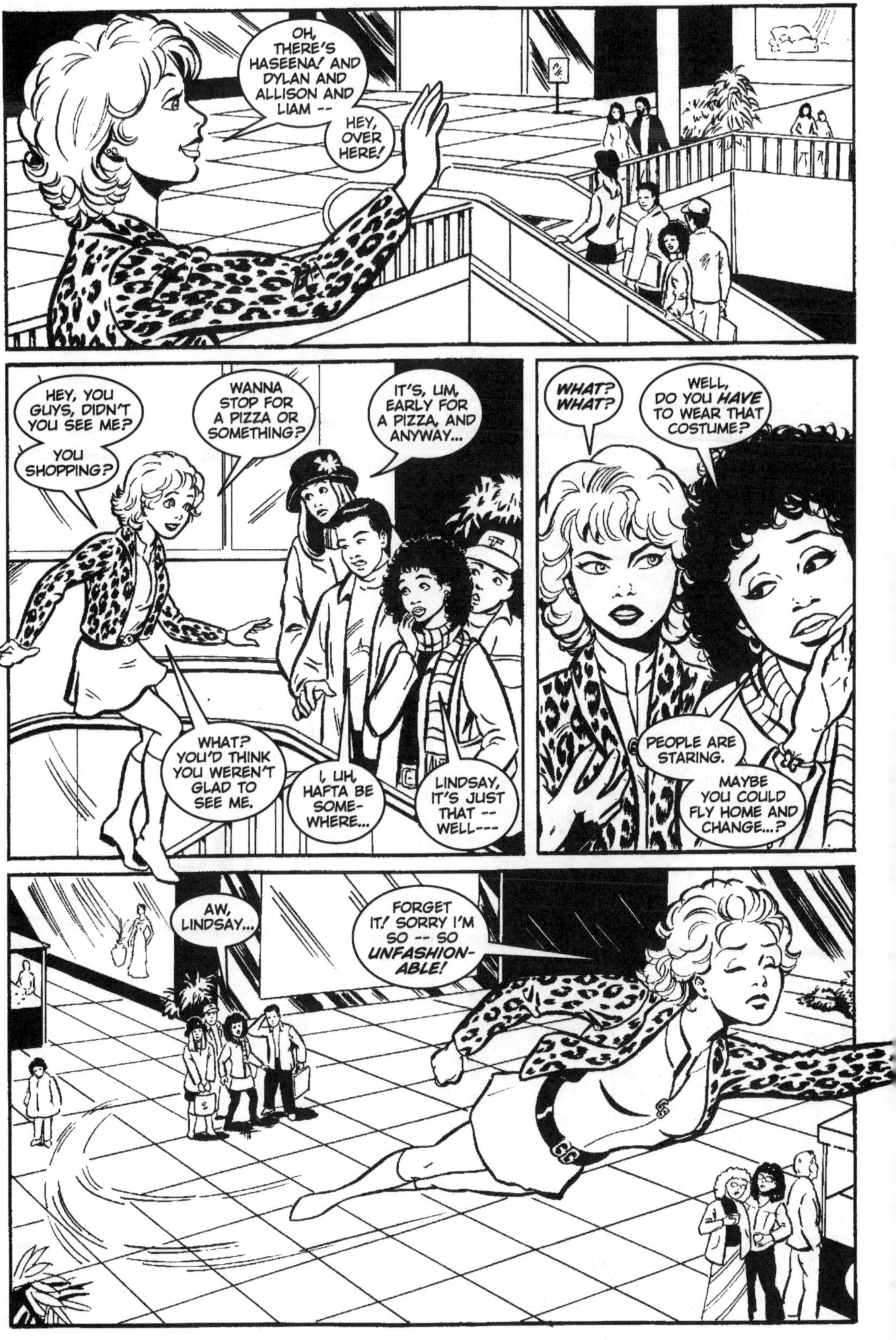

OH, THERE'S HASEENA! AND DYLAN AND ALLISON AND LIAM --
HEY, OVER HERE!
HEY, YOU GUYS, DIDN'T YOU SEE ME?
YOU SHOPPING?
WANNA STOP FOR A PIZZA OR SOMETHING?
IT'S, UM, EARLY FOR A PIZZA, AND ANYWAY...
WHAT? YOU'D THINK YOU WEREN'T GLAD TO SEE ME.
I, UH, HAFTA BE SOME-WHERE...
LINDSAY, IT'S JUST THAT -- WELL---
WHAT? WHAT?
WELL, DO YOU HAVE TO WEAR THAT COSTUME?
PEOPLE ARE STARING.
MAYBE YOU COULD FLY HOME AND CHANGE...?
AW, LINDSAY...
FORGET IT! SORRY I'M SO -- SO UNFASHION-ABLE!

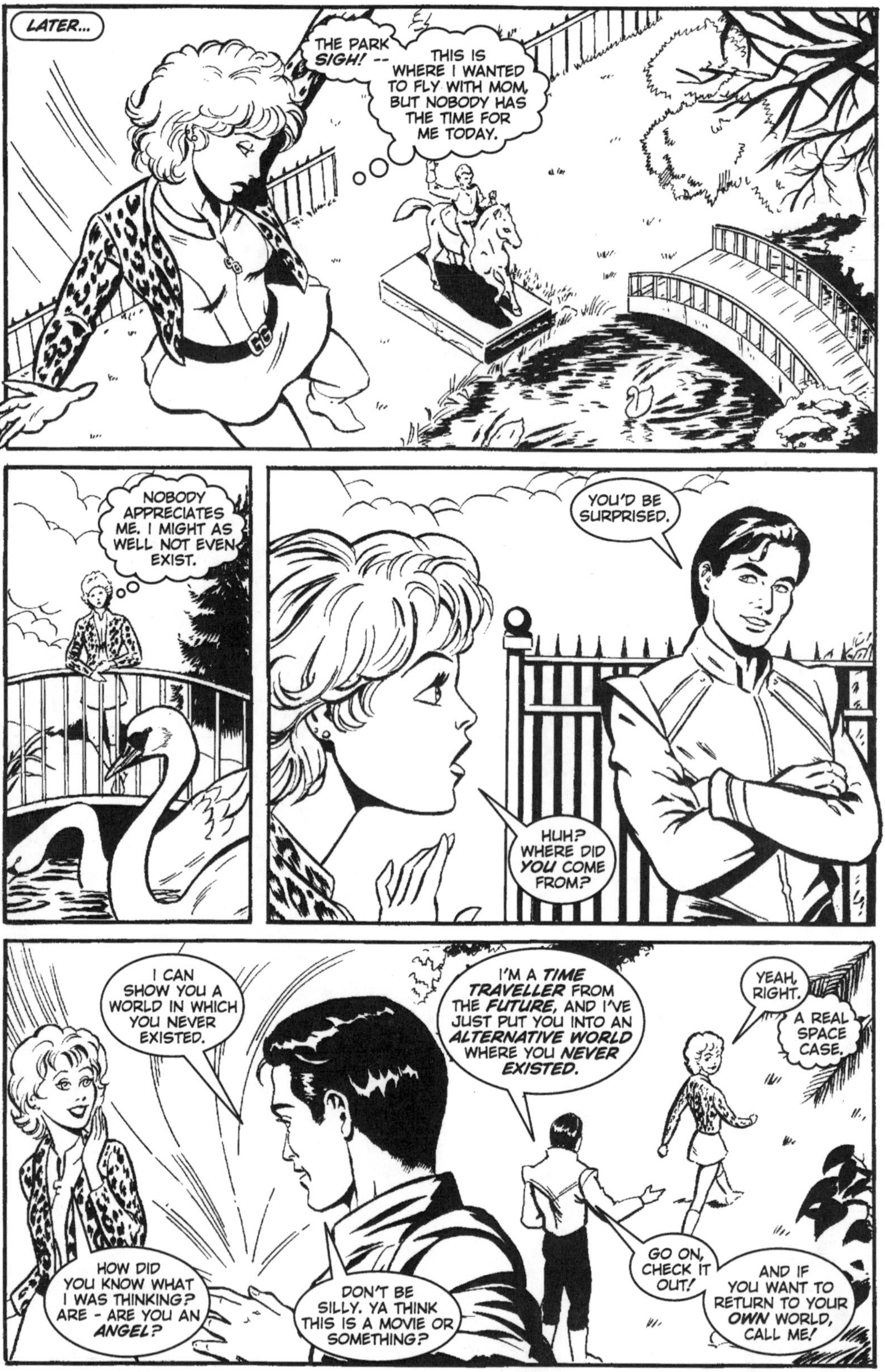
LATER...
THE PARK SIGH! --
THIS IS WHERE I WANTED TO FLY WITH MOM, BUT NOBODY HAS THE TIME FOR ME TODAY.
NOBODY APPRECIATES ME. I MIGHT AS WELL NOT EVEN EXIST.
YOU'D BE SURPRISED.
HUH? WHERE DID YOU COME FROM?
I CAN SHOW YOU A WORLD IN WHICH YOU NEVER EXISTED.
HOW DID YOU KNOW WHAT I WAS THINKING? ARE - ARE YOU AN ANGEL?
DON'T BE SILLY. YA THINK THIS IS A MOVIE OR SOMETHING?
I'M A TIME TRAVELLER FROM THE FUTURE, AND I'VE JUST PUT YOU INTO AN ALTERNATIVE WORLD WHERE YOU NEVER EXISTED.
GO ON, CHECK IT OUT!
AND IF YOU WANT TO RETURN TO YOUR OWN WORLD, CALL ME!
YEAH, RIGHT.
A REAL SPACE CASE.

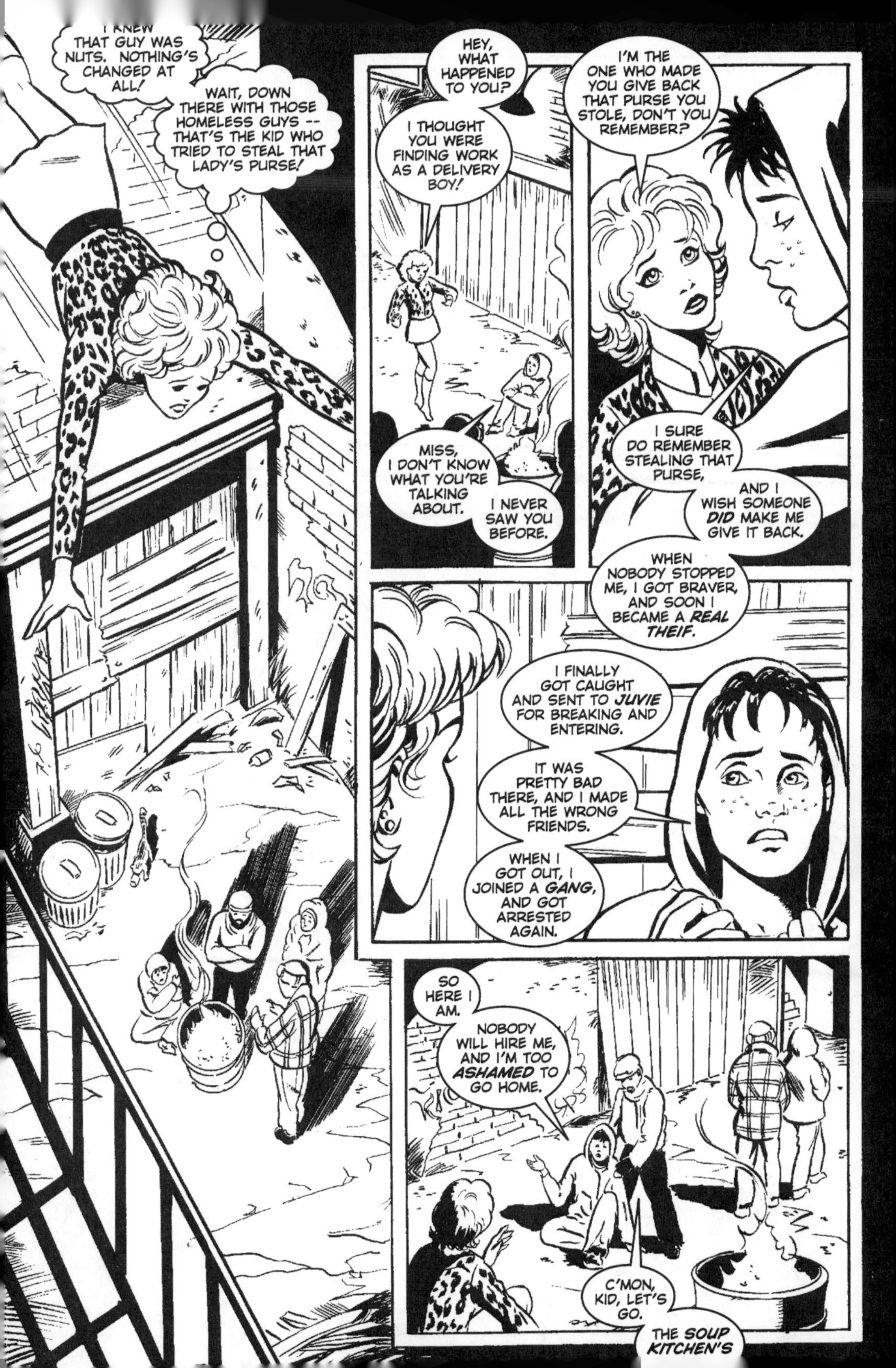

I KNEW THAT GUY WAS NUTS. NOTHING'S CHANGED AT ALL!
WAIT, DOWN THERE WITH THOSE HOMELESS GUYS -- THAT'S THE KID WHO TRIED TO STEAL THAT LADY'S PURSE!
HEY, WHAT HAPPENED TO YOU?
I THOUGHT YOU WERE FINDING WORK AS A DELIVERY BOY!
MISS, I DON'T KNOW WHAT YOU'RE TALKING ABOUT.
I NEVER SAW YOU BEFORE.
I'M THE ONE WHO MADE YOU GIVE BACK THAT PURSE YOU STOLE, DON'T YOU REMEMBER?
I SURE DO REMEMBER STEALING THAT PURSE,
AND I WISH SOMEONE DID MAKE ME GIVE IT BACK.
WHEN NOBODY STOPPED ME, I GOT BRAVER, AND SOON I BECAME A REAL THEIF.
I FINALLY GOT CAUGHT AND SENT TO JUVIE FOR BREAKING AND ENTERING.
IT WAS PRETTY BAD THERE, AND I MADE ALL THE WRONG FRIENDS.
WHEN I GOT OUT, I JOINED A GANG, AND GOT ARRESTED AGAIN.
SO HERE I AM.
NOBODY WILL HIRE ME, AND I'M TOO ASHAMED TO GO HOME.
C'MON, KID, LET'S GO.
THE SOUP KITCHEN'S

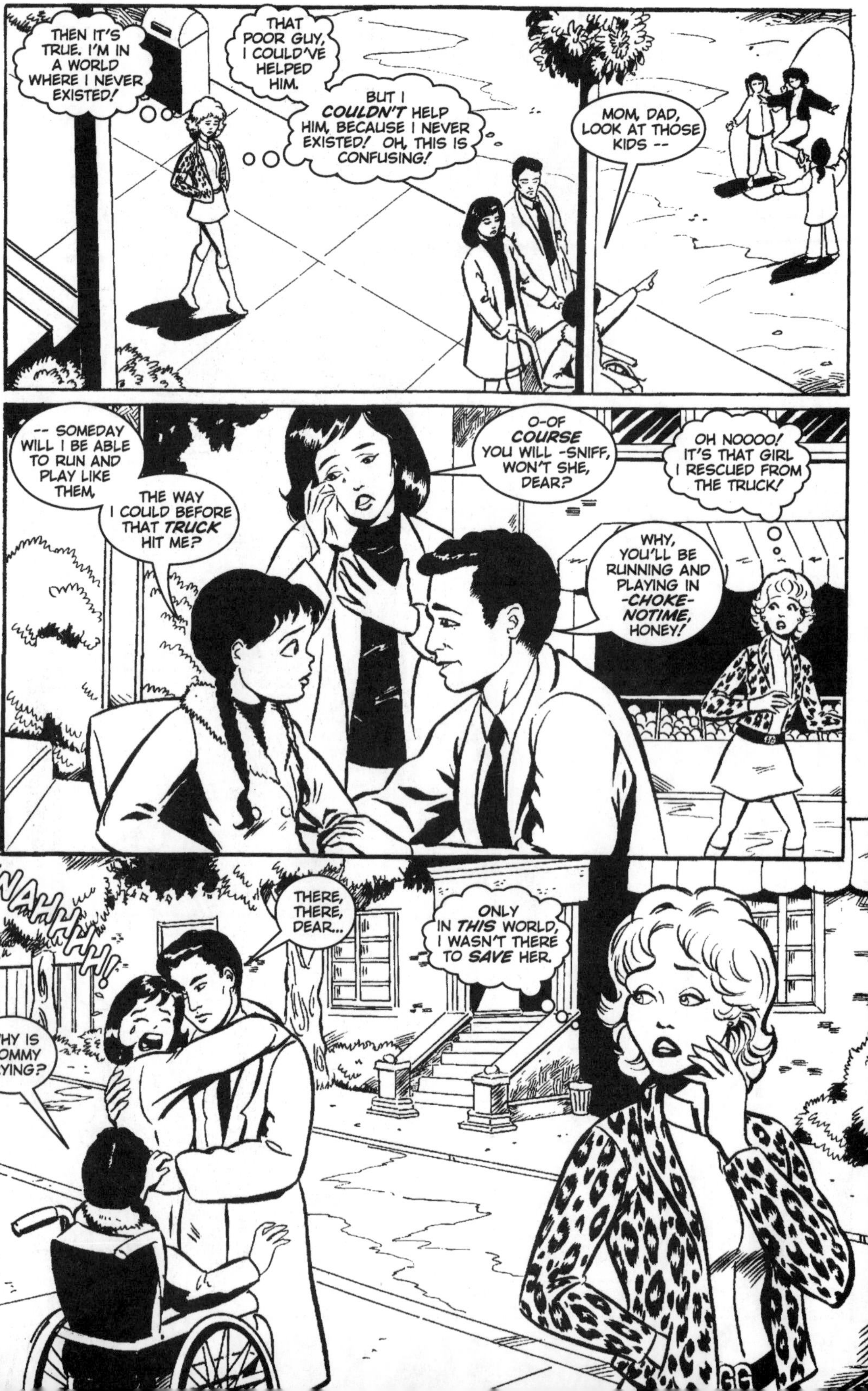
THEN IT'S TRUE. I'M IN A WORLD WHERE I NEVER EXISTED!
THAT POOR GUY, I COULD'VE HELPED HIM.
BUT I COULDN'T HELP HIM, BECAUSE I NEVER EXISTED! OH, THIS IS CONFUSING!
MOM, DAD, LOOK AT THOSE KIDS --
-- SOMEDAY WILL I BE ABLE TO RUN AND PLAY LIKE THEM,
THE WAY I COULD BEFORE THAT TRUCK HIT ME?
O-OF COURSE YOU WILL -SNIFF, WON'T SHE, DEAR?
OH NOOOO! IT'S THAT GIRL I RESCUED FROM THE TRUCK!
WHY, YOU'LL BE RUNNING AND PLAYING IN -CHOKE- NOTIME, HONEY!
WAHHHHH!
THERE, THERE, DEAR...
ONLY IN THIS WORLD, I WASN'T THERE TO SAVE HER.
WHY IS MOMMY CRYING?

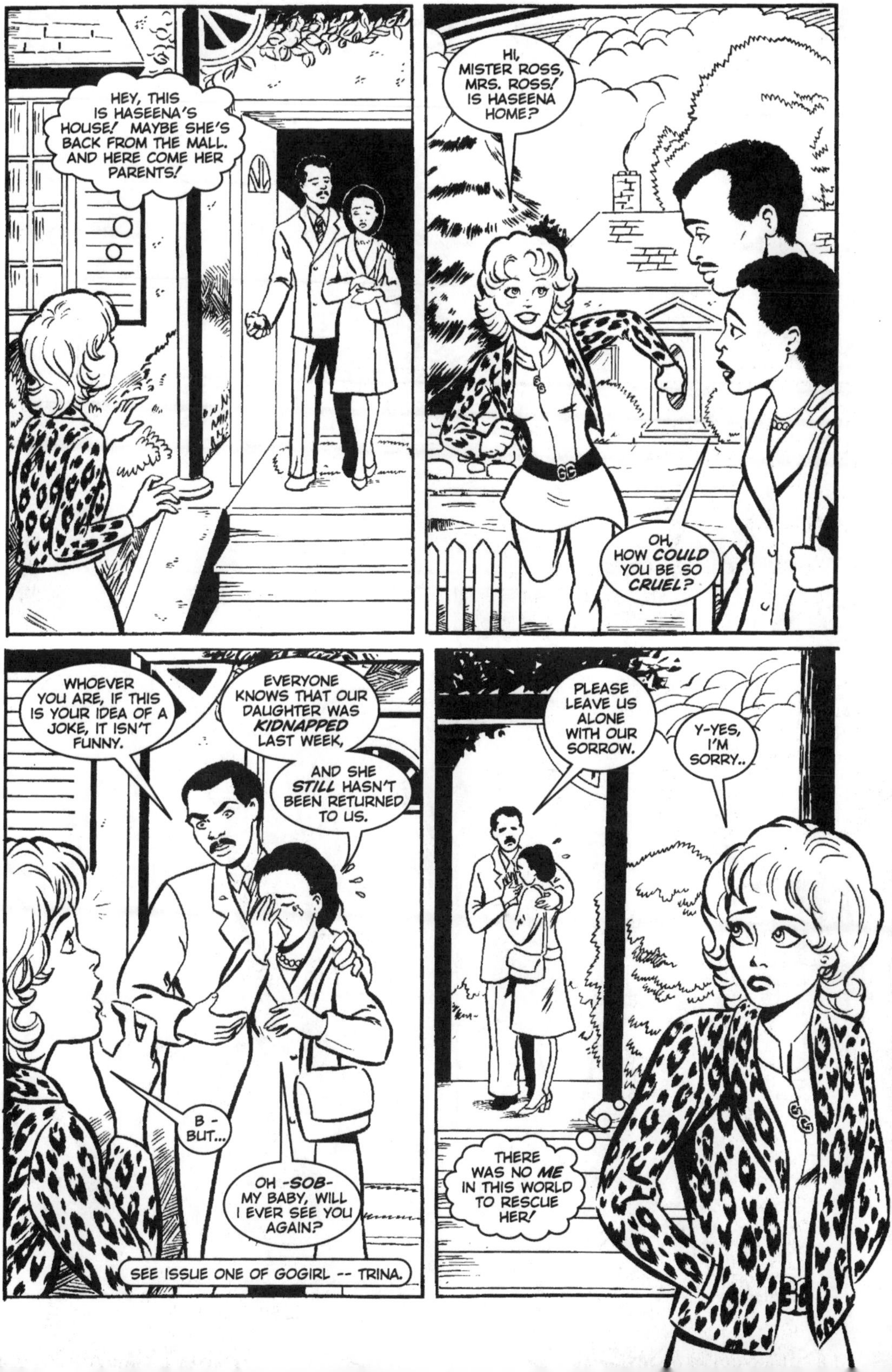
HEY, THIS IS HASEENA'S HOUSE! MAYBE SHE'S BACK FROM THE MALL. AND HERE COME HER PARENTS!
HI, MISTER ROSS, MRS. ROSS! IS HASEENA HOME?
OH, HOW COULD YOU BE SO CRUEL?
WHOEVER YOU ARE, IF THIS IS YOUR IDEA OF A JOKE, IT ISN'T FUNNY.
EVERYONE KNOWS THAT OUR DAUGHTER WAS KIDNAPPED LAST WEEK,
AND SHE STILL HASN'T BEEN RETURNED TO US.
B - BUT...
OH -SOB- MY BABY, WILL I EVER SEE YOU AGAIN?
SEE ISSUE ONE OF GOGIRL -- TRINA.
PLEASE LEAVE US ALONE WITH OUR SORROW.
Y-YES, I'M SORRY..
THERE WAS NO ME IN THIS WORLD TO RESCUE HER!

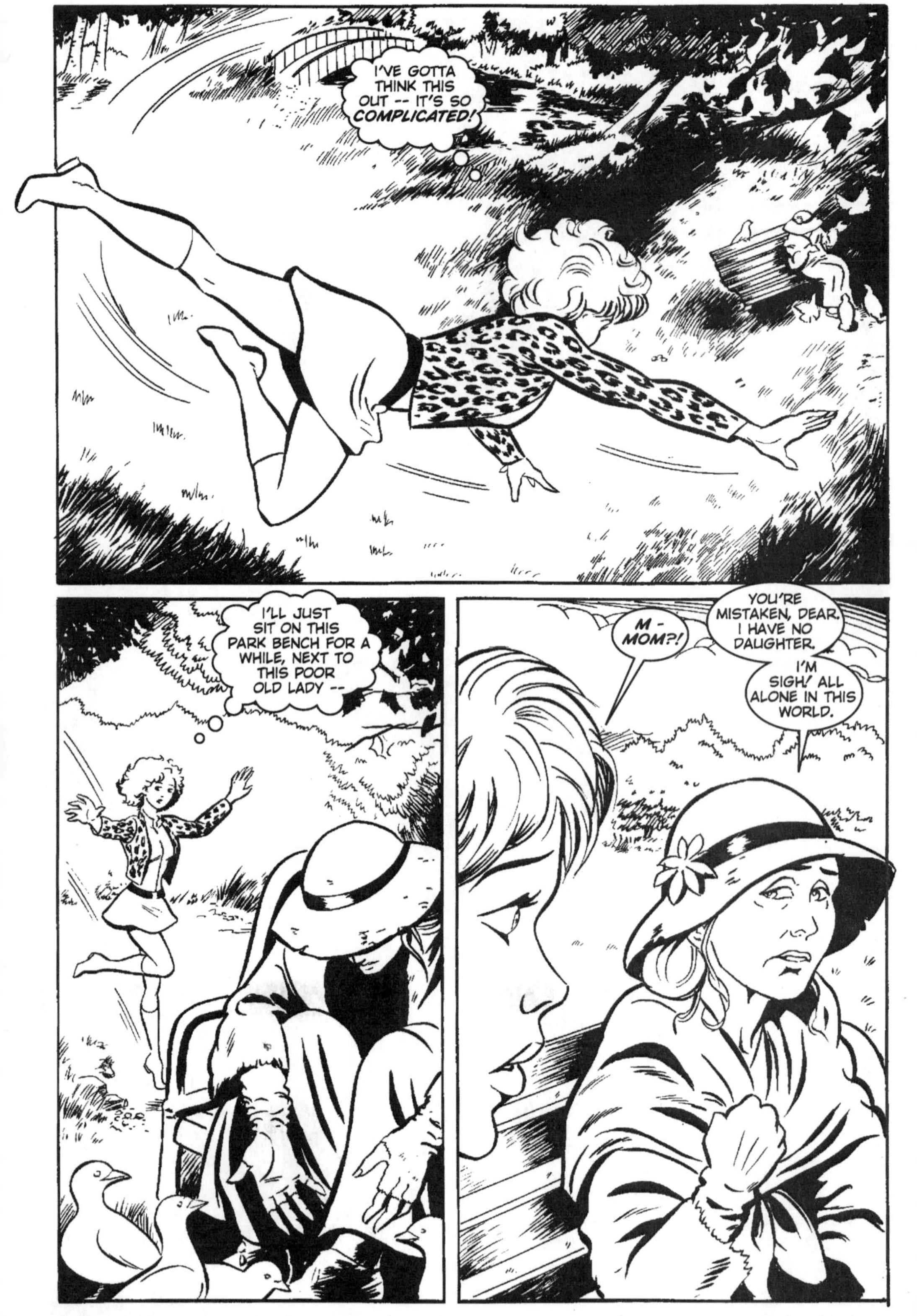
I'VE GOTTA THINK THIS OUT -- IT'S SO COMPLICATED!
I'LL JUST SIT ON THIS PARK BENCH FOR A WHILE, NEXT TO THIS POOR OLD LADY --
M - MOM?!
YOU'RE MISTAKEN, DEAR. I HAVE NO DAUGHTER.
I'M SIGH! ALL ALONE IN THIS WORLD.

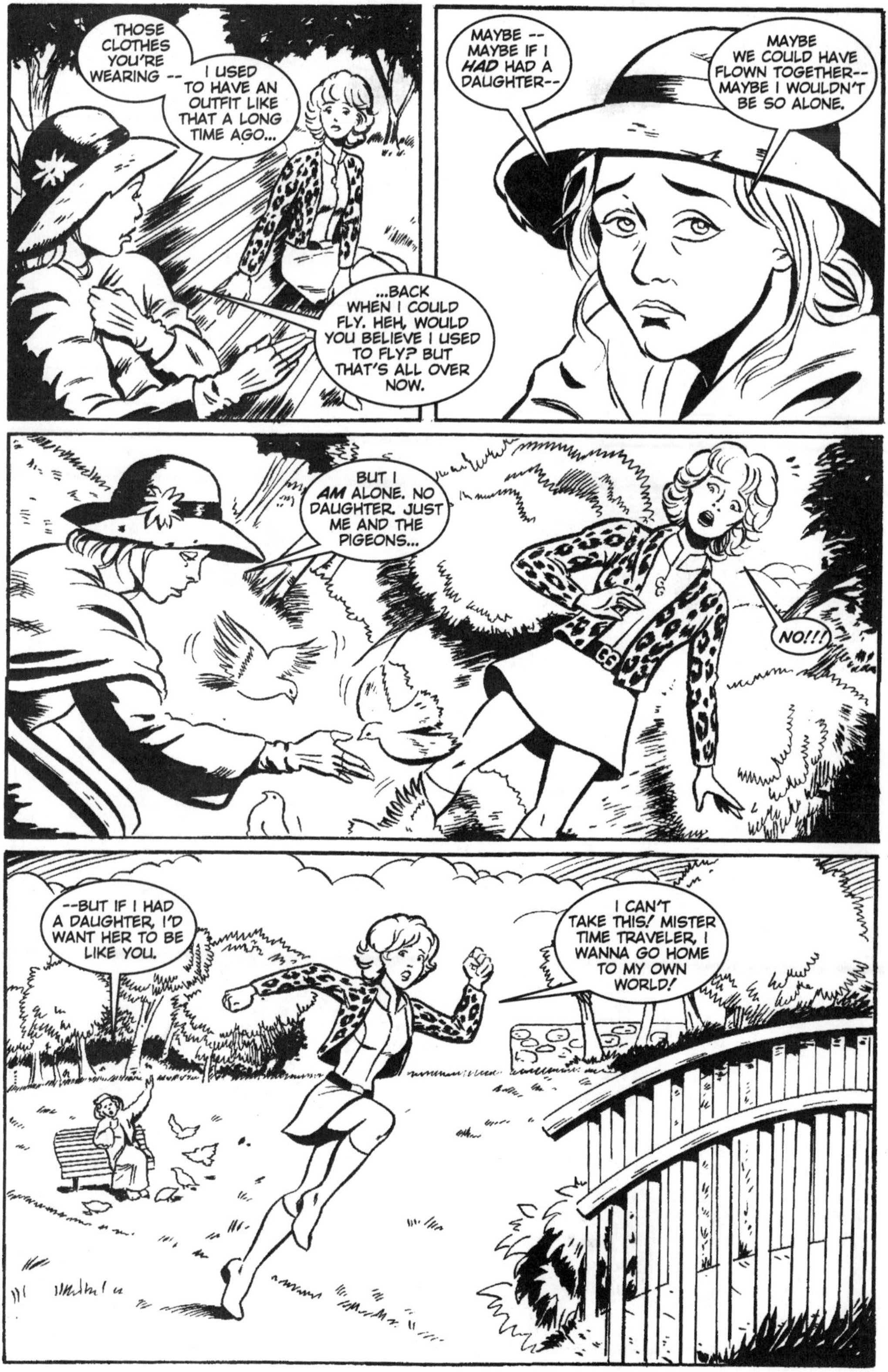
THOSE CLOTHES YOU'RE WEARING --
I USED TO HAVE AN OUTFIT LIKE THAT A LONG TIME AGO...
...BACK WHEN I COULD FLY. HEH, WOULD YOU BELIEVE I USED TO FLY? BUT THAT'S ALL OVER NOW.
MAYBE -- MAYBE IF I HAD HAD A DAUGHTER--
MAYBE WE COULD HAVE FLOWN TOGETHER-- MAYBE I WOULDN'T BE SO ALONE.
BUT I AM ALONE. NO DAUGHTER. JUST ME AND THE PIGEONS...
NO!!!
--BUT IF I HAD A DAUGHTER, I'D WANT HER TO BE LIKE YOU.
I CAN'T TAKE THIS! MISTER TIME TRAVELER, I WANNA GO HOME TO MY OWN WORLD!

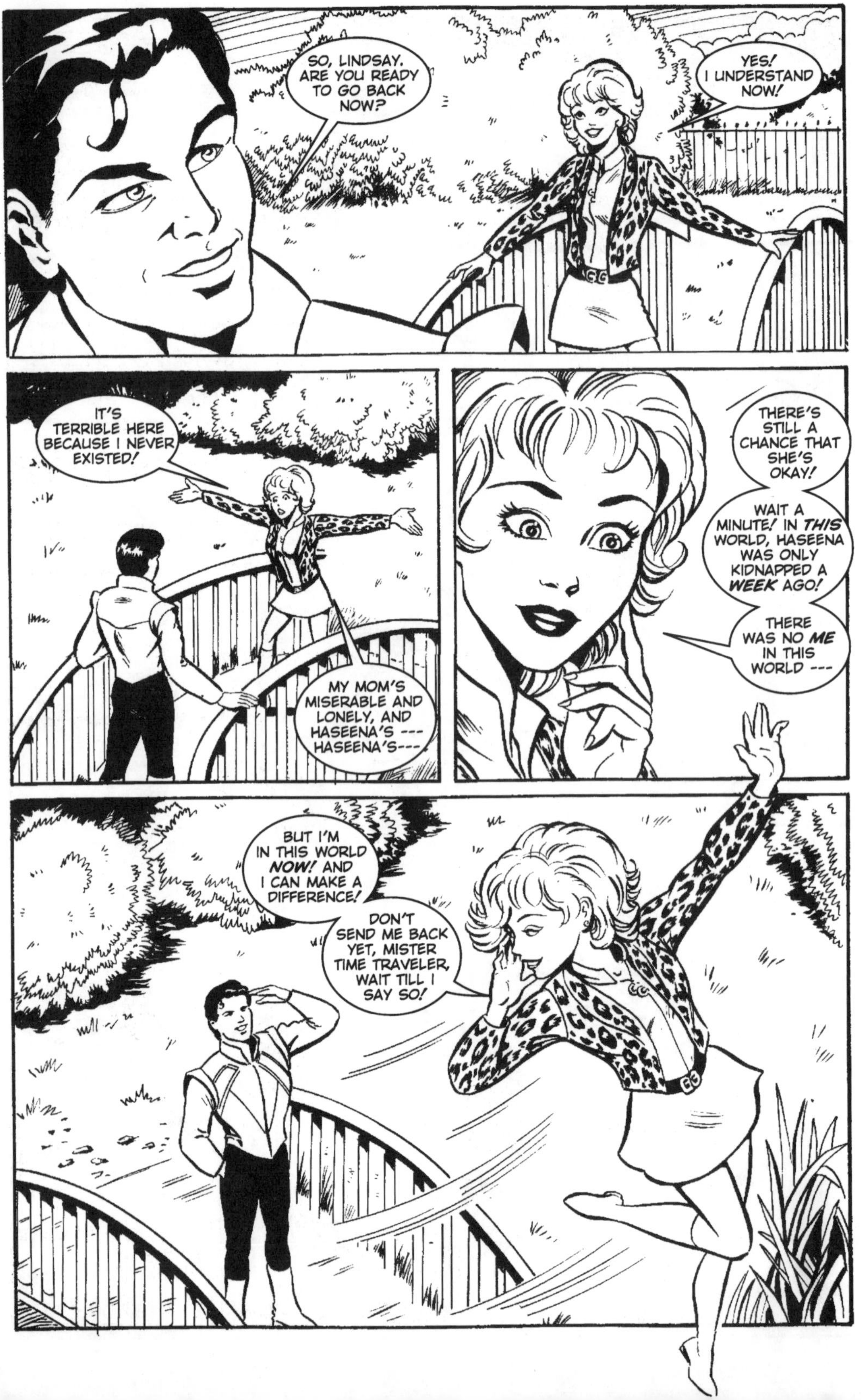
SO, LINDSAY. ARE YOU READY TO GO BACK NOW?
YES! I UNDERSTAND NOW!
IT'S TERRIBLE HERE BECAUSE I NEVER EXISTED!
MY MOM'S MISERABLE AND LONELY, AND HASEENA'S --- HASEENA'S---
THERE'S STILL A CHANCE THAT SHE'S OKAY!
WAIT A MINUTE! IN *THIS* WORLD, HASEENA WAS ONLY KIDNAPPED A *WEEK* AGO!
THERE WAS NO *ME* IN THIS WORLD ---
BUT I'M IN THIS WORLD *NOW!* AND I CAN MAKE A DIFFERENCE!
DON'T SEND ME BACK YET, MISTER TIME TRAVELER, WAIT TILL I SAY SO!

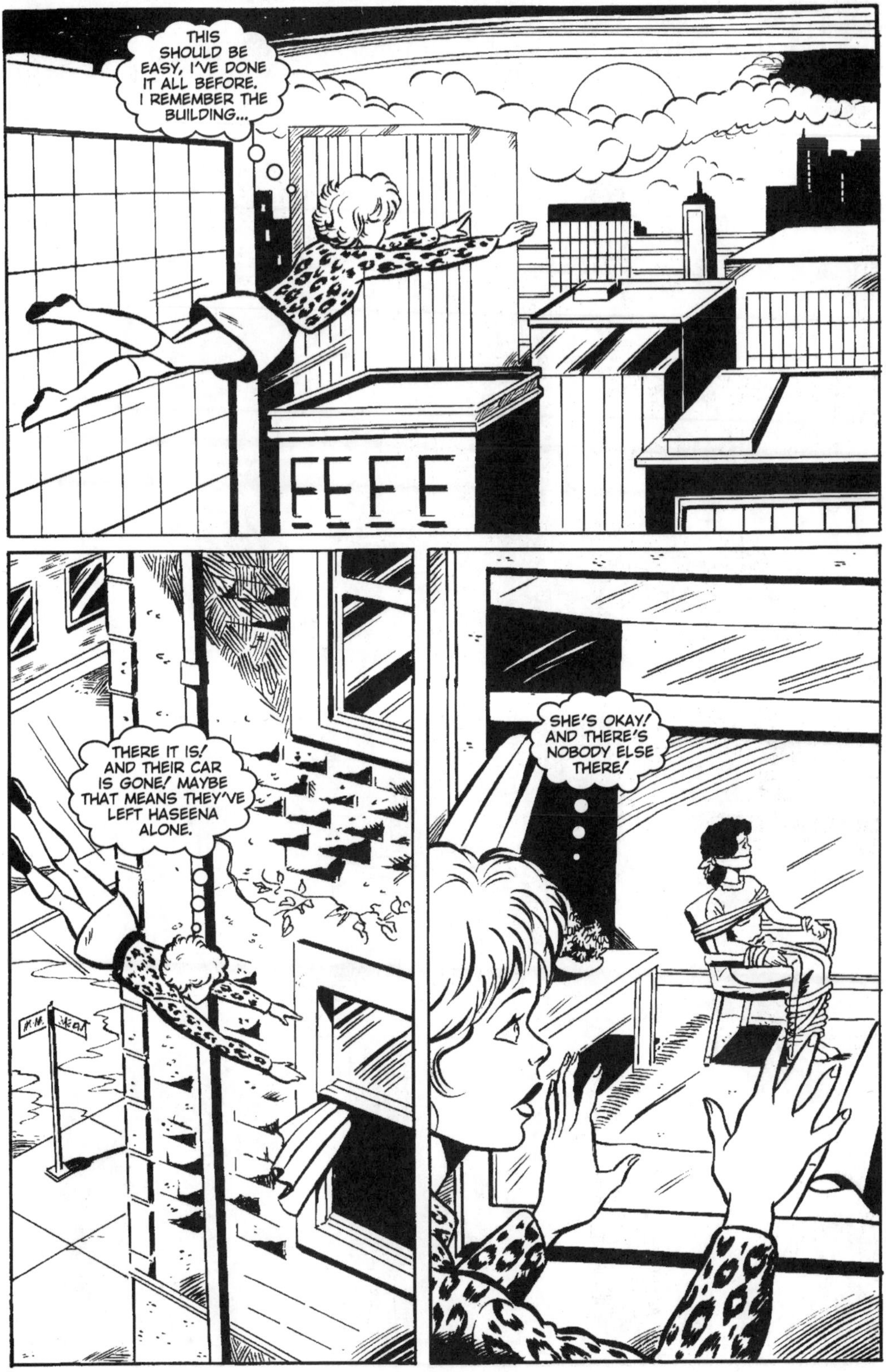
THIS SHOULD BE EASY, I'VE DONE IT ALL BEFORE. I REMEMBER THE BUILDING...
THERE IT IS! AND THEIR CAR IS GONE! MAYBE THAT MEANS THEY'VE LEFT HASEENA ALONE.
SHE'S OKAY! AND THERE'S NOBODY ELSE THERE!

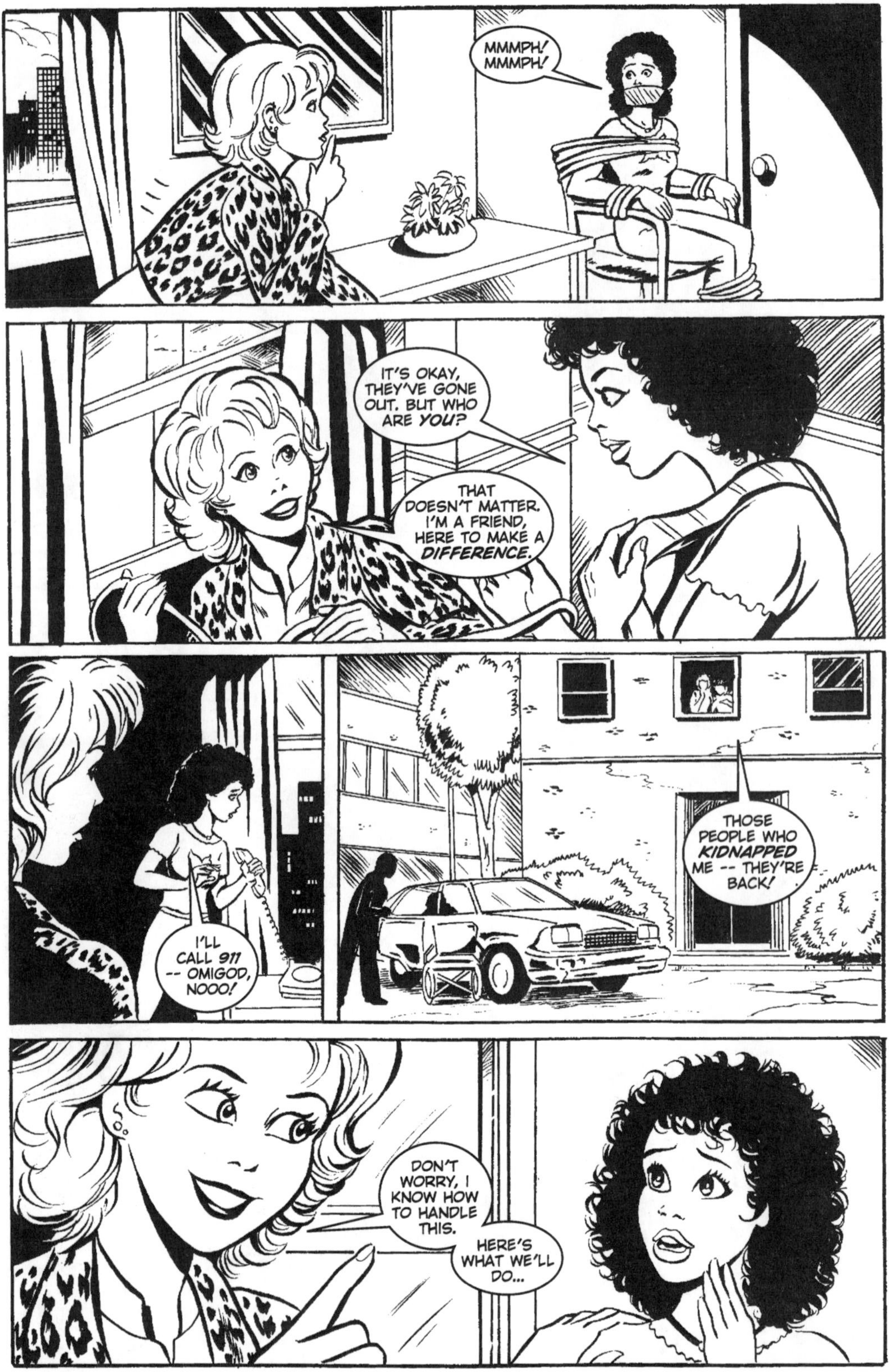
MMMPH! MMMPH!
IT'S OKAY, THEY'VE GONE OUT. BUT WHO ARE *YOU*?
THAT DOESN'T MATTER. I'M A FRIEND, HERE TO MAKE A *DIFFERENCE.*
I'LL CALL 911 -- OMIGOD, NOOO!
THOSE PEOPLE WHO *KIDNAPPED* ME -- THEY'RE BACK!
DON'T WORRY, I KNOW HOW TO HANDLE THIS.
HERE'S WHAT WE'LL DO...

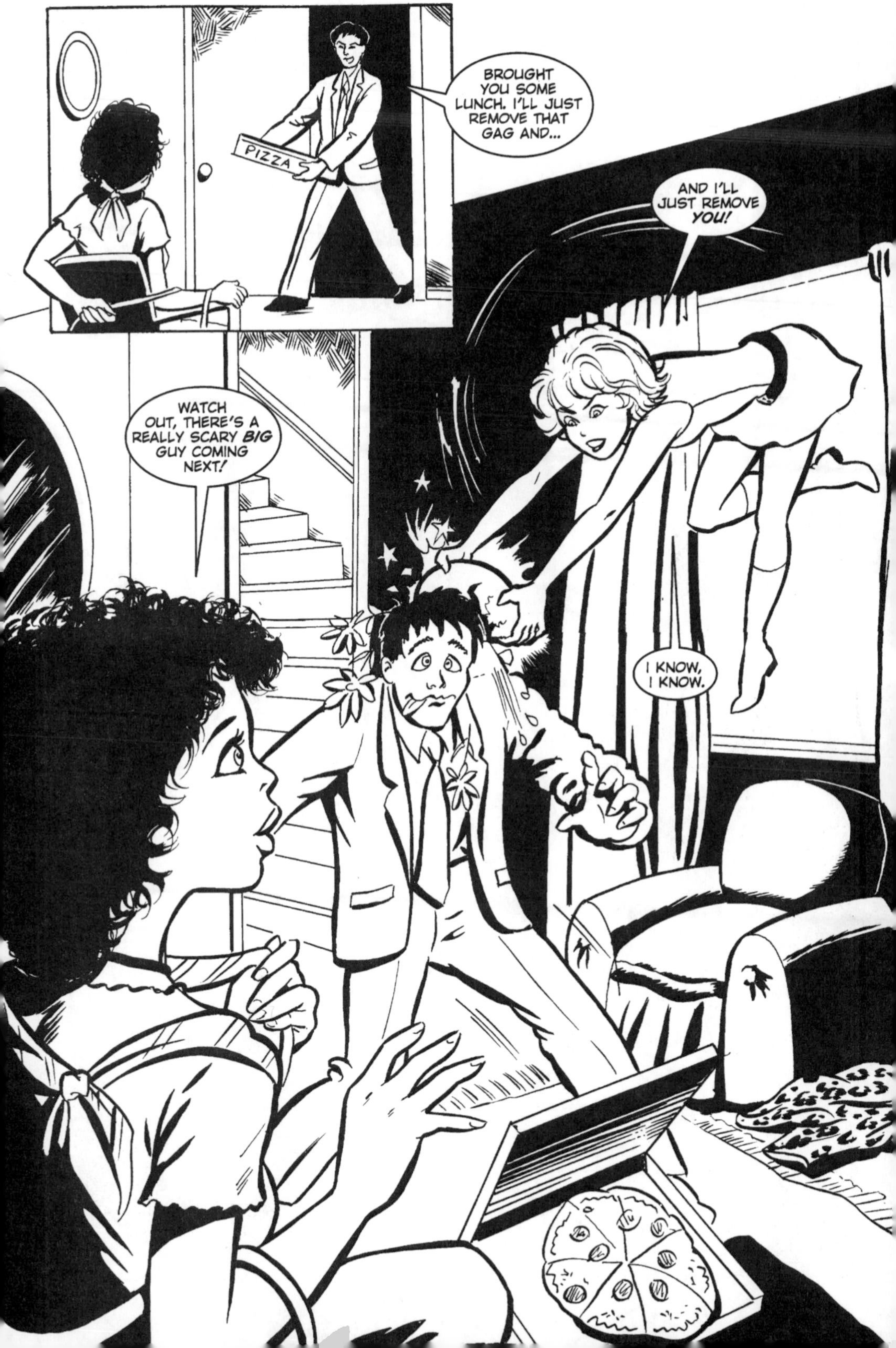
BROUGHT YOU SOME LUNCH. I'LL JUST REMOVE THAT GAG AND...
PIZZA
AND I'LL JUST REMOVE *YOU!*
WATCH OUT, THERE'S A REALLY SCARY *BIG* GUY COMING NEXT!
I KNOW, I KNOW.

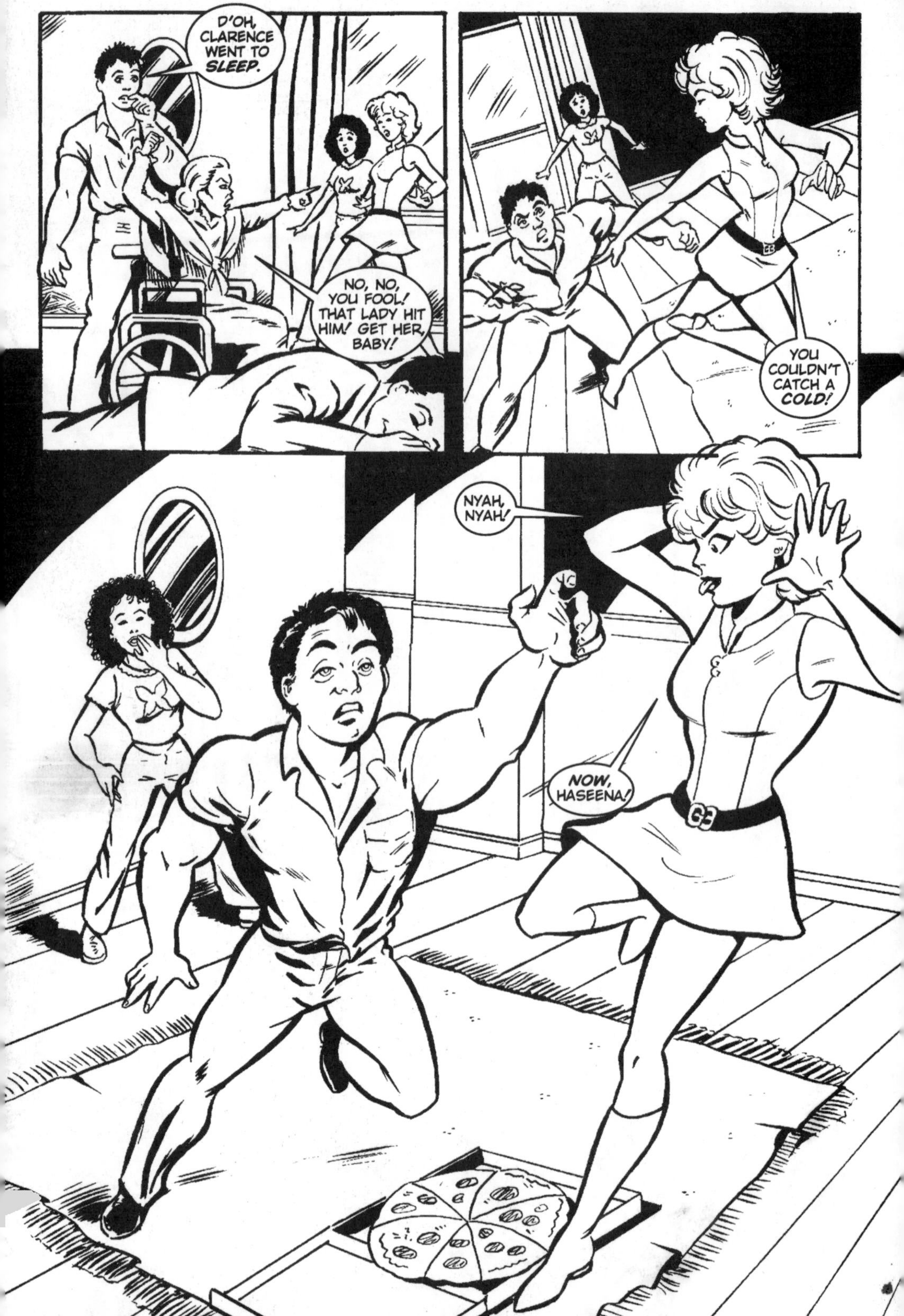
D'OH, CLARENCE WENT TO SLEEP.
NO, NO, YOU FOOL! THAT LADY HIT HIM! GET HER, BABY!
YOU COULDN'T CATCH A COLD!
NYAH, NYAH!
NOW, HASEENA!

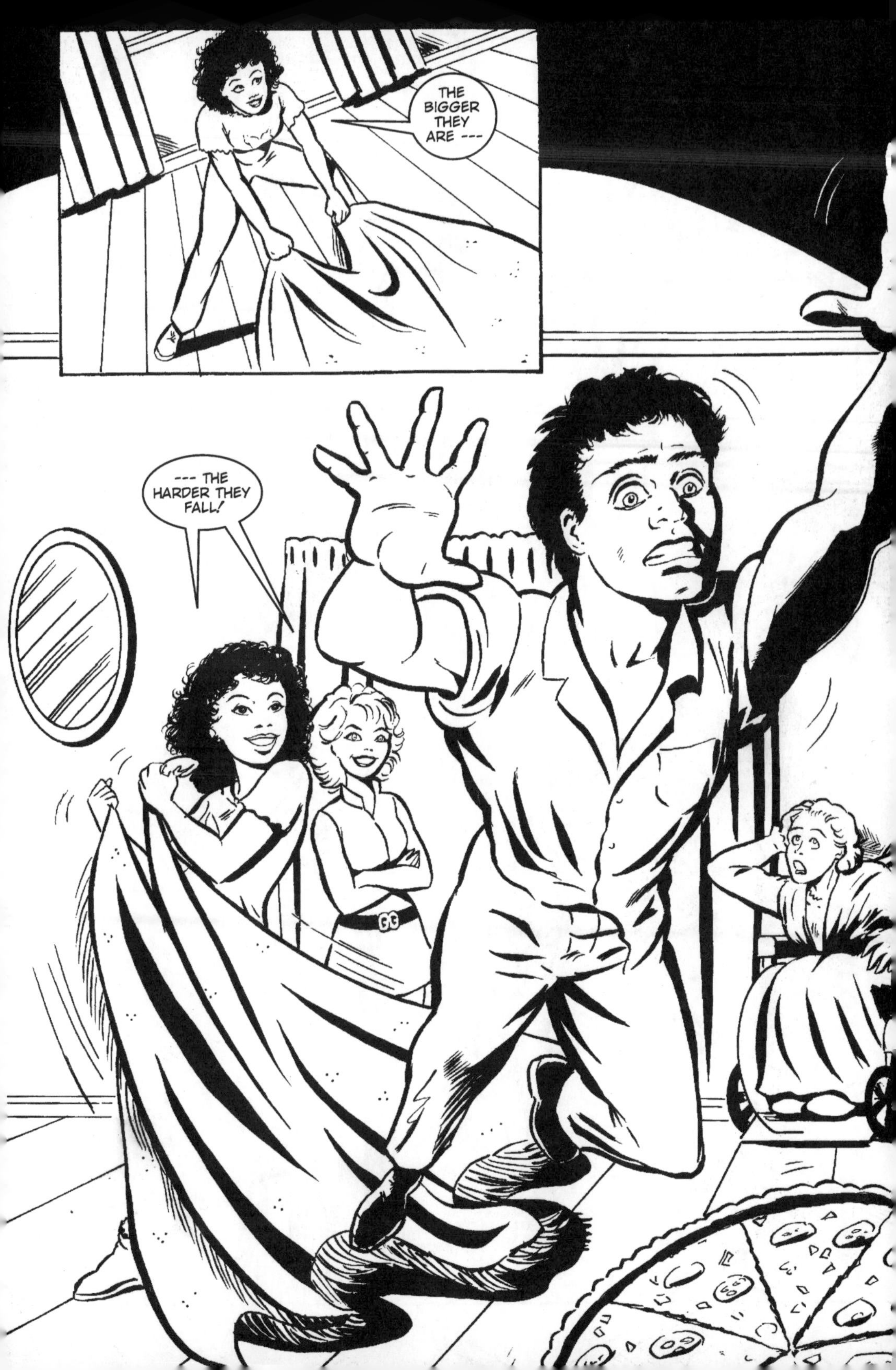
THE BIGGER THEY ARE ---
--- THE HARDER THEY FALL!

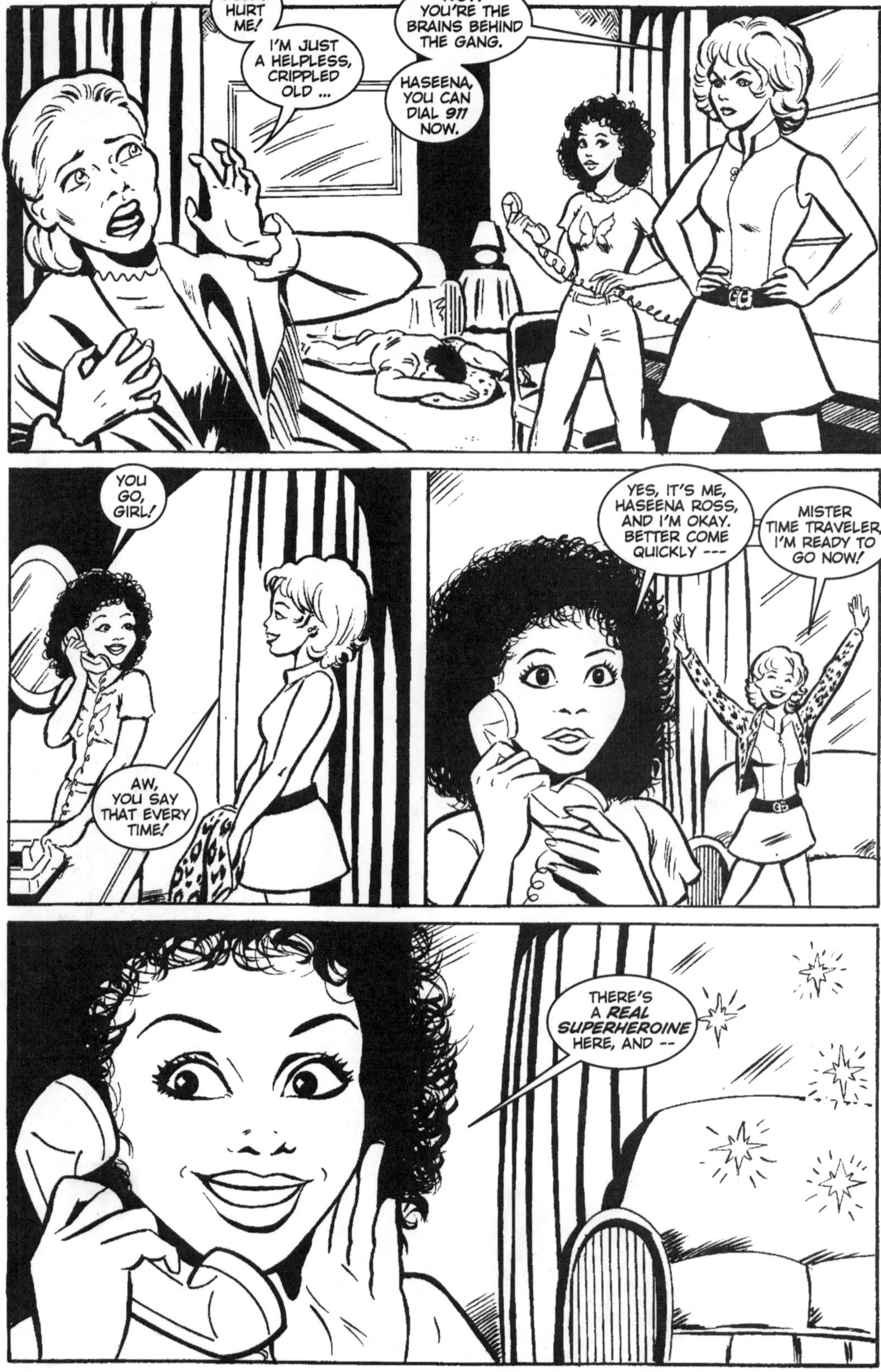
DON'T HURT ME!
I'M JUST A HELPLESS, CRIPPLED OLD ...
NOT! YOU'RE THE BRAINS BEHIND THE GANG.
HASEENA, YOU CAN DIAL 911 NOW.
YOU GO, GIRL!
AW, YOU SAY THAT EVERY TIME!
YES, IT'S ME, HASEENA ROSS, AND I'M OKAY. BETTER COME QUICKLY ---
MISTER TIME TRAVELER, I'M READY TO GO NOW!
THERE'S A REAL SUPERHEROINE HERE, AND --

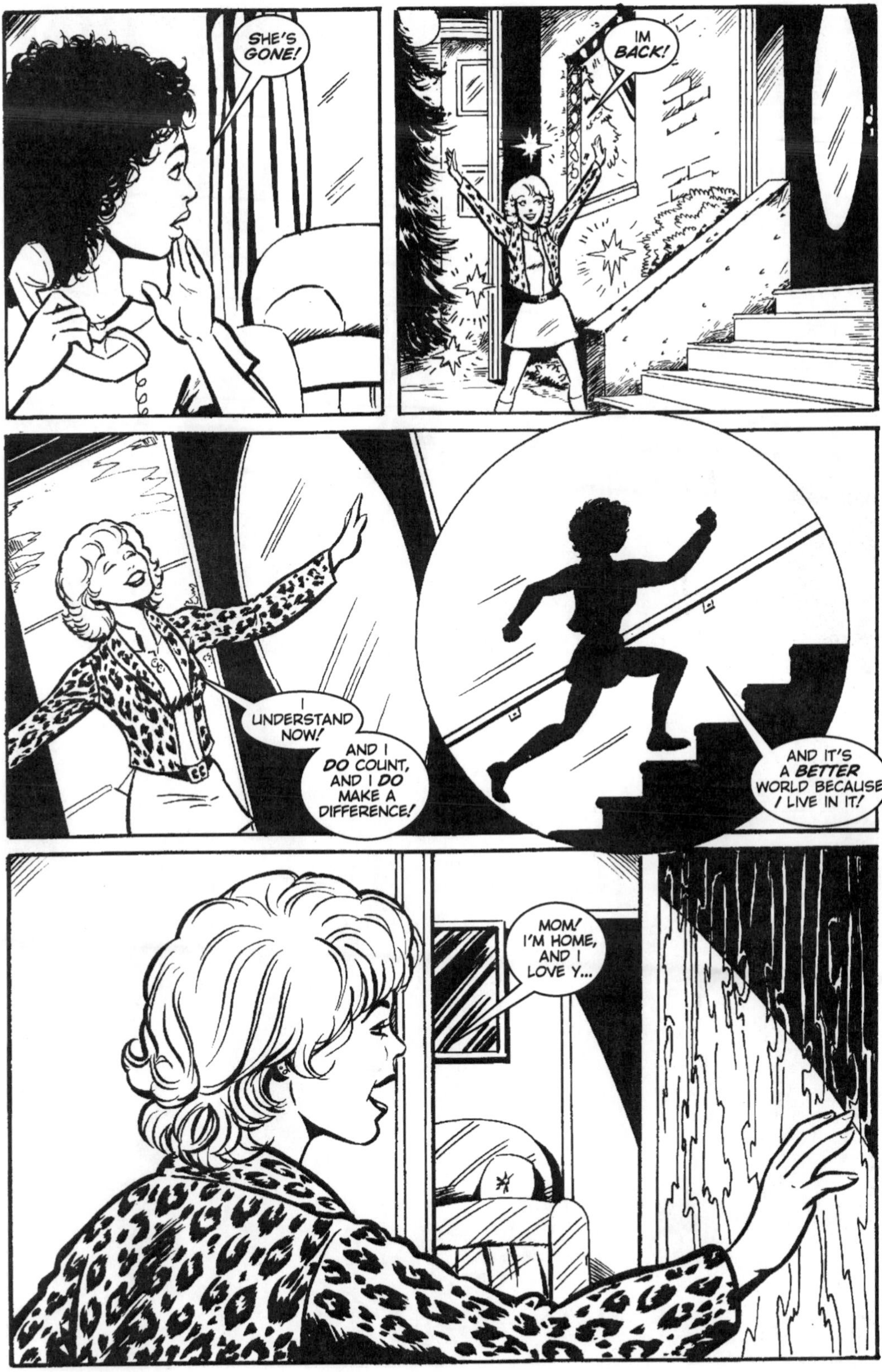
SHE'S GONE!
IM BACK!
I UNDERSTAND NOW!
AND I DO COUNT, AND I DO MAKE A DIFFERENCE!
AND IT'S A BETTER WORLD BECAUSE I LIVE IN IT!
MOM! I'M HOME, AND I LOVE Y...

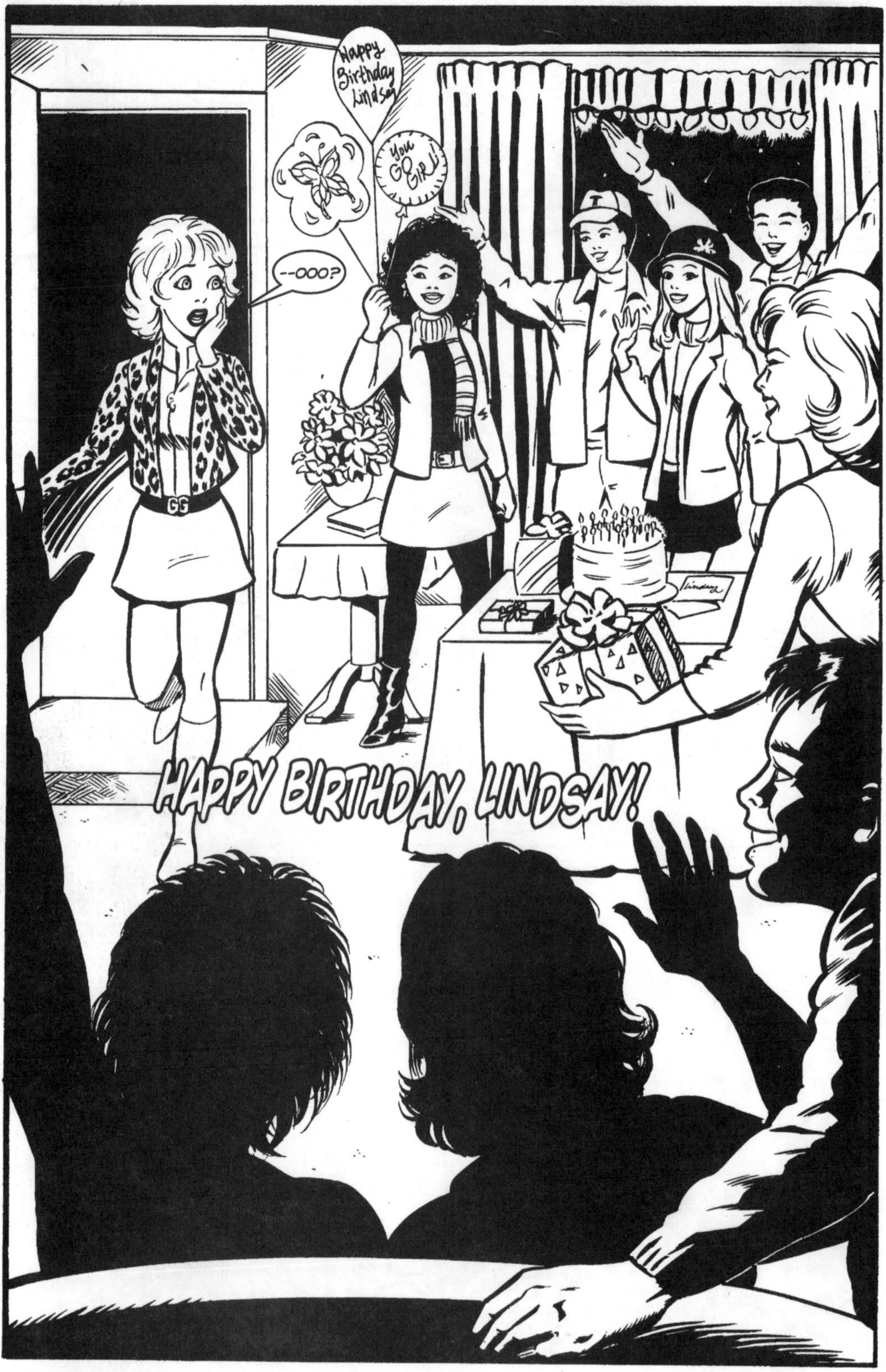
Happy Birthday Lindsay
You GO GIRL!
--OOO?
HAPPY BIRTHDAY, LINDSAY!

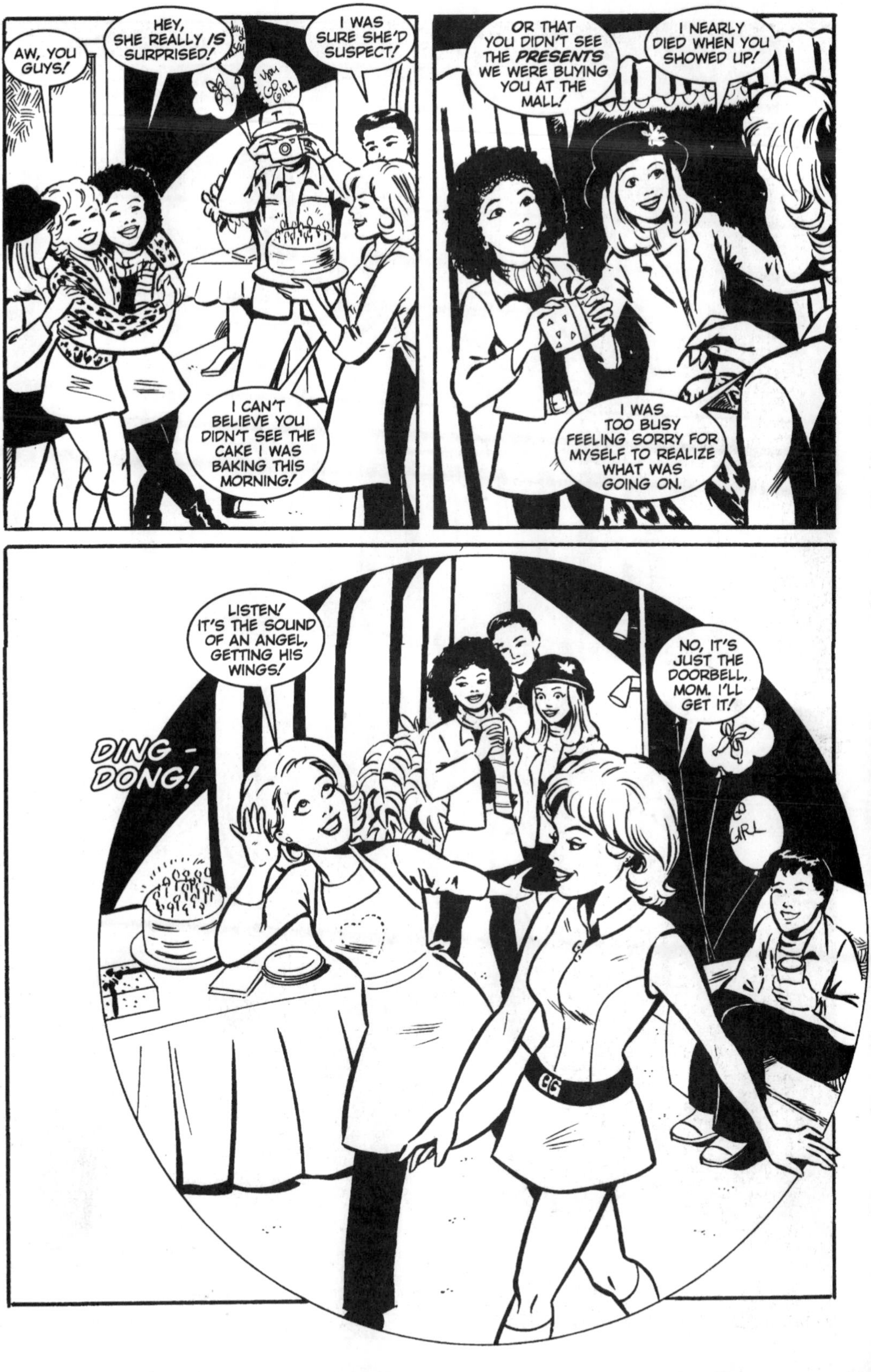
AW, YOU GUYS!
HEY, SHE REALLY IS SURPRISED!
I WAS SURE SHE'D SUSPECT!
I CAN'T BELIEVE YOU DIDN'T SEE THE CAKE I WAS BAKING THIS MORNING!
OR THAT YOU DIDN'T SEE THE PRESENTS WE WERE BUYING YOU AT THE MALL!
I NEARLY DIED WHEN YOU SHOWED UP!
I WAS TOO BUSY FEELING SORRY FOR MYSELF TO REALIZE WHAT WAS GOING ON.
DING - DONG!
LISTEN! IT'S THE SOUND OF AN ANGEL, GETTING HIS WINGS!
NO, IT'S JUST THE DOORBELL, MOM. I'LL GET IT!

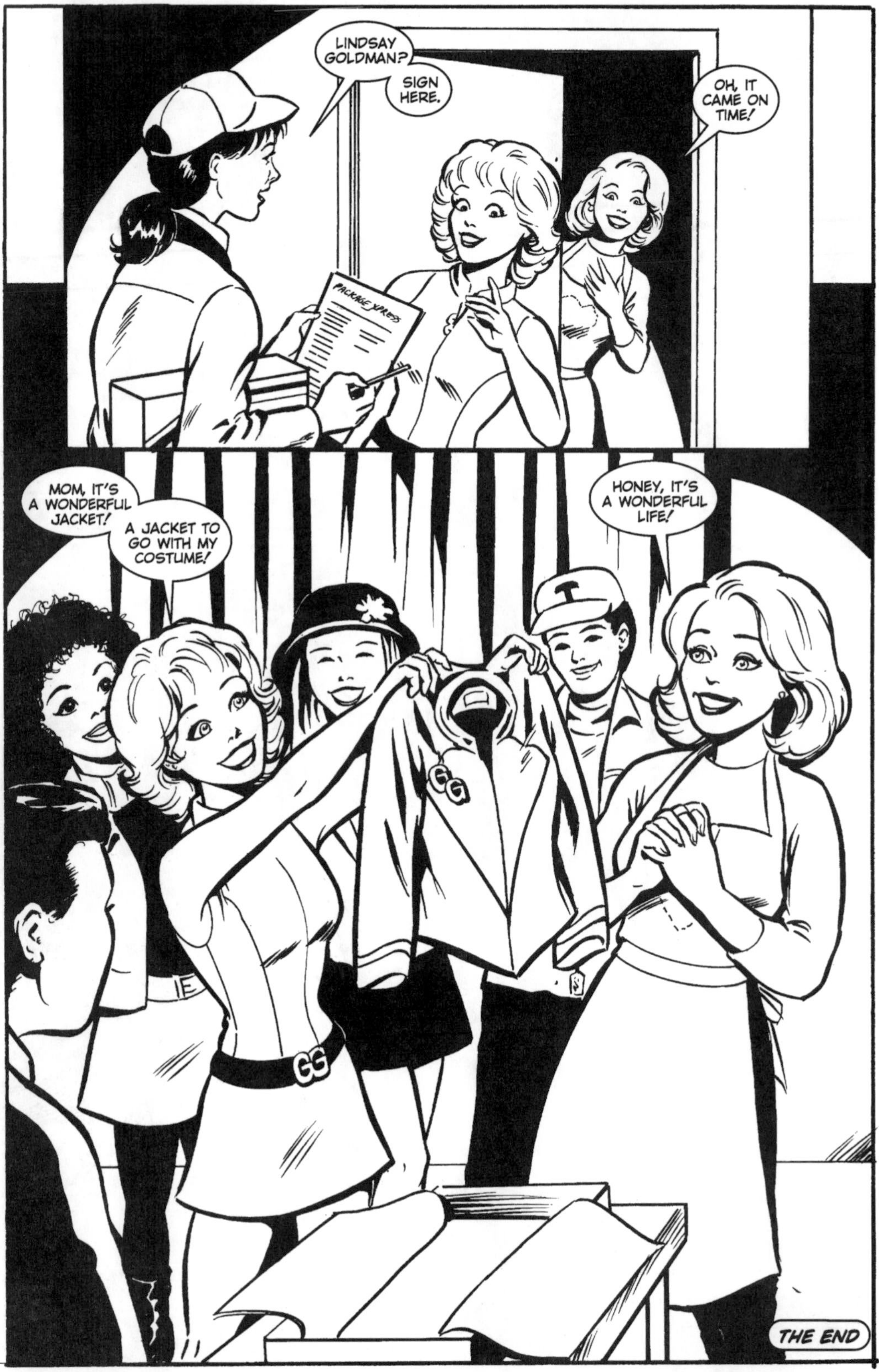
LINDSAY GOLDMAN?
SIGN HERE.
OH, IT CAME ON TIME!
PACKAGE XPRESS
MOM, IT'S A WONDERFUL JACKET!
A JACKET TO GO WITH MY COSTUME!
HONEY, IT'S A WONDERFUL LIFE!
THE END

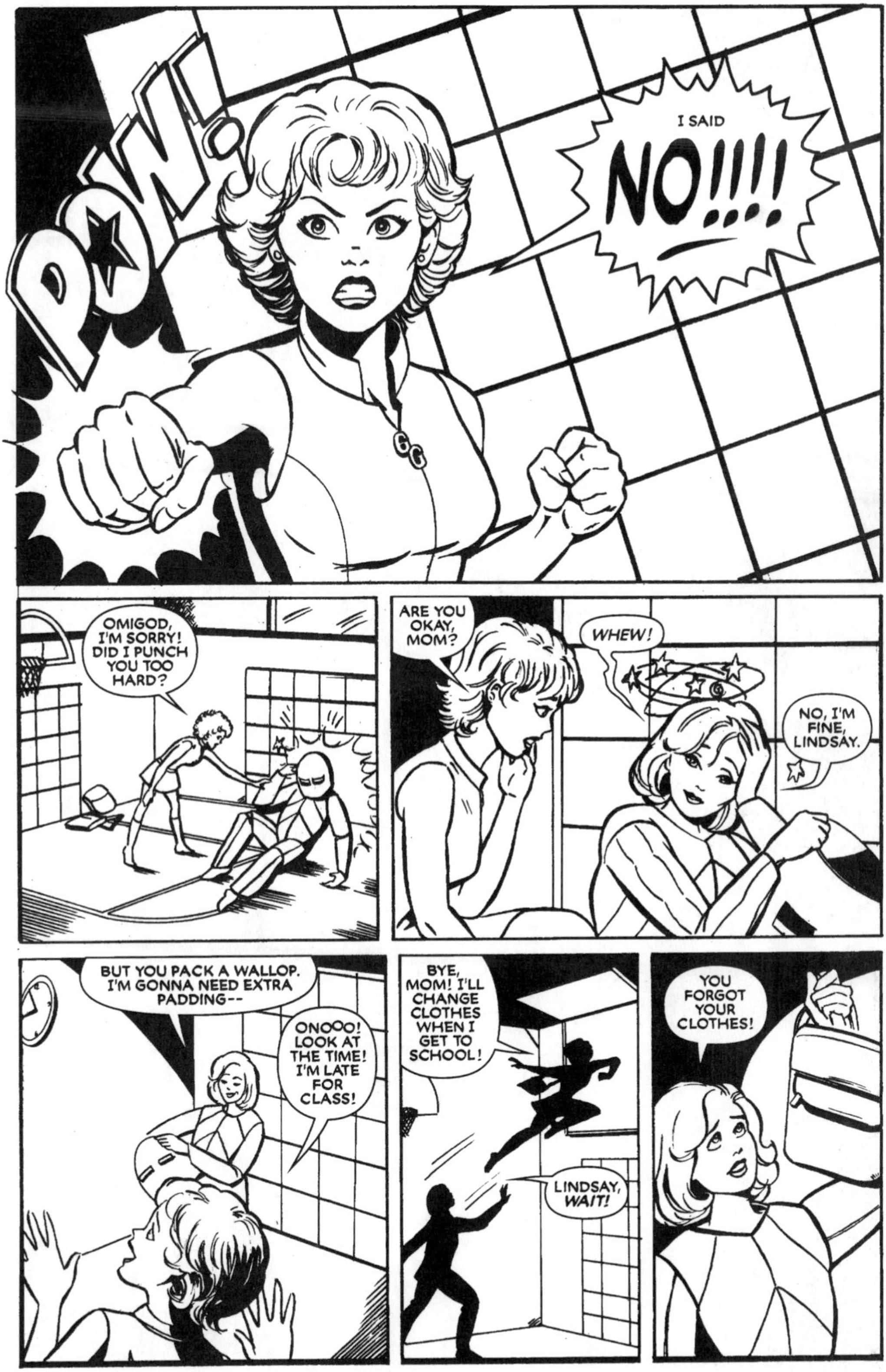
POW!
I SAID NO!!!!!
OMIGOD, I'M SORRY! DID I PUNCH YOU TOO HARD?
ARE YOU OKAY, MOM?
WHEW!
NO, I'M FINE, LINDSAY.
BUT YOU PACK A WALLOP. I'M GONNA NEED EXTRA PADDING--
ONOOO! LOOK AT THE TIME! I'M LATE FOR CLASS!
BYE, MOM! I'LL CHANGE CLOTHES WHEN I GET TO SCHOOL!
LINDSAY, WAIT!
YOU FORGOT YOUR CLOTHES!

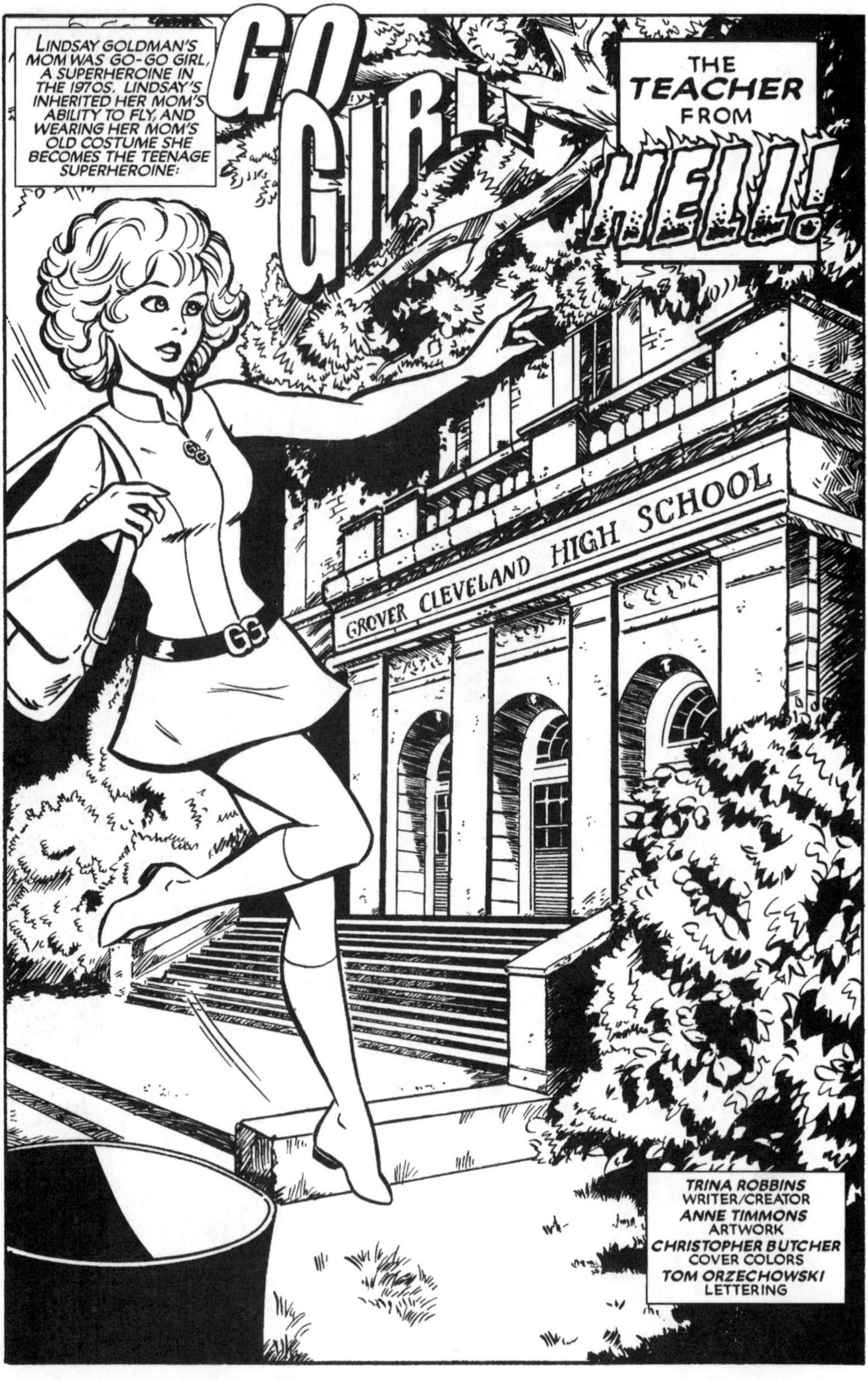
LINDSAY GOLDMAN'S MOM WAS GO-GO GIRL, A SUPERHEROINE IN THE 1970S. LINDSAY'S INHERITED HER MOM'S ABILITY TO FLY, AND WEARING HER MOM'S OLD COSTUME SHE BECOMES THE TEENAGE SUPERHEROINE:
GO GIRL!
THE TEACHER FROM HELL!
GROVER CLEVELAND HIGH SCHOOL
TRINA ROBBINS WRITER/CREATOR
ANNE TIMMONS ARTWORK
CHRISTOPHER BUTCHER COVER COLORS
TOM ORZECHOWSKI LETTERING

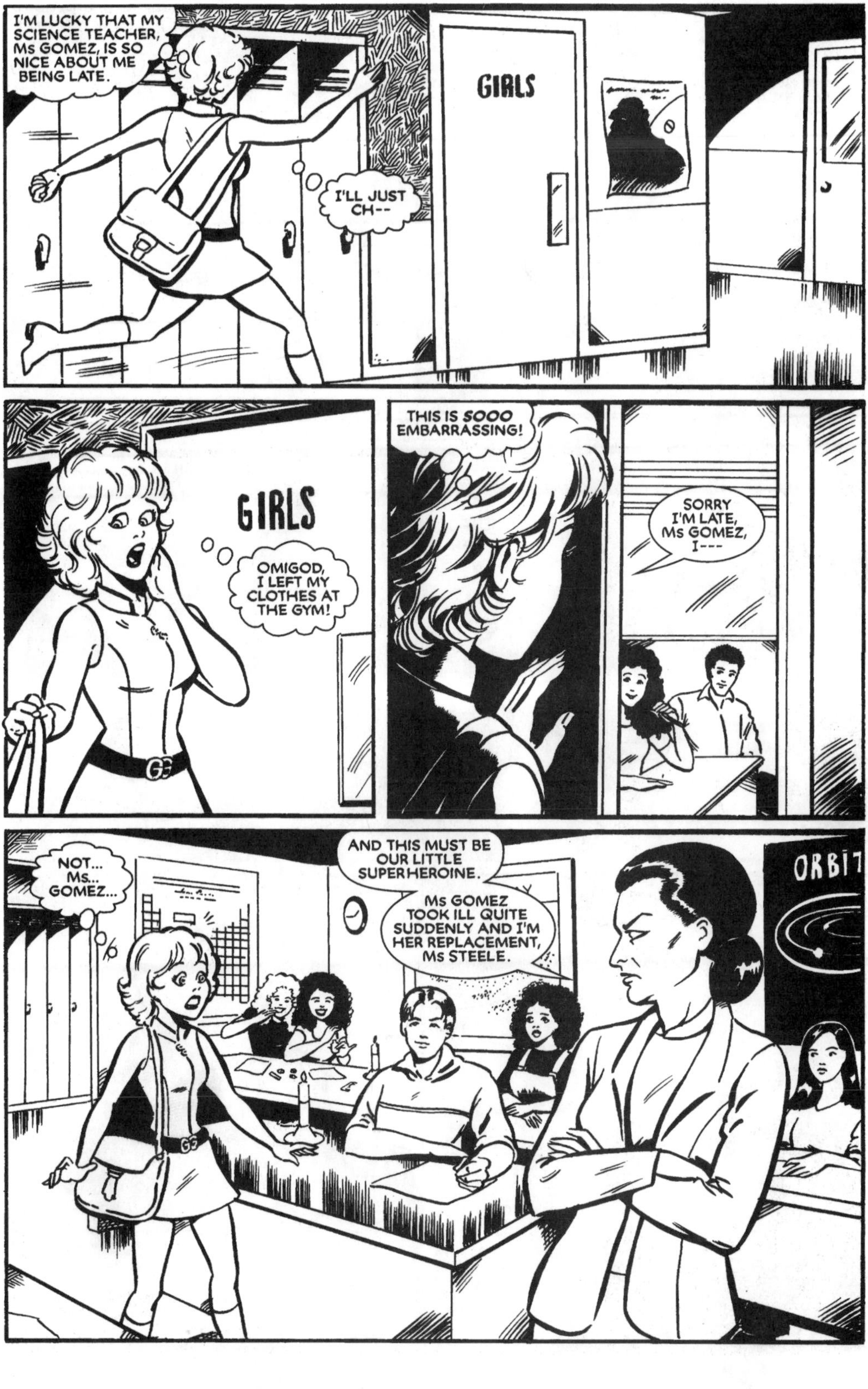
I'M LUCKY THAT MY SCIENCE TEACHER, Ms GOMEZ, IS SO NICE ABOUT ME BEING LATE.
I'LL JUST CH--
GIRLS
GIRLS
OMIGOD, I LEFT MY CLOTHES AT THE GYM!
THIS IS SOOO EMBARRASSING!
SORRY I'M LATE, Ms GOMEZ, I---
NOT... Ms... GOMEZ...
AND THIS MUST BE OUR LITTLE SUPERHEROINE.
Ms GOMEZ TOOK ILL QUITE SUDDENLY AND I'M HER REPLACEMENT, Ms STEELE.
ORBIT

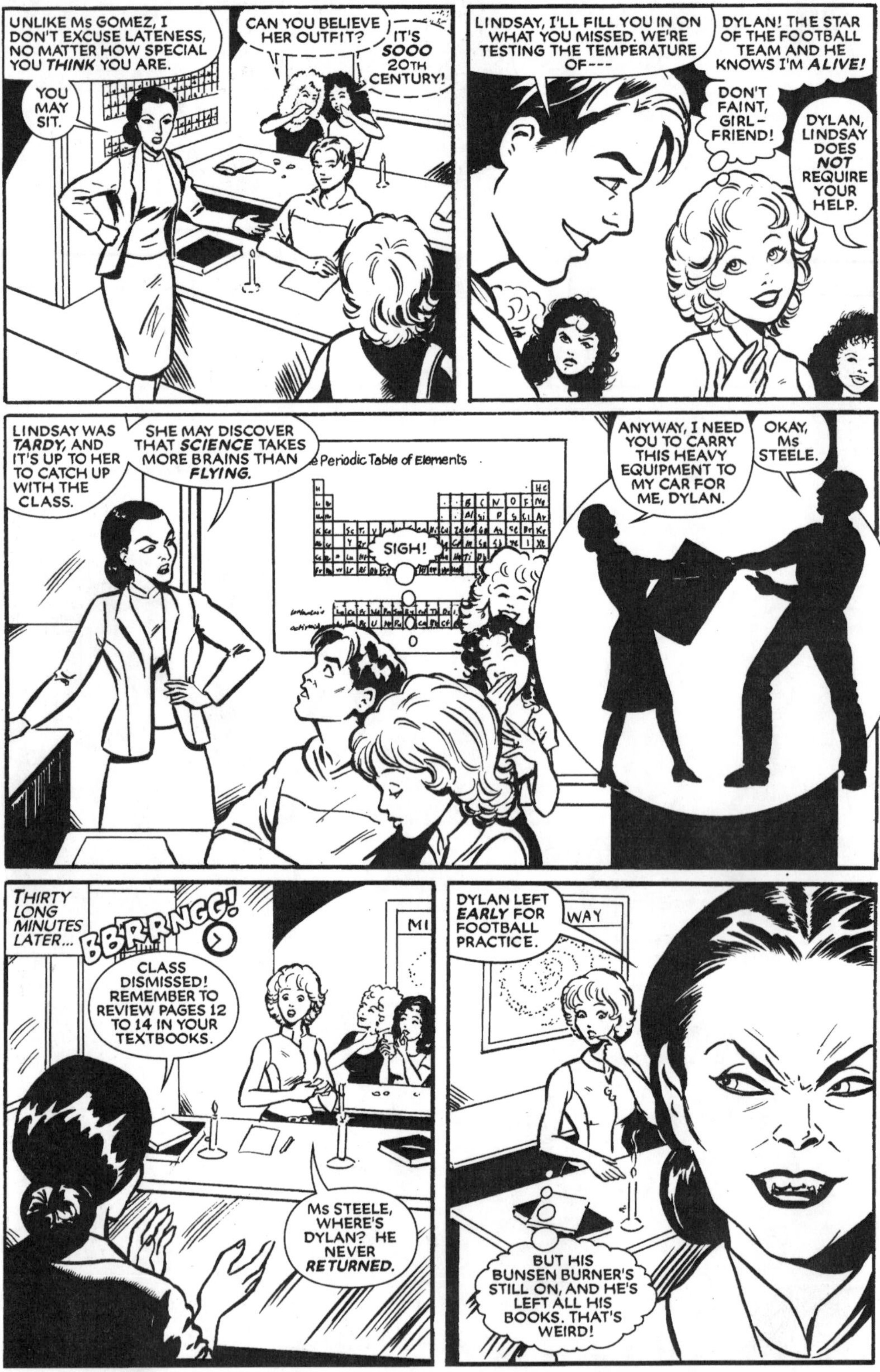
UNLIKE Ms GOMEZ, I DON'T EXCUSE LATENESS, NO MATTER HOW SPECIAL YOU *THINK* YOU ARE.
YOU MAY SIT.
CAN YOU BELIEVE HER OUTFIT?
IT'S *SOOO* 20TH CENTURY!
LINDSAY, I'LL FILL YOU IN ON WHAT YOU MISSED. WE'RE TESTING THE TEMPERATURE OF---
DYLAN! THE STAR OF THE FOOTBALL TEAM AND HE KNOWS I'M *ALIVE!*
DON'T FAINT, GIRL-FRIEND!
DYLAN, LINDSAY DOES *NOT* REQUIRE YOUR HELP.
LINDSAY WAS *TARDY,* AND IT'S UP TO HER TO CATCH UP WITH THE CLASS.
SHE MAY DISCOVER THAT *SCIENCE* TAKES MORE BRAINS THAN *FLYING.*
The Periodic Table of Elements
SIGH!
ANYWAY, I NEED YOU TO CARRY THIS HEAVY EQUIPMENT TO MY CAR FOR ME, DYLAN.
OKAY, Ms STEELE.
THIRTY LONG MINUTES LATER...
BBRRRNGG!
CLASS DISMISSED! REMEMBER TO REVIEW PAGES 12 TO 14 IN YOUR TEXTBOOKS.
Ms STEELE, WHERE'S DYLAN? HE NEVER *RETURNED.*
DYLAN LEFT *EARLY* FOR FOOTBALL PRACTICE.
BUT HIS BUNSEN BURNER'S STILL ON, AND HE'S LEFT ALL HIS BOOKS. THAT'S WEIRD!

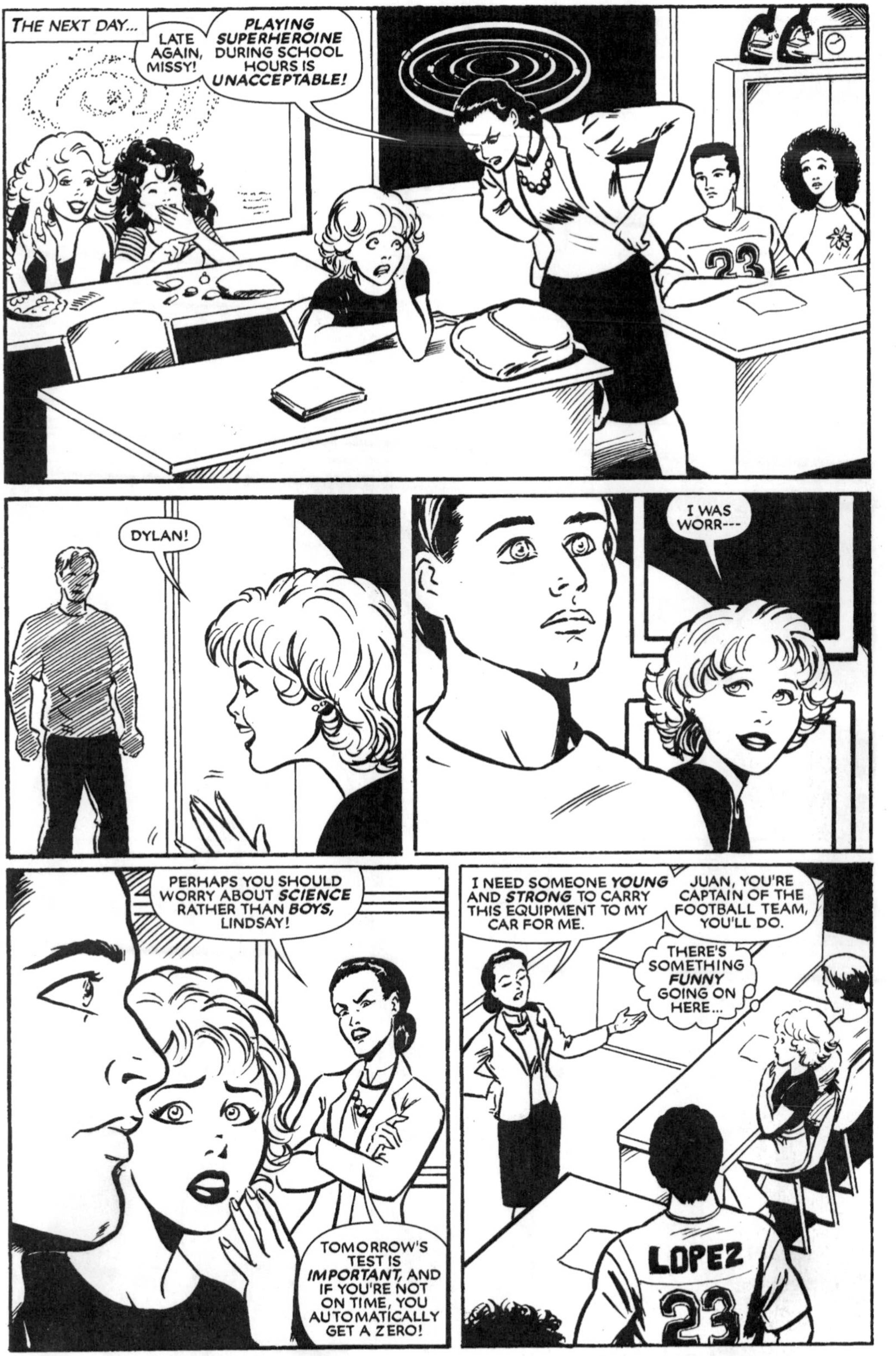
THE NEXT DAY...
LATE AGAIN, MISSY!
PLAYING SUPERHEROINE DURING SCHOOL HOURS IS UNACCEPTABLE!
DYLAN!
I WAS WORR---
PERHAPS YOU SHOULD WORRY ABOUT SCIENCE RATHER THAN BOYS, LINDSAY!
TOMORROW'S TEST IS IMPORTANT, AND IF YOU'RE NOT ON TIME, YOU AUTOMATICALLY GET A ZERO!
I NEED SOMEONE YOUNG AND STRONG TO CARRY THIS EQUIPMENT TO MY CAR FOR ME.
JUAN, YOU'RE CAPTAIN OF THE FOOTBALL TEAM, YOU'LL DO.
THERE'S SOMETHING FUNNY GOING ON HERE...
LOPEZ
23

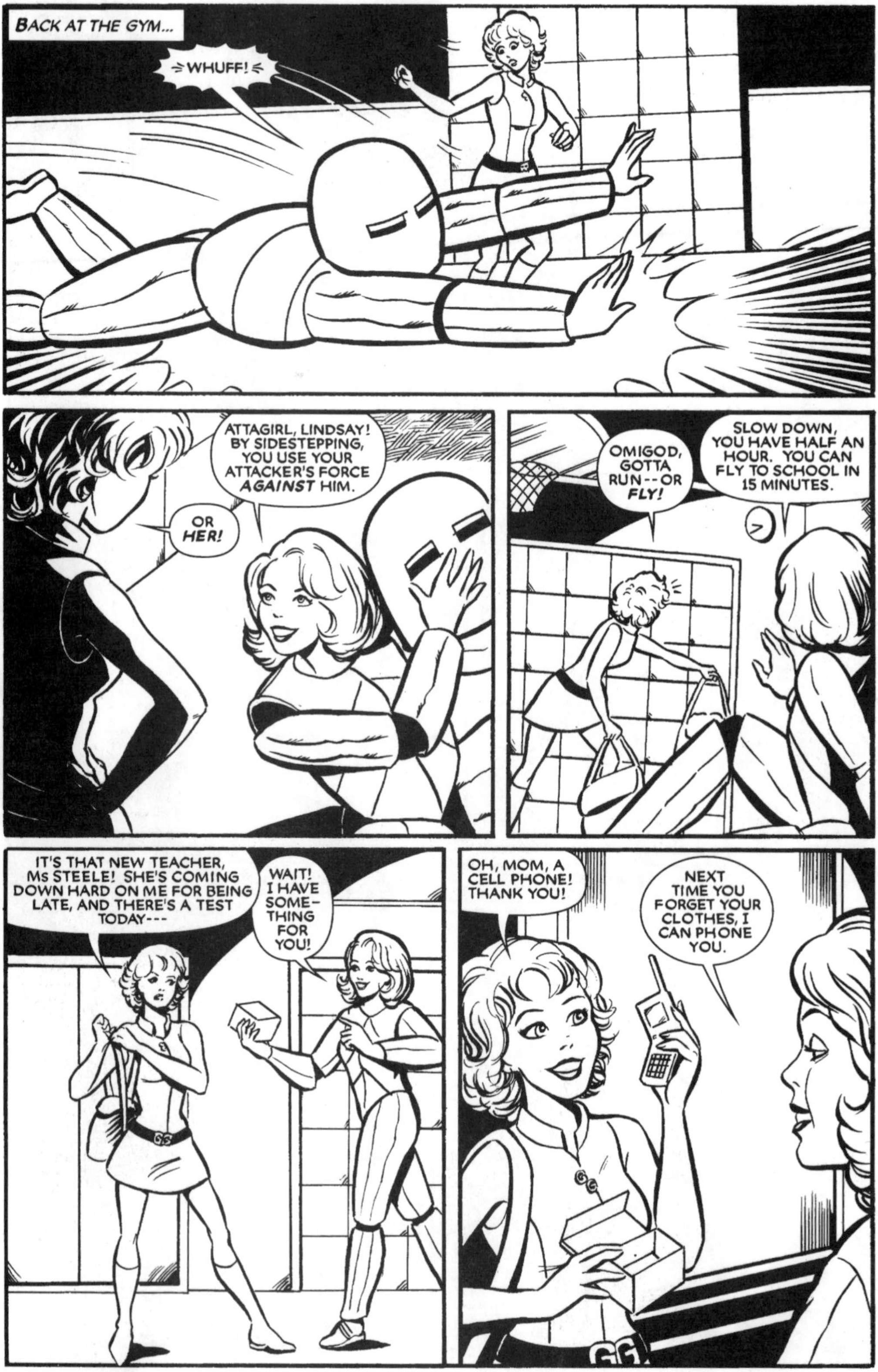
BACK AT THE GYM...
WHUFF!
OR HER!
ATTAGIRL, LINDSAY! BY SIDESTEPPING, YOU USE YOUR ATTACKER'S FORCE AGAINST HIM.
OMIGOD, GOTTA RUN--OR FLY!
SLOW DOWN, YOU HAVE HALF AN HOUR. YOU CAN FLY TO SCHOOL IN 15 MINUTES.
IT'S THAT NEW TEACHER, Ms STEELE! SHE'S COMING DOWN HARD ON ME FOR BEING LATE, AND THERE'S A TEST TODAY---
WAIT! I HAVE SOME-THING FOR YOU!
OH, MOM, A CELL PHONE! THANK YOU!
NEXT TIME YOU FORGET YOUR CLOTHES, I CAN PHONE YOU.

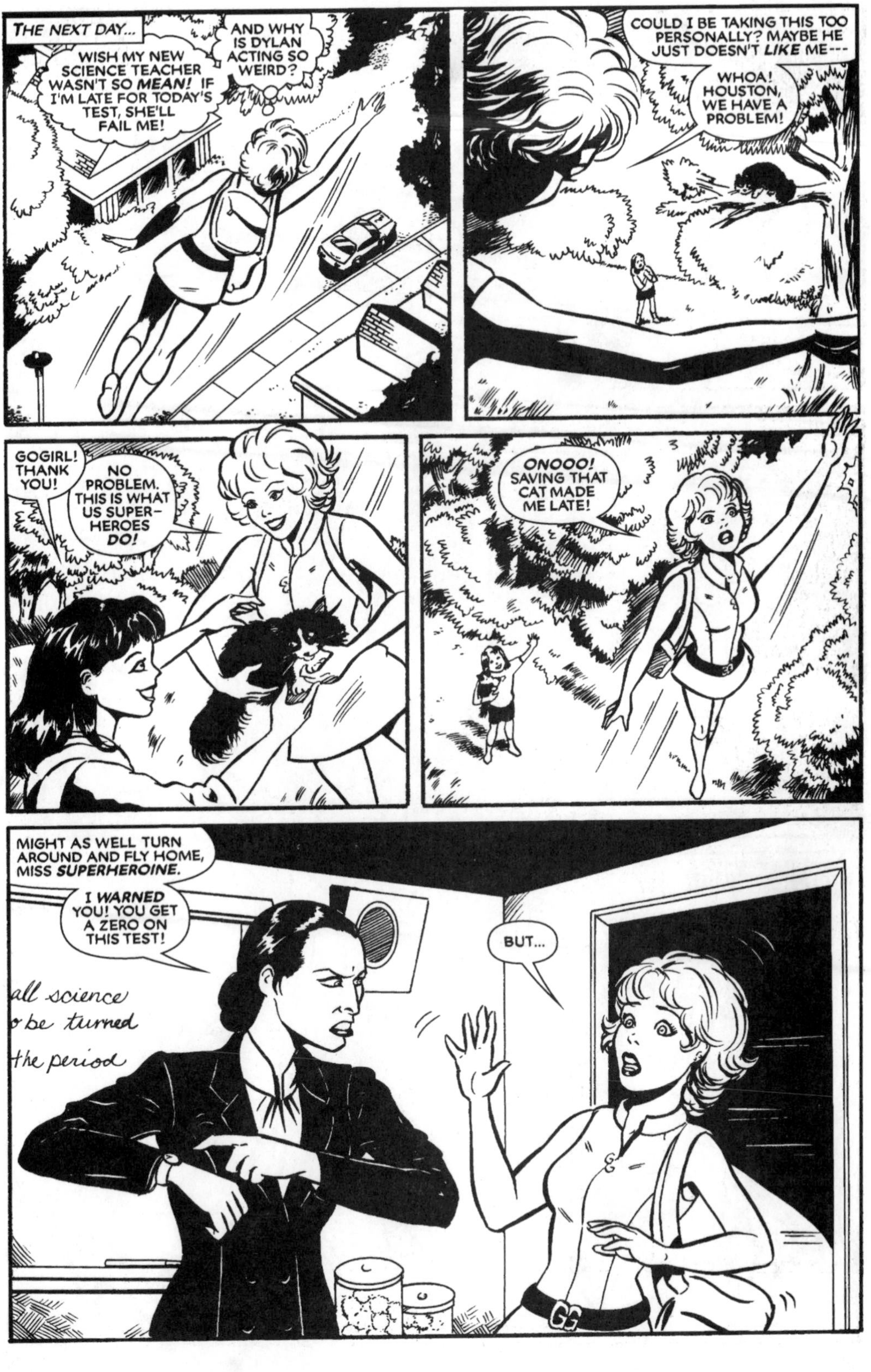
THE NEXT DAY...
WISH MY NEW SCIENCE TEACHER WASN'T SO MEAN! IF I'M LATE FOR TODAY'S TEST, SHE'LL FAIL ME!
AND WHY IS DYLAN ACTING SO WEIRD?
COULD I BE TAKING THIS TOO PERSONALLY? MAYBE HE JUST DOESN'T LIKE ME---
WHOA! HOUSTON, WE HAVE A PROBLEM!
GOGIRL! THANK YOU!
NO PROBLEM. THIS IS WHAT US SUPER-HEROES DO!
ONOOO! SAVING THAT CAT MADE ME LATE!
MIGHT AS WELL TURN AROUND AND FLY HOME, MISS SUPERHEROINE.
I WARNED YOU! YOU GET A ZERO ON THIS TEST!
BUT...
all science
o be turned
the period

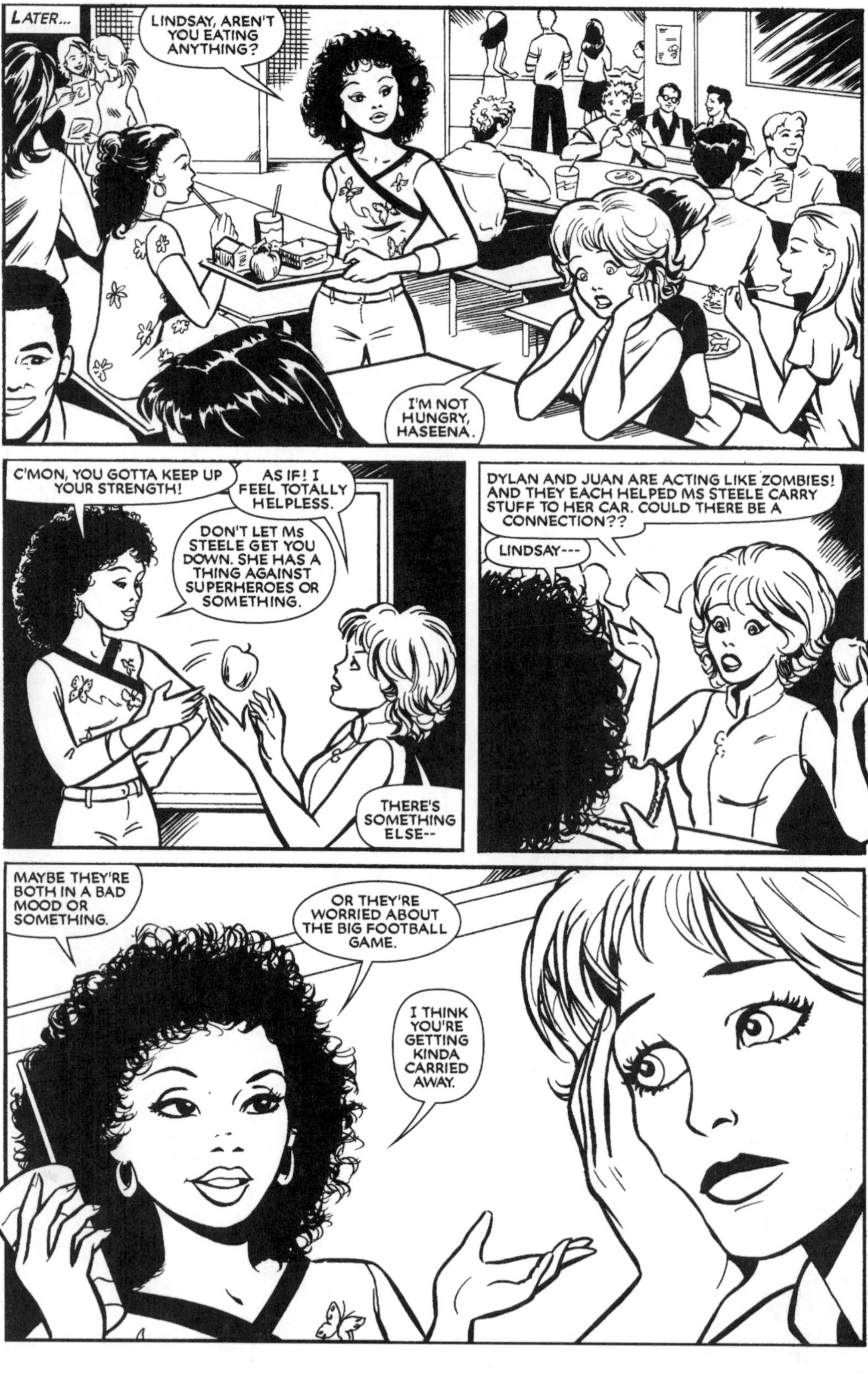
LATER...
LINDSAY, AREN'T YOU EATING ANYTHING?
I'M NOT HUNGRY, HASEENA.
C'MON, YOU GOTTA KEEP UP YOUR STRENGTH!
AS IF! I FEEL TOTALLY HELPLESS.
DON'T LET Ms STEELE GET YOU DOWN. SHE HAS A THING AGAINST SUPERHEROES OR SOMETHING.
THERE'S SOMETHING ELSE--
DYLAN AND JUAN ARE ACTING LIKE ZOMBIES! AND THEY EACH HELPED MS STEELE CARRY STUFF TO HER CAR. COULD THERE BE A CONNECTION??
LINDSAY---
MAYBE THEY'RE BOTH IN A BAD MOOD OR SOMETHING.
OR THEY'RE WORRIED ABOUT THE BIG FOOTBALL GAME.
I THINK YOU'RE GETTING KINDA CARRIED AWAY.

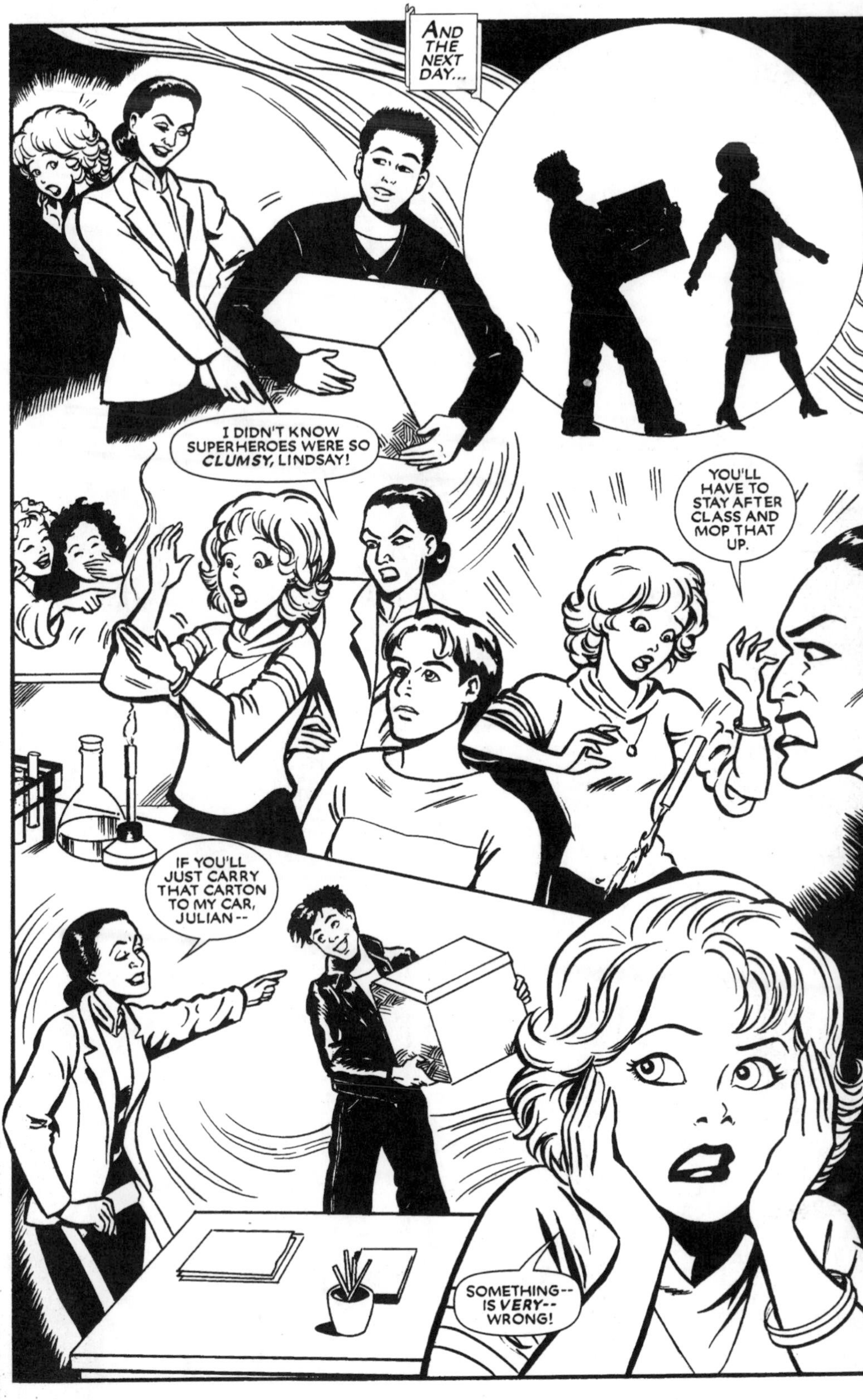
AND THE NEXT DAY...
I DIDN'T KNOW SUPERHEROES WERE SO CLUMSY, LINDSAY!
YOU'LL HAVE TO STAY AFTER CLASS AND MOP THAT UP.
IF YOU'LL JUST CARRY THAT CARTON TO MY CAR, JULIAN--
SOMETHING-- IS VERY-- WRONG!

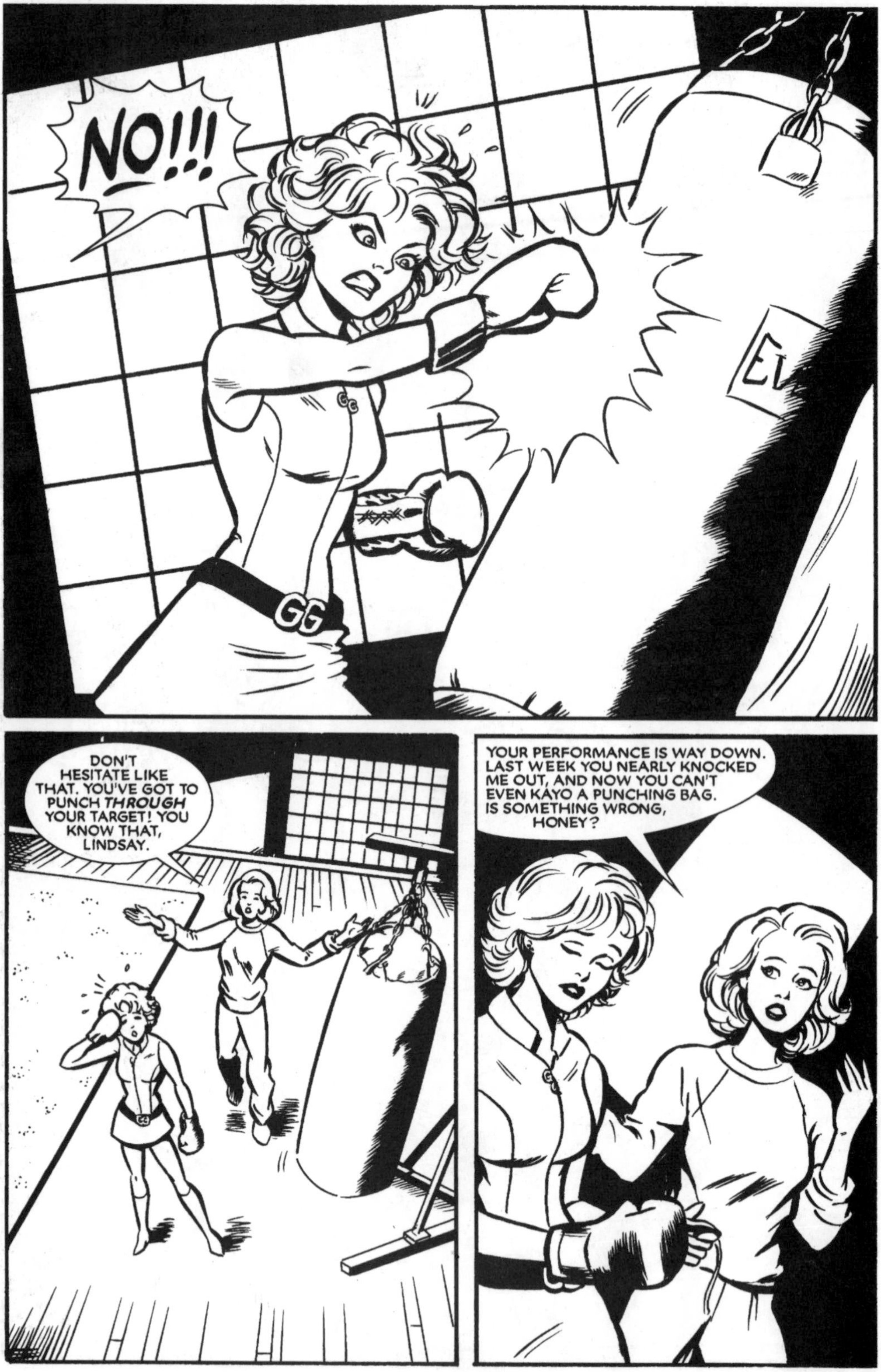
NO!!!
DON'T HESITATE LIKE THAT. YOU'VE GOT TO PUNCH *THROUGH* YOUR TARGET! YOU KNOW THAT, LINDSAY.
YOUR PERFORMANCE IS WAY DOWN. LAST WEEK YOU NEARLY KNOCKED ME OUT, AND NOW YOU CAN'T EVEN KAYO A PUNCHING BAG. IS SOMETHING WRONG, HONEY?

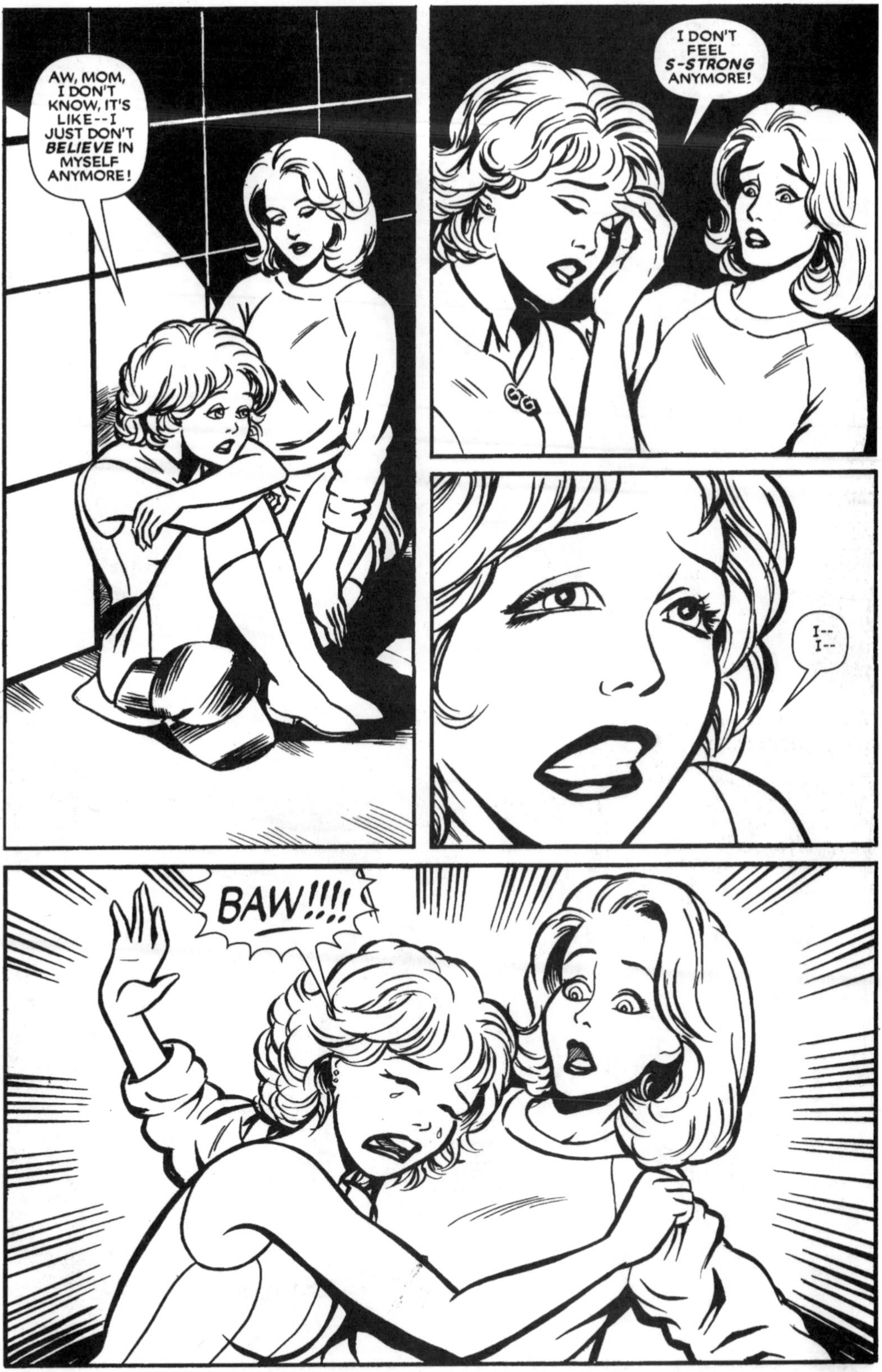
AW, MOM, I DON'T KNOW, IT'S LIKE--I JUST DON'T BELIEVE IN MYSELF ANYMORE!
I DON'T FEEL S-STRONG ANYMORE!
I-- I--
BAW!!!!

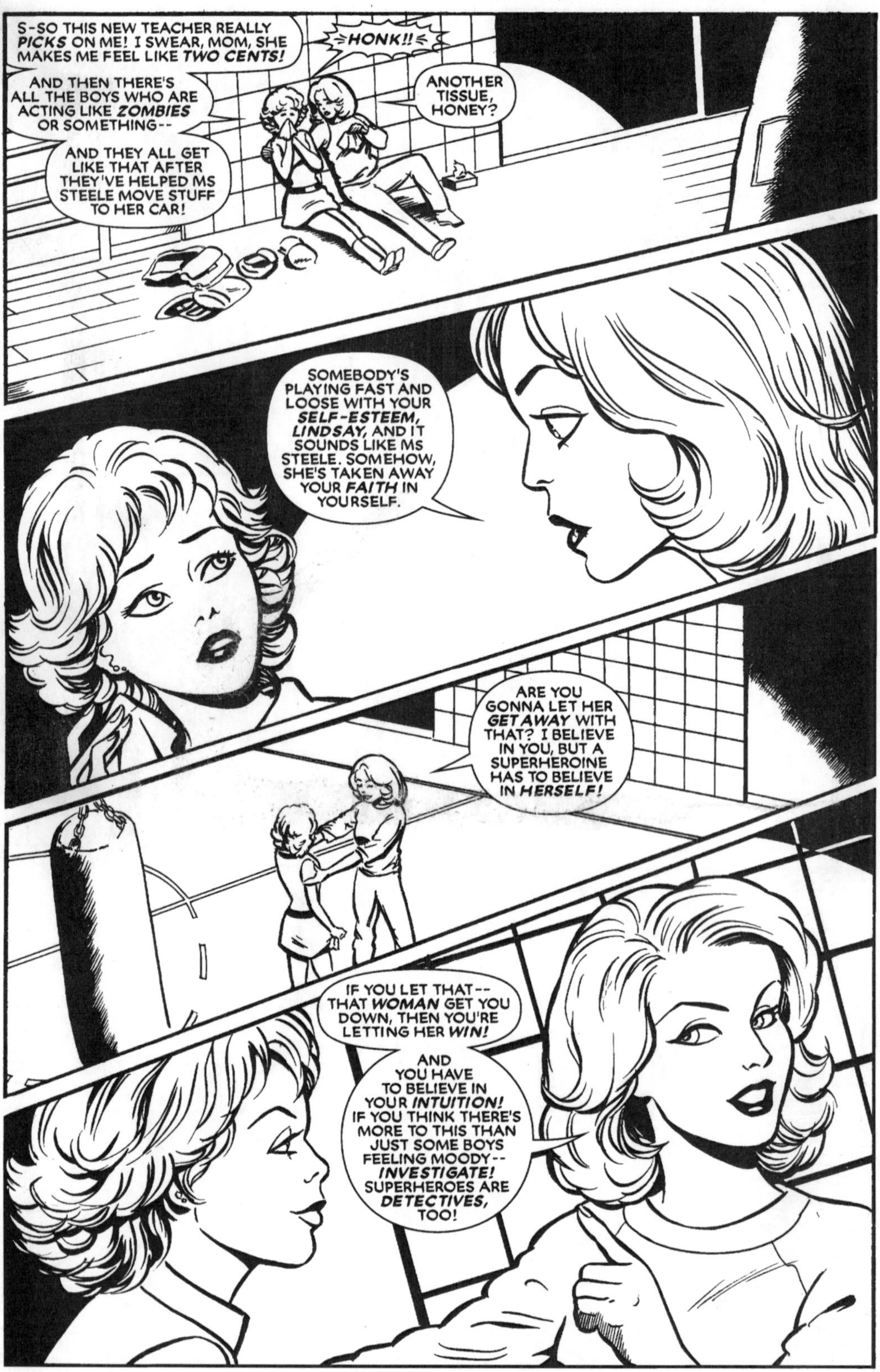

S-SO THIS NEW TEACHER REALLY *PICKS* ON ME! I SWEAR, MOM, SHE MAKES ME FEEL LIKE *TWO CENTS!*
HONK!!
AND THEN THERE'S ALL THE BOYS WHO ARE ACTING LIKE *ZOMBIES* OR SOMETHING--
ANOTHER TISSUE, HONEY?
AND THEY ALL GET LIKE THAT AFTER THEY'VE HELPED MS STEELE MOVE STUFF TO HER CAR!
SOMEBODY'S PLAYING FAST AND LOOSE WITH YOUR *SELF-ESTEEM, LINDSAY,* AND IT SOUNDS LIKE MS STEELE. SOMEHOW, SHE'S TAKEN AWAY YOUR *FAITH* IN YOURSELF.
ARE YOU GONNA LET HER *GET AWAY* WITH THAT? I BELIEVE IN YOU, BUT A SUPERHEROINE HAS TO BELIEVE IN *HERSELF!*
IF YOU LET THAT-- THAT *WOMAN* GET YOU DOWN, THEN YOU'RE LETTING HER *WIN!*
AND YOU HAVE TO BELIEVE IN YOUR *INTUITION!* IF YOU THINK THERE'S MORE TO THIS THAN JUST SOME BOYS FEELING MOODY-- *INVESTIGATE!* SUPERHEROES ARE *DETECTIVES,* TOO!

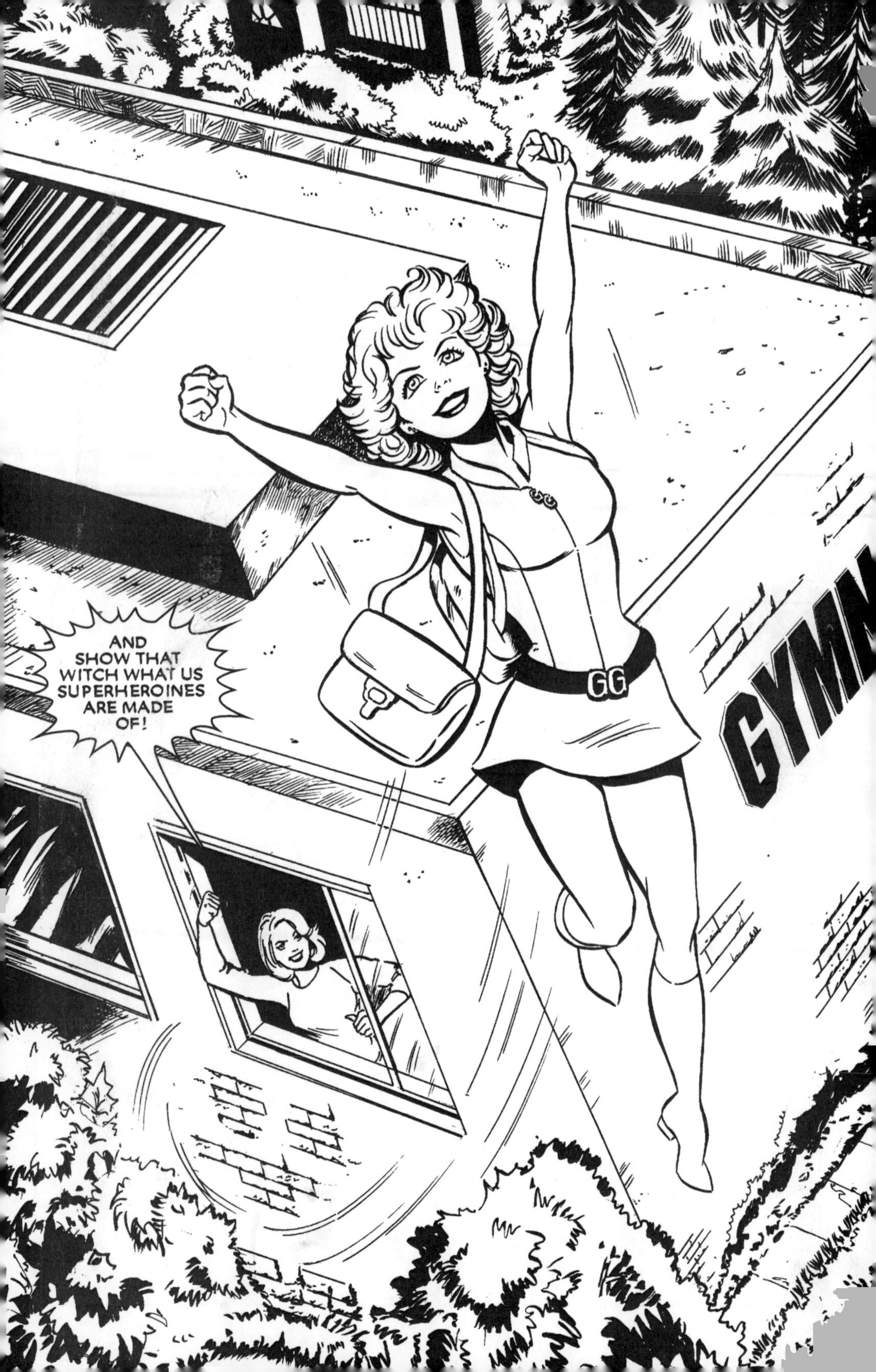
AND SHOW THAT WITCH WHAT US SUPERHEROINES ARE MADE OF!

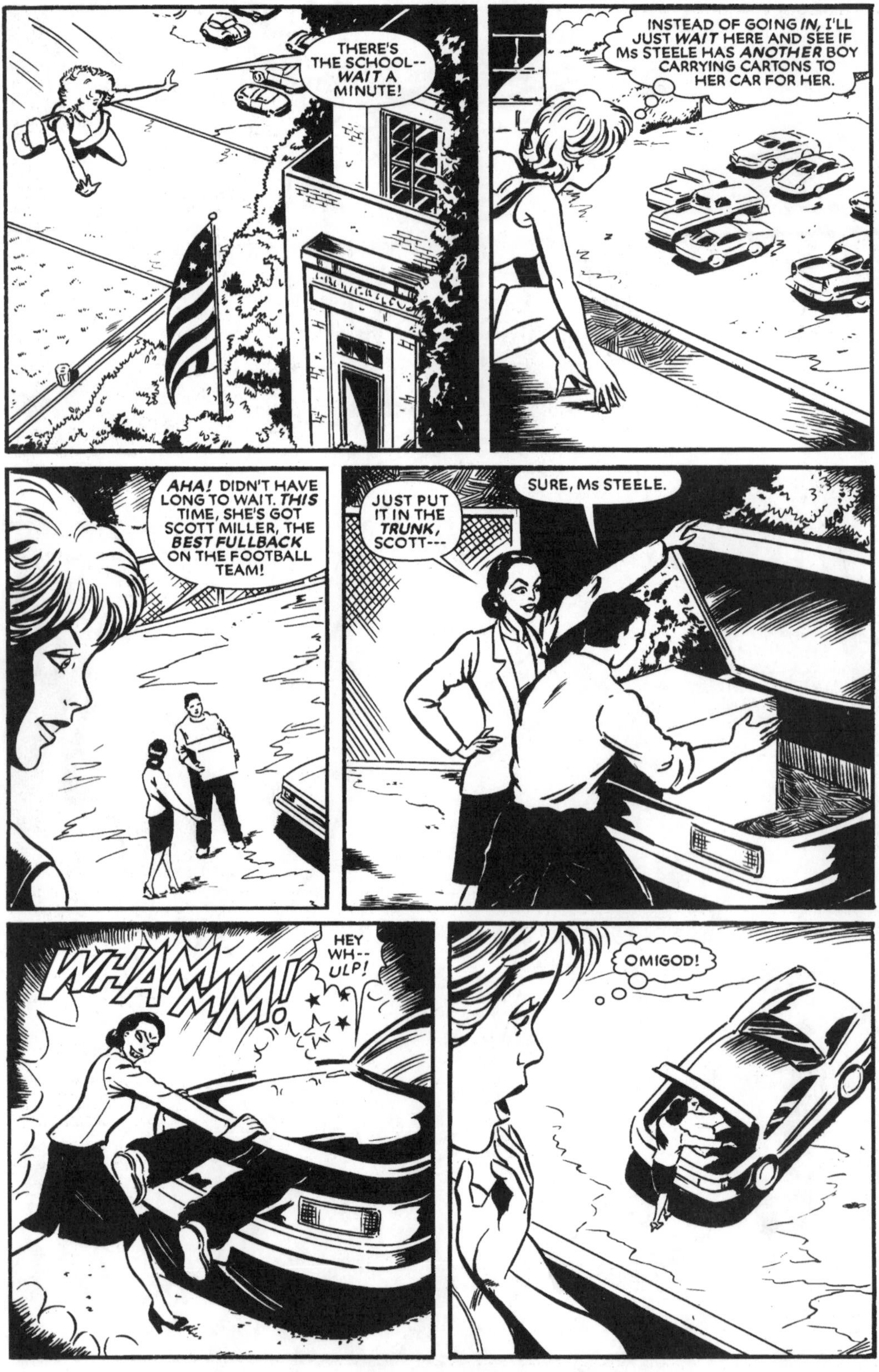
THERE'S THE SCHOOL-- WAIT A MINUTE!
INSTEAD OF GOING IN, I'LL JUST WAIT HERE AND SEE IF Ms STEELE HAS ANOTHER BOY CARRYING CARTONS TO HER CAR FOR HER.
AHA! DIDN'T HAVE LONG TO WAIT. THIS TIME, SHE'S GOT SCOTT MILLER, THE BEST FULLBACK ON THE FOOTBALL TEAM!
JUST PUT IT IN THE TRUNK, SCOTT---
SURE, Ms STEELE.
WHAMMM!
HEY WH-- ULP!
OMIGOD!

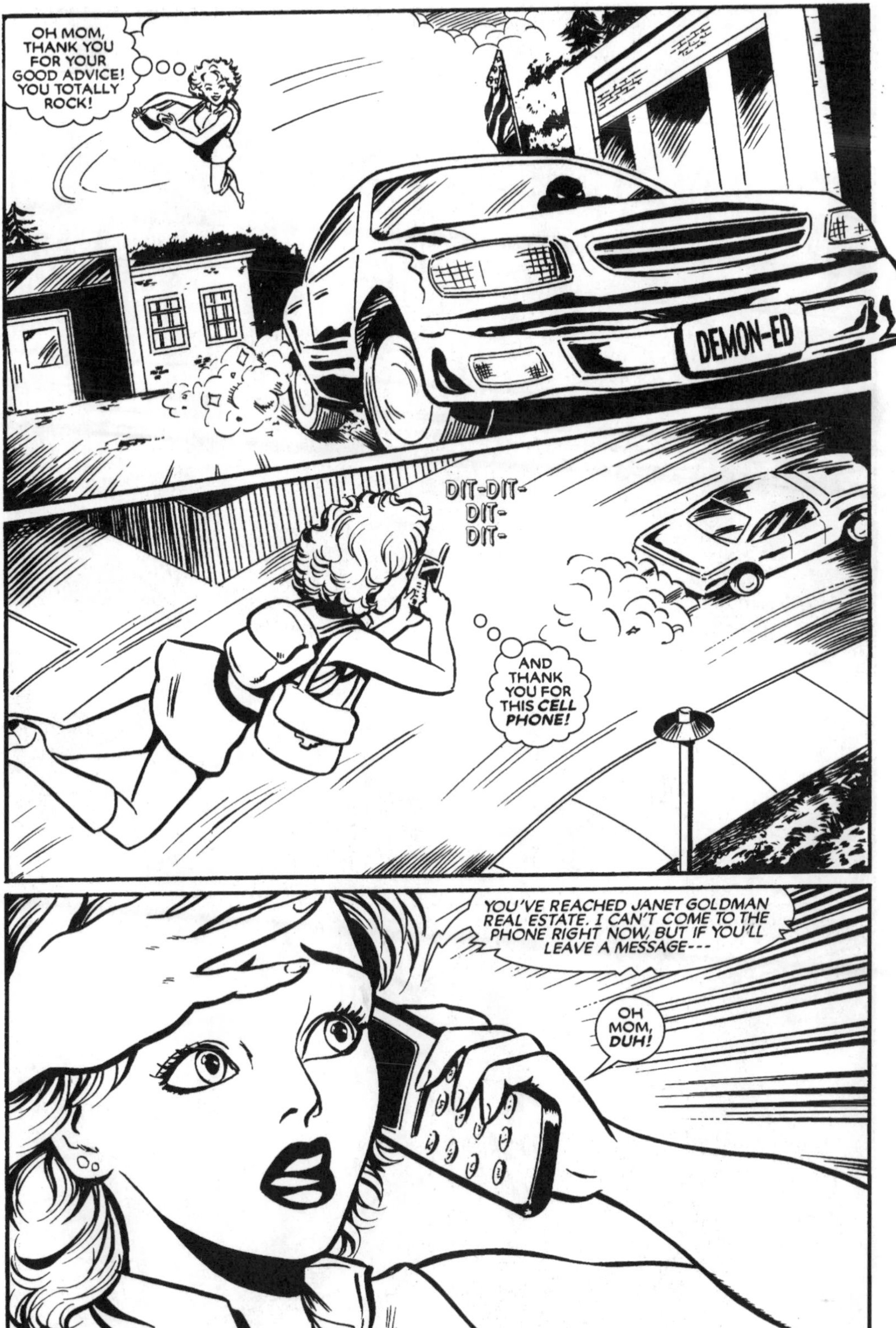
OH MOM, THANK YOU FOR YOUR GOOD ADVICE! YOU TOTALLY ROCK!
DEMON-ED
DIT-DIT-DIT-DIT-
AND THANK YOU FOR THIS CELL PHONE!
YOU'VE REACHED JANET GOLDMAN REAL ESTATE. I CAN'T COME TO THE PHONE RIGHT NOW, BUT IF YOU'LL LEAVE A MESSAGE---
OH MOM, DUH!

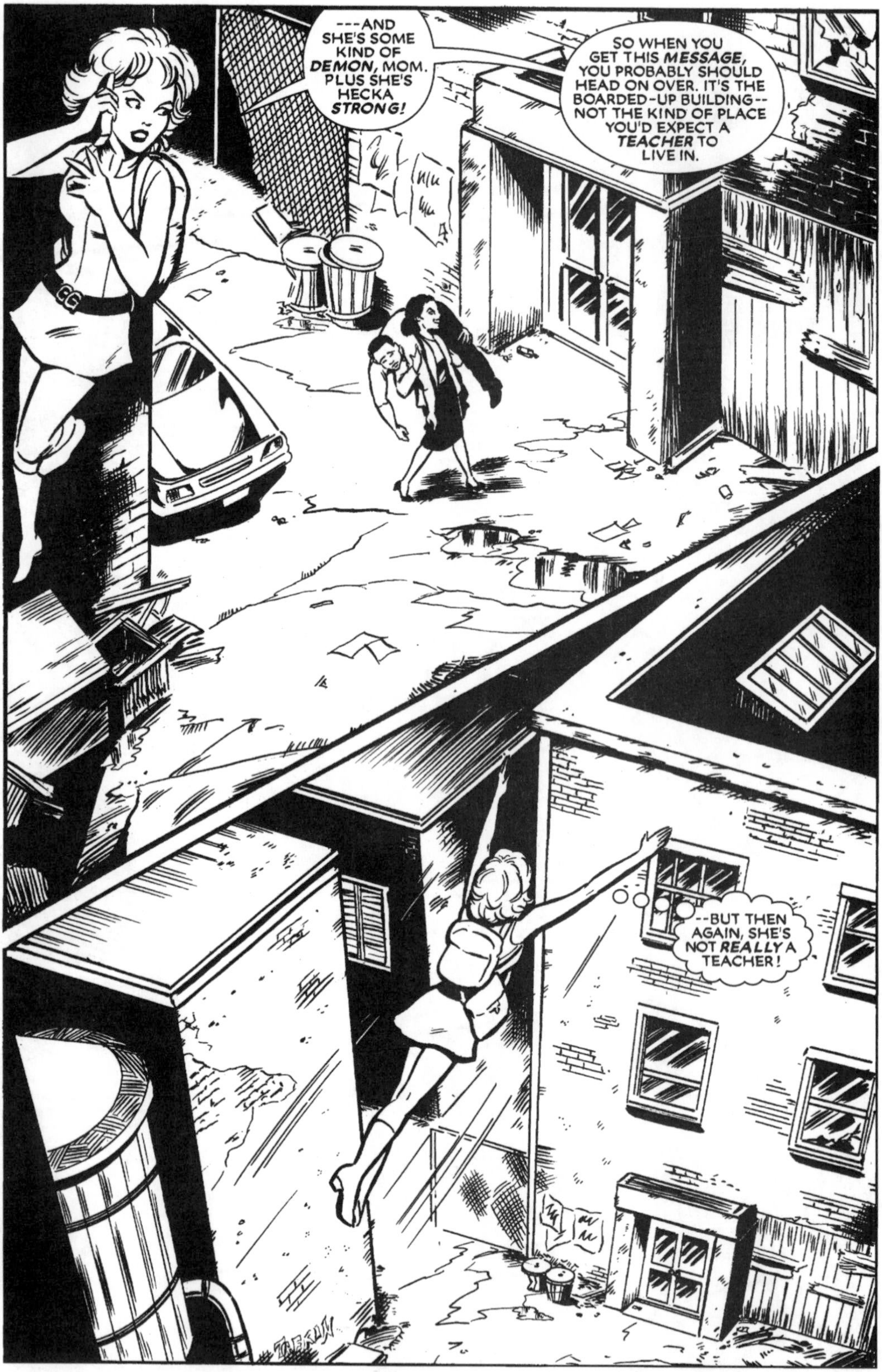
---AND SHE'S SOME KIND OF DEMON, MOM. PLUS SHE'S HECKA STRONG!
SO WHEN YOU GET THIS MESSAGE, YOU PROBABLY SHOULD HEAD ON OVER. IT'S THE BOARDED-UP BUILDING-- NOT THE KIND OF PLACE YOU'D EXPECT A TEACHER TO LIVE IN.
--BUT THEN AGAIN, SHE'S NOT REALLY A TEACHER!

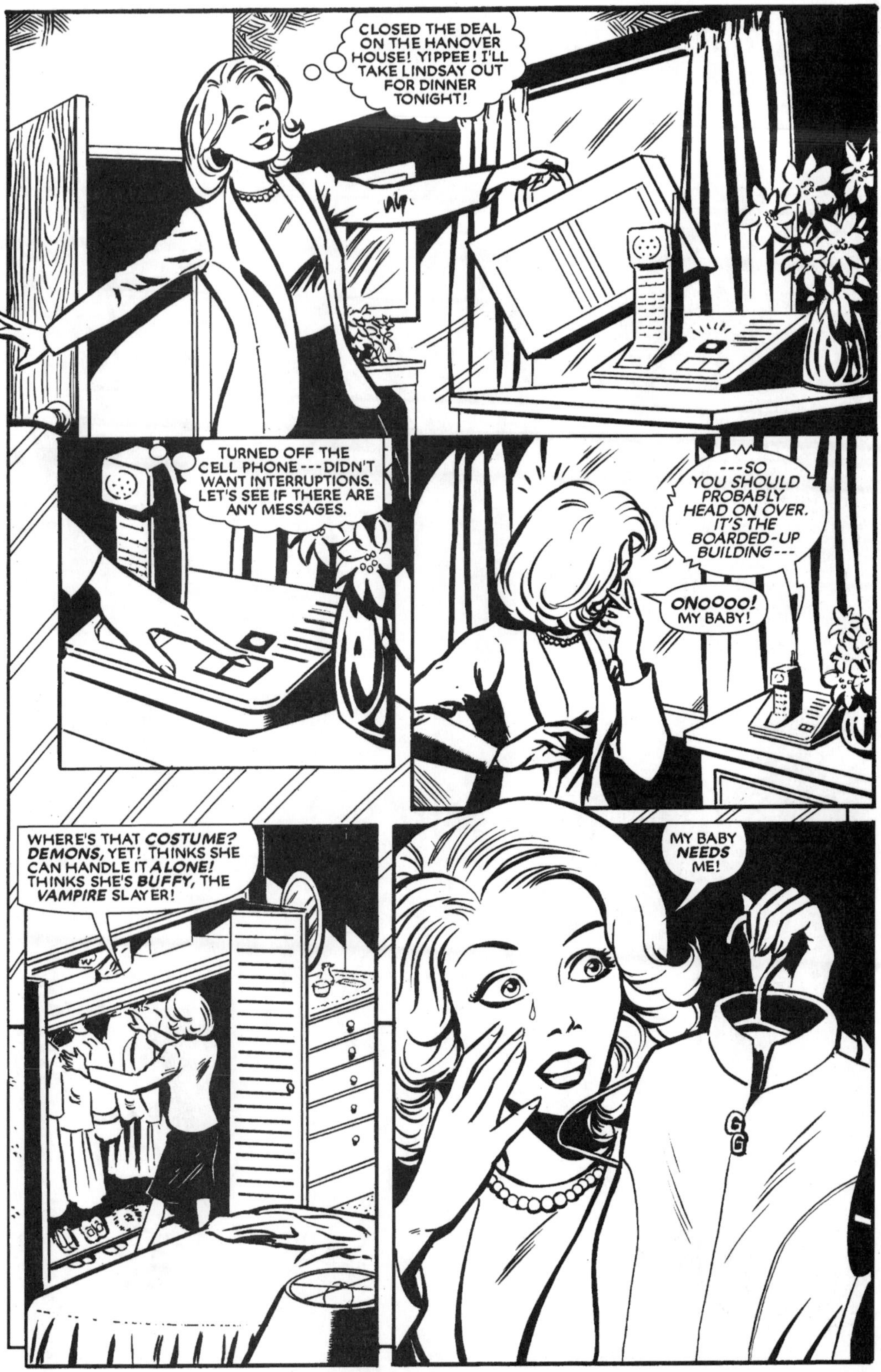
CLOSED THE DEAL ON THE HANOVER HOUSE! YIPPEE! I'LL TAKE LINDSAY OUT FOR DINNER TONIGHT!
TURNED OFF THE CELL PHONE---DIDN'T WANT INTERRUPTIONS. LET'S SEE IF THERE ARE ANY MESSAGES.
---SO YOU SHOULD PROBABLY HEAD ON OVER. IT'S THE BOARDED-UP BUILDING---
ONOOOO! MY BABY!
WHERE'S THAT COSTUME? DEMONS, YET! THINKS SHE CAN HANDLE IT ALONE! THINKS SHE'S BUFFY, THE VAMPIRE SLAYER!
MY BABY NEEDS ME!

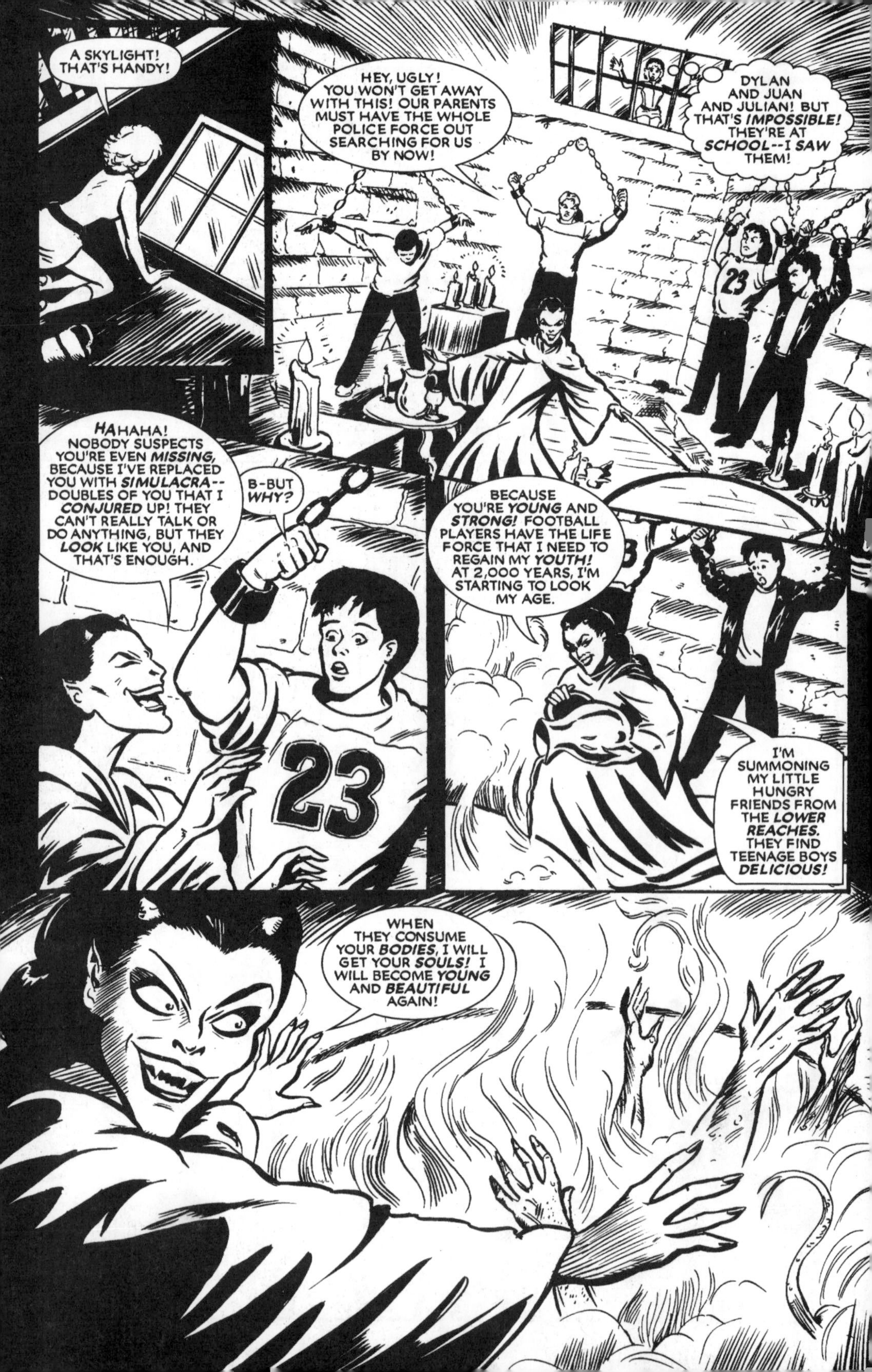
A SKYLIGHT! THAT'S HANDY!
HEY, UGLY! YOU WON'T GET AWAY WITH THIS! OUR PARENTS MUST HAVE THE WHOLE POLICE FORCE OUT SEARCHING FOR US BY NOW!
DYLAN AND JUAN AND JULIAN! BUT THAT'S IMPOSSIBLE! THEY'RE AT SCHOOL--I SAW THEM!
HAHAHA! NOBODY SUSPECTS YOU'RE EVEN MISSING, BECAUSE I'VE REPLACED YOU WITH SIMULACRA-- DOUBLES OF YOU THAT I CONJURED UP! THEY CAN'T REALLY TALK OR DO ANYTHING, BUT THEY LOOK LIKE YOU, AND THAT'S ENOUGH.
B-BUT WHY?
BECAUSE YOU'RE YOUNG AND STRONG! FOOTBALL PLAYERS HAVE THE LIFE FORCE THAT I NEED TO REGAIN MY YOUTH! AT 2,000 YEARS, I'M STARTING TO LOOK MY AGE.
I'M SUMMONING MY LITTLE HUNGRY FRIENDS FROM THE LOWER REACHES. THEY FIND TEENAGE BOYS DELICIOUS!
WHEN THEY CONSUME YOUR BODIES, I WILL GET YOUR SOULS! I WILL BECOME YOUNG AND BEAUTIFUL AGAIN!

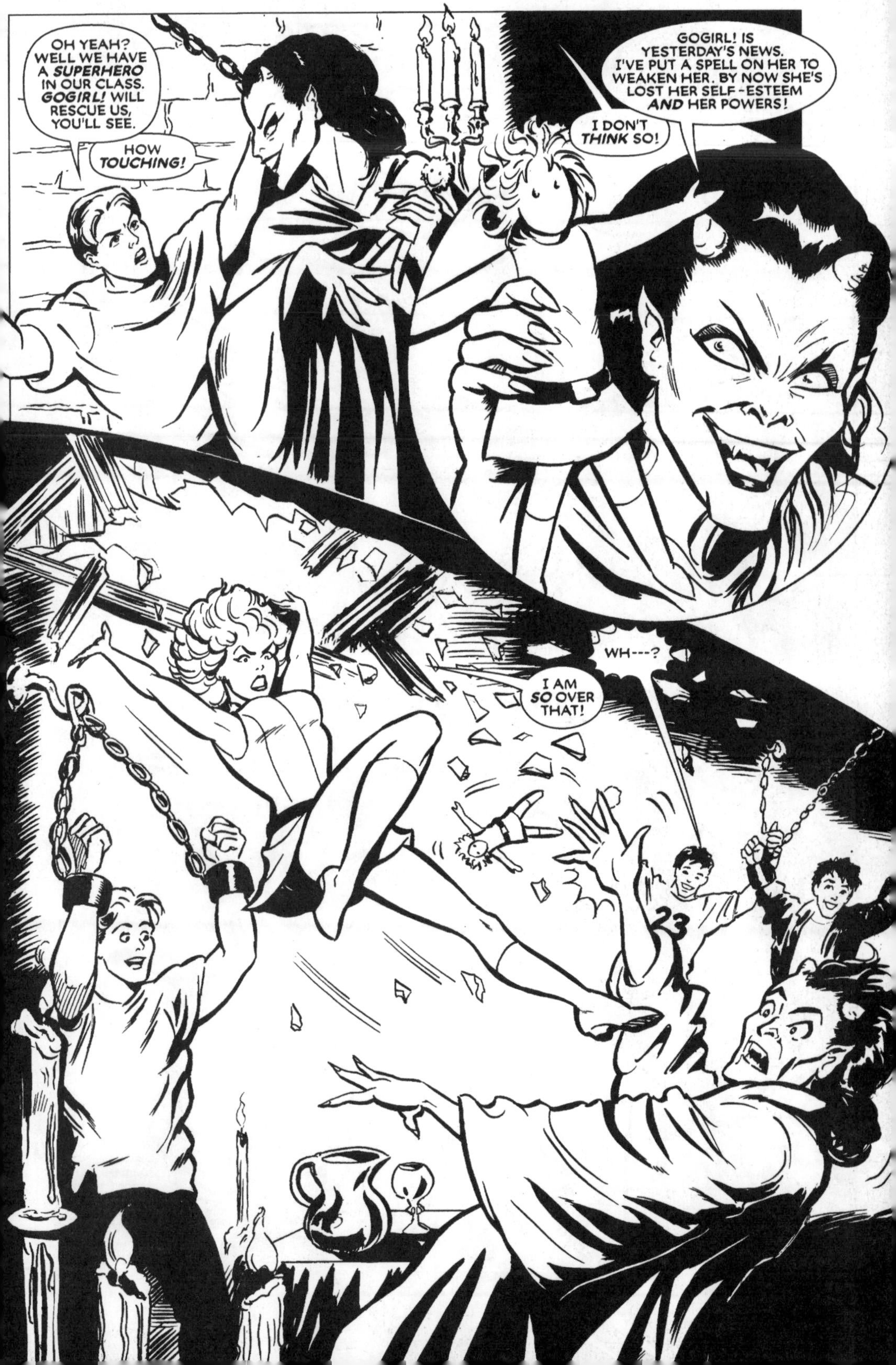

OH YEAH? WELL WE HAVE A SUPERHERO IN OUR CLASS. GOGIRL! WILL RESCUE US, YOU'LL SEE.
HOW TOUCHING!
I DON'T THINK SO!
GOGIRL! IS YESTERDAY'S NEWS. I'VE PUT A SPELL ON HER TO WEAKEN HER. BY NOW SHE'S LOST HER SELF-ESTEEM AND HER POWERS!
I AM SO OVER THAT!
WH---?
23

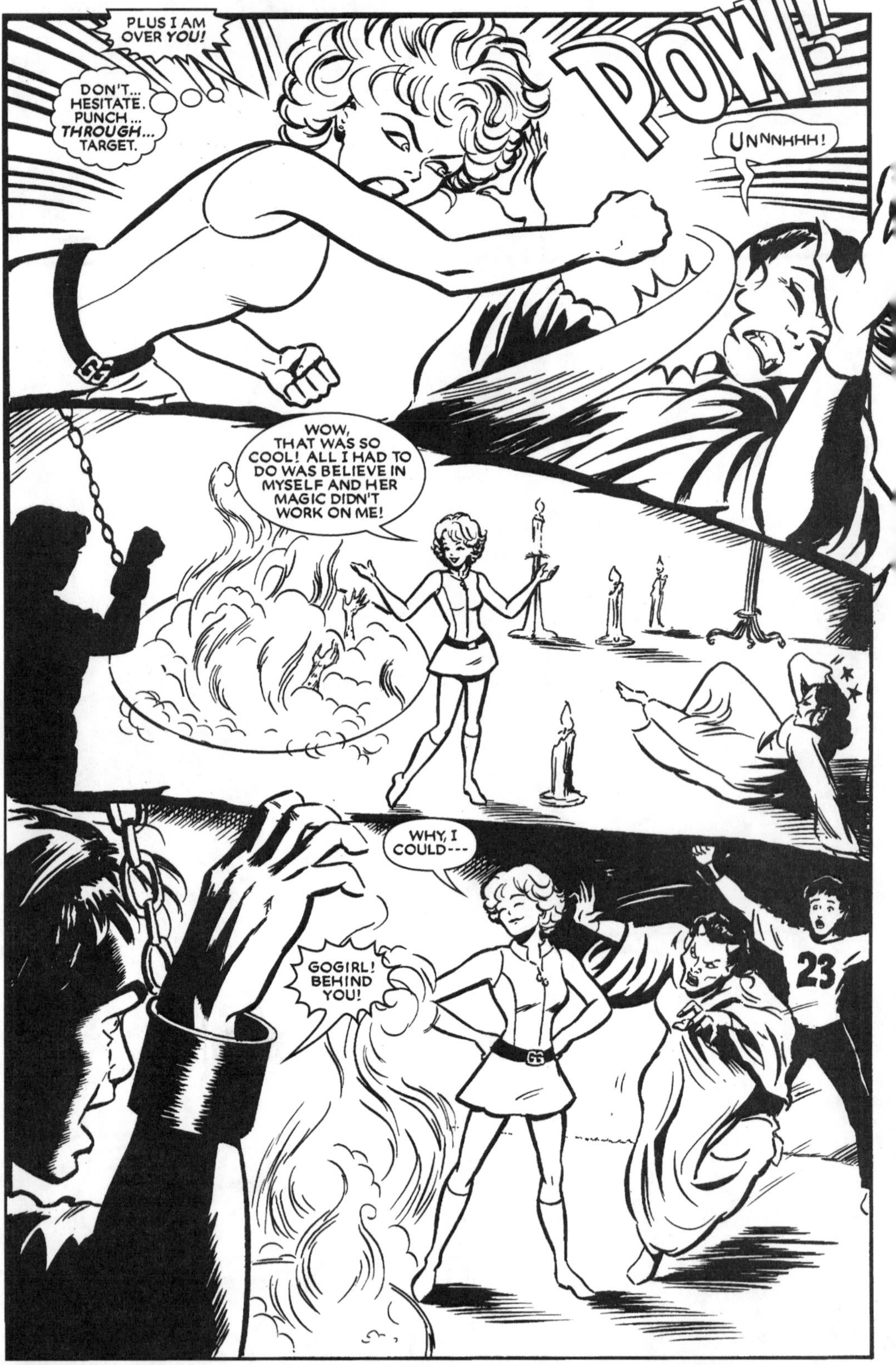
PLUS I AM OVER YOU!
DON'T... HESITATE. PUNCH... THROUGH... TARGET.
POW!
UNNNHHH!
WOW, THAT WAS SO COOL! ALL I HAD TO DO WAS BELIEVE IN MYSELF AND HER MAGIC DIDN'T WORK ON ME!
WHY, I COULD---
GOGIRL! BEHIND YOU!
23

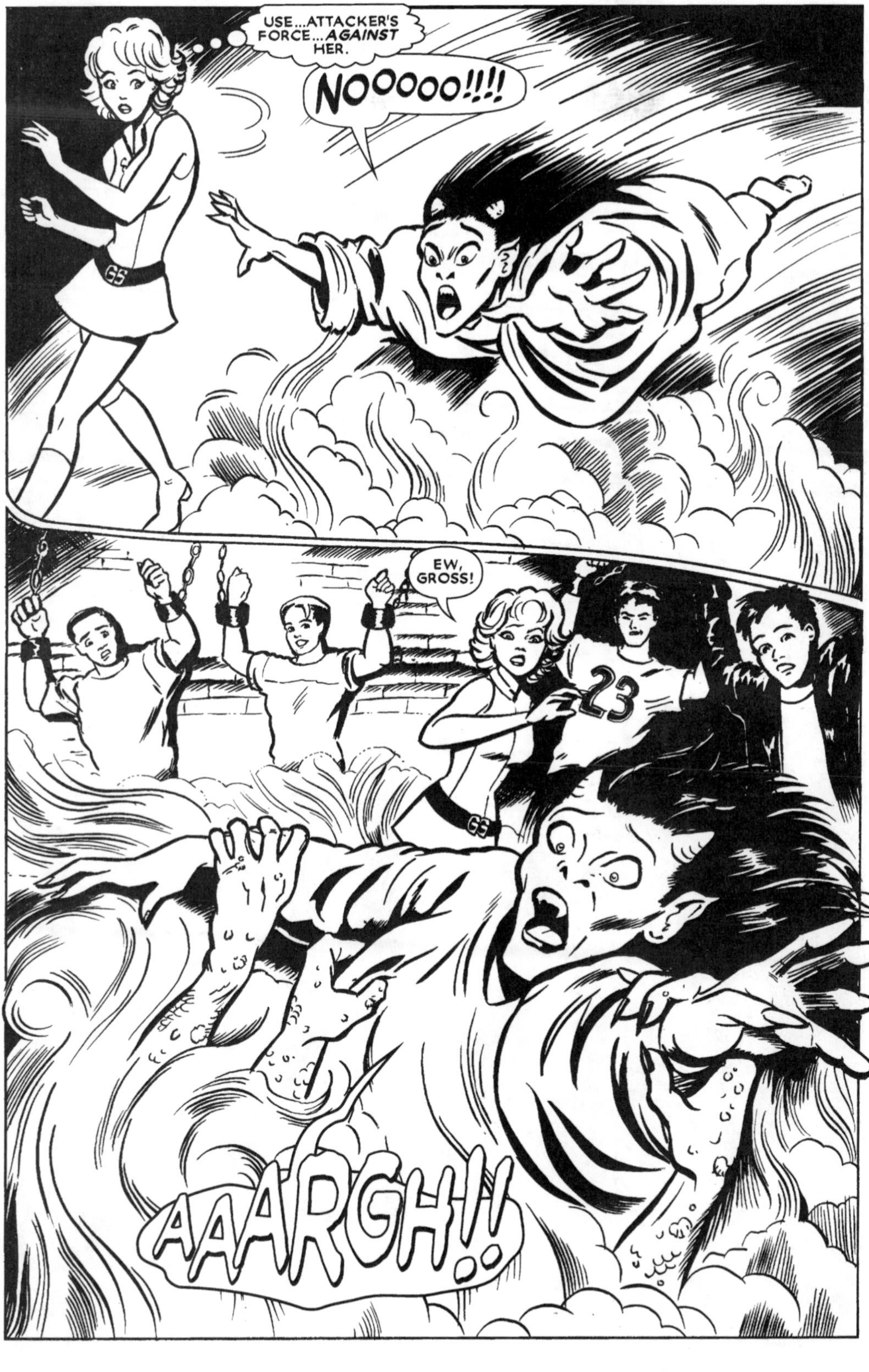
USE...ATTACKER'S FORCE...AGAINST HER.
NOOOOO!!!!
EW, GROSS!
AAARGH!!!

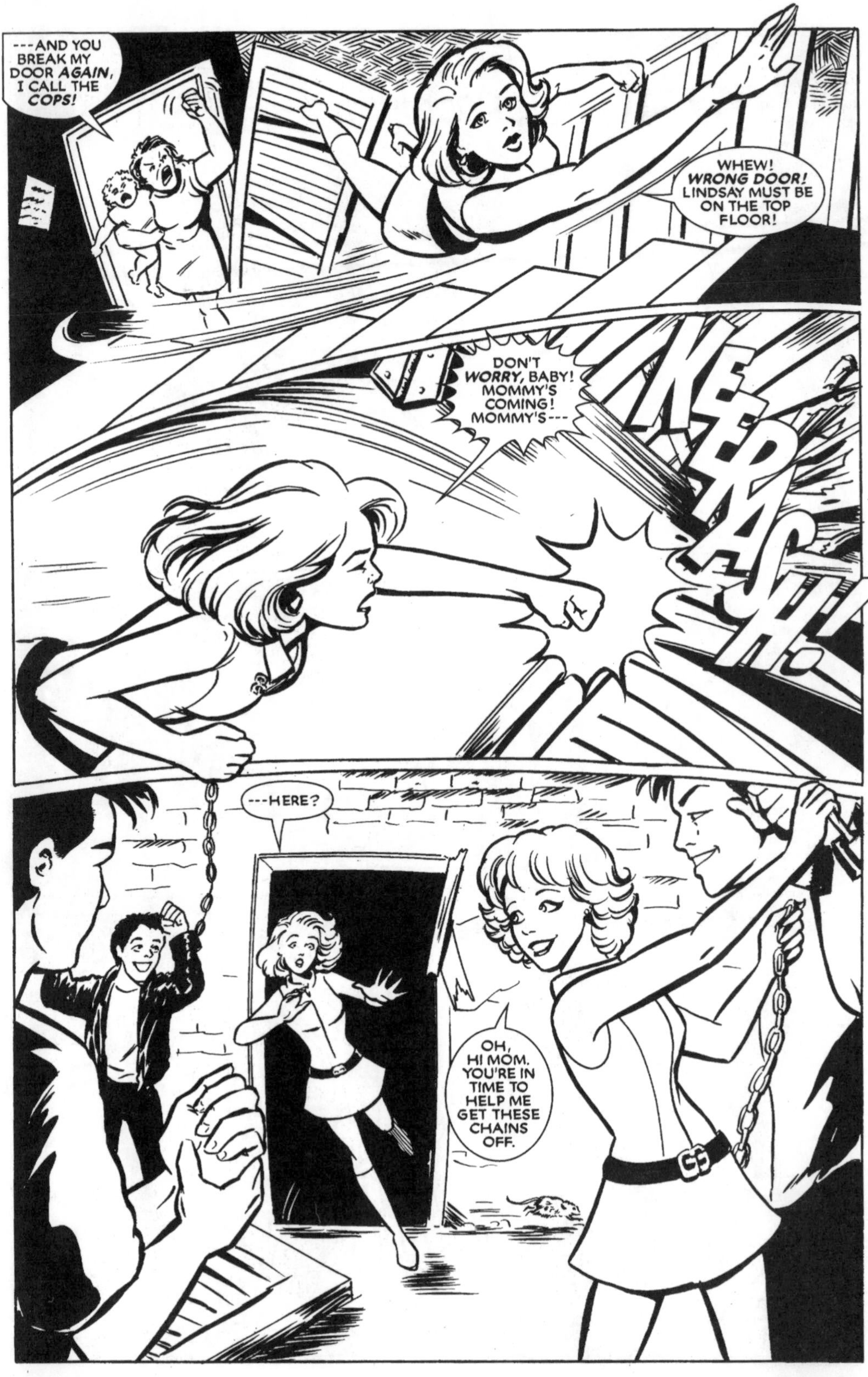
---AND YOU BREAK MY DOOR AGAIN, I CALL THE COPS!
WHEW! WRONG DOOR! LINDSAY MUST BE ON THE TOP FLOOR!
DON'T WORRY, BABY! MOMMY'S COMING! MOMMY'S---
KKERASH!!
---HERE?
OH, HI MOM. YOU'RE IN TIME TO HELP ME GET THESE CHAINS OFF.

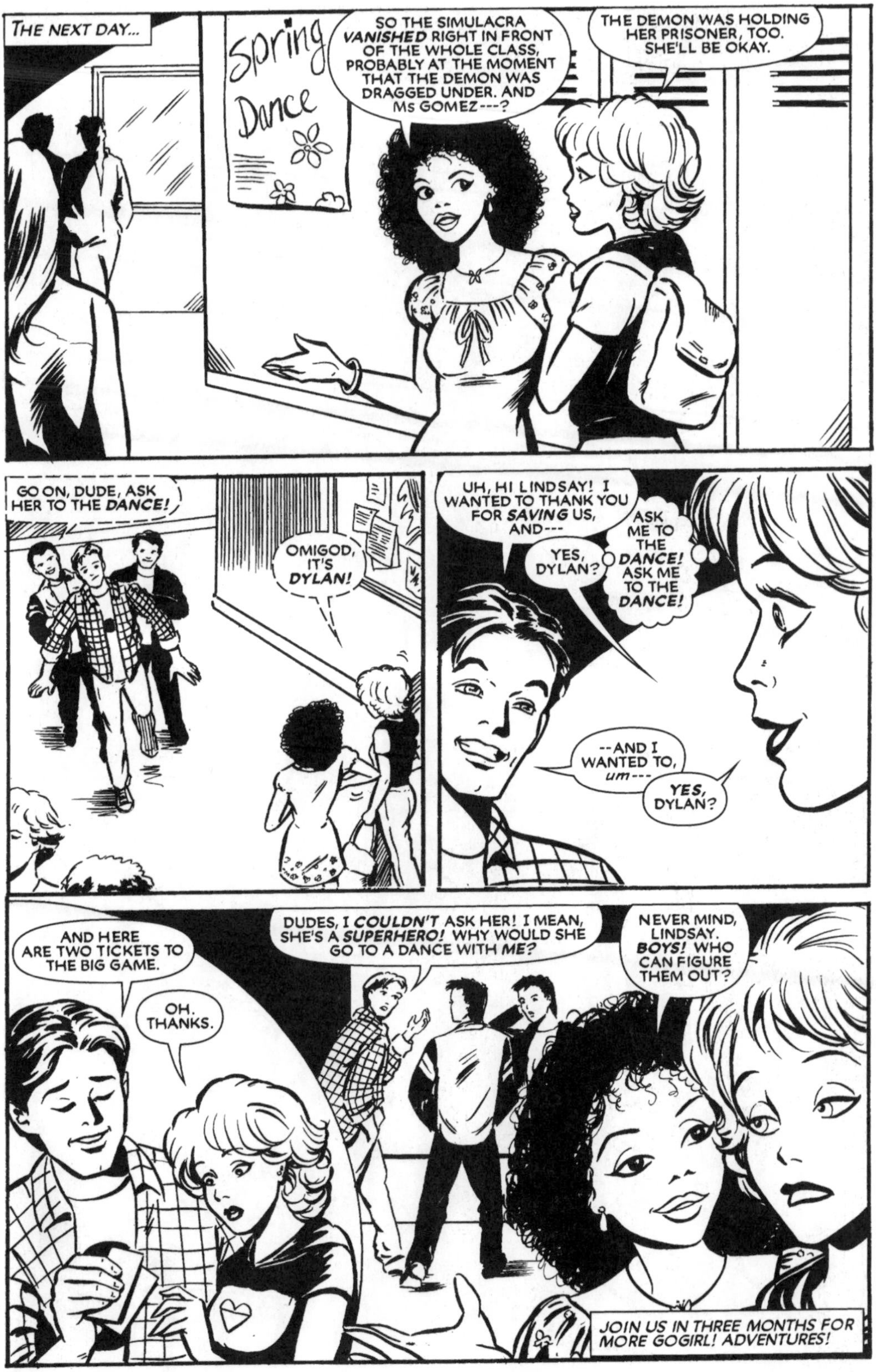
THE NEXT DAY...
Spring Dance
SO THE SIMULACRA VANISHED RIGHT IN FRONT OF THE WHOLE CLASS, PROBABLY AT THE MOMENT THAT THE DEMON WAS DRAGGED UNDER. AND Ms GOMEZ---?
THE DEMON WAS HOLDING HER PRISONER, TOO. SHE'LL BE OKAY.
GO ON, DUDE, ASK HER TO THE DANCE!
OMIGOD, IT'S DYLAN!
UH, HI LINDSAY! I WANTED TO THANK YOU FOR SAVING US, AND---
YES, DYLAN?
ASK ME TO THE DANCE! ASK ME TO THE DANCE!
--AND I WANTED TO, um---
YES, DYLAN?
AND HERE ARE TWO TICKETS TO THE BIG GAME.
OH. THANKS.
DUDES, I COULDN'T ASK HER! I MEAN, SHE'S A SUPERHERO! WHY WOULD SHE GO TO A DANCE WITH ME?
NEVER MIND, LINDSAY. BOYS! WHO CAN FIGURE THEM OUT?
JOIN US IN THREE MONTHS FOR MORE GOGIRL! ADVENTURES!

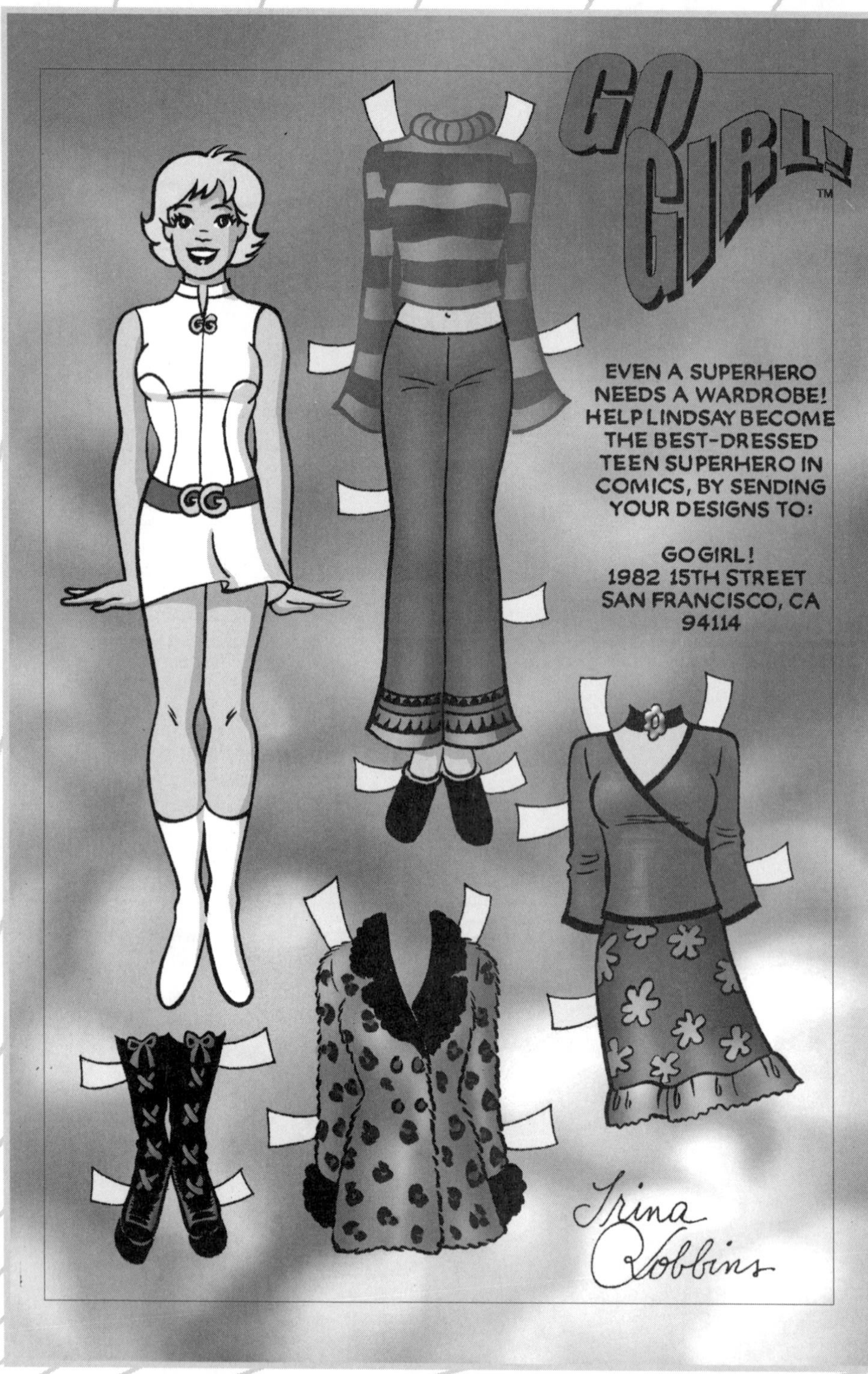
GO GIRL!!
EVEN A SUPERHERO NEEDS A WARDROBE! HELP LINDSAY BECOME THE BEST-DRESSED TEEN SUPERHERO IN COMICS, BY SENDING YOUR DESIGNS TO:
GO GIRL!
1982 15TH STREET
SAN FRANCISCO, CA
94114
Trina Robbins

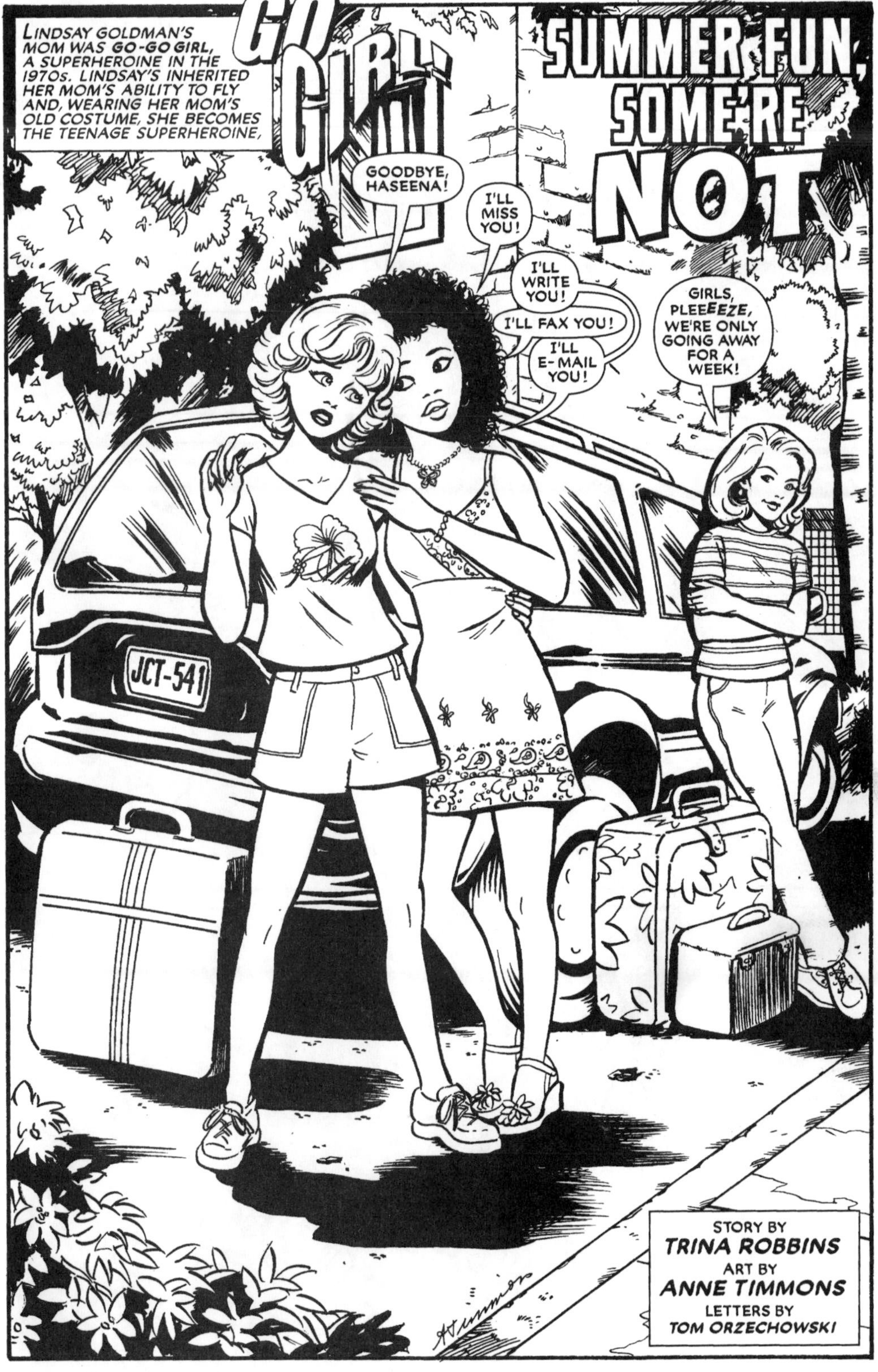
LINDSAY GOLDMAN'S MOM WAS GO-GO GIRL, A SUPERHEROINE IN THE 1970s. LINDSAY'S INHERITED HER MOM'S ABILITY TO FLY AND, WEARING HER MOM'S OLD COSTUME, SHE BECOMES THE TEENAGE SUPERHEROINE,
GO GIRL!
SUMMER FUN, SOME'RE NOT
GOODBYE, HASEENA!
I'LL MISS YOU!
I'LL WRITE YOU!
I'LL FAX YOU!
I'LL E-MAIL YOU!
GIRLS, PLEEEEEZE, WE'RE ONLY GOING AWAY FOR A WEEK!
JCT-541
STORY BY TRINA ROBBINS
ART BY ANNE TIMMONS
LETTERS BY TOM ORZECHOWSKI

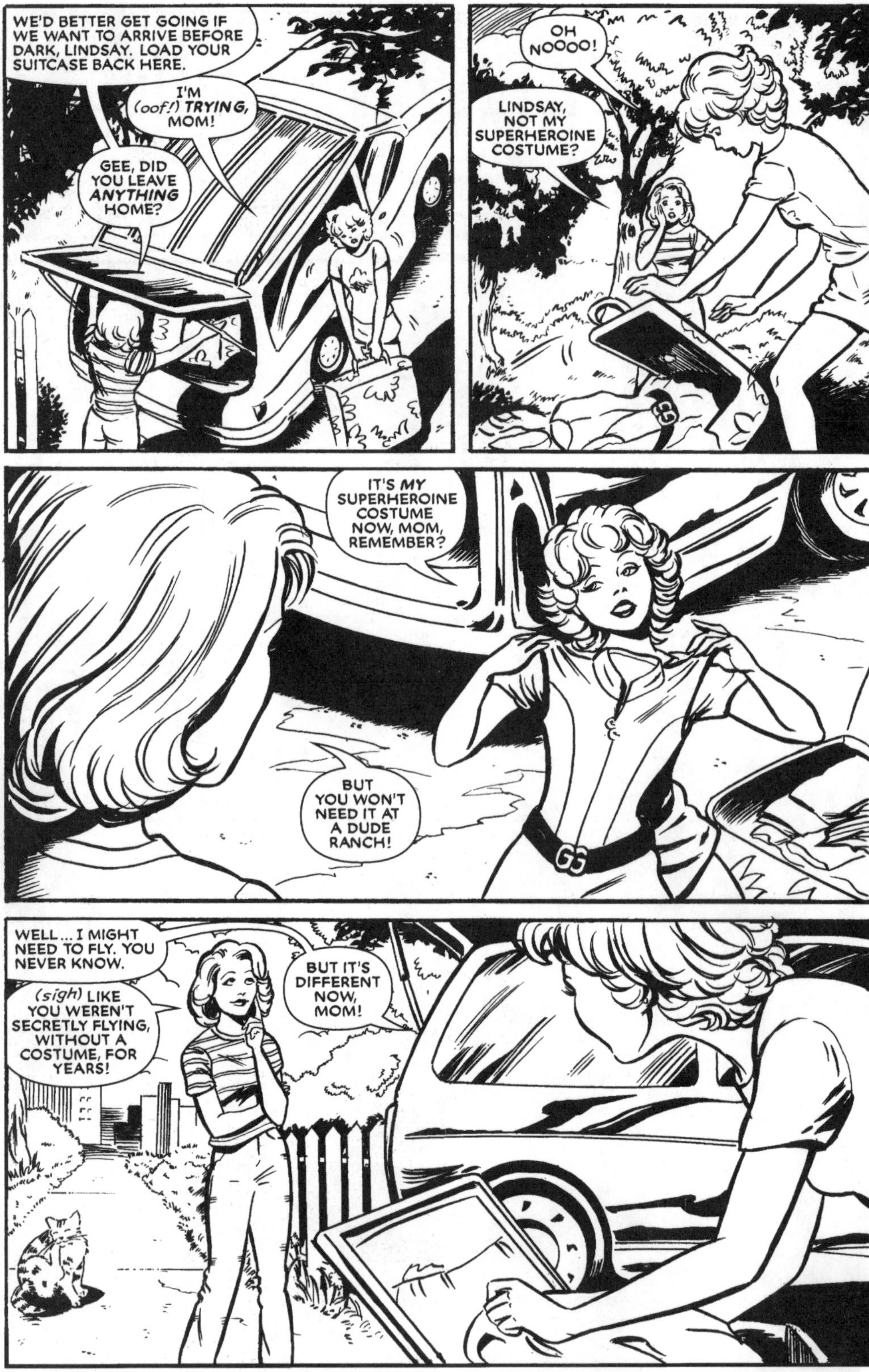
WE'D BETTER GET GOING IF WE WANT TO ARRIVE BEFORE DARK, LINDSAY. LOAD YOUR SUITCASE BACK HERE.
I'M (oof!) TRYING, MOM!
GEE, DID YOU LEAVE ANYTHING HOME?
OH NOOOO!
LINDSAY, NOT MY SUPERHEROINE COSTUME?
IT'S MY SUPERHEROINE COSTUME NOW, MOM, REMEMBER?
BUT YOU WON'T NEED IT AT A DUDE RANCH!
WELL... I MIGHT NEED TO FLY. YOU NEVER KNOW.
(sigh) LIKE YOU WEREN'T SECRETLY FLYING, WITHOUT A COSTUME, FOR YEARS!
BUT IT'S DIFFERENT NOW, MOM!

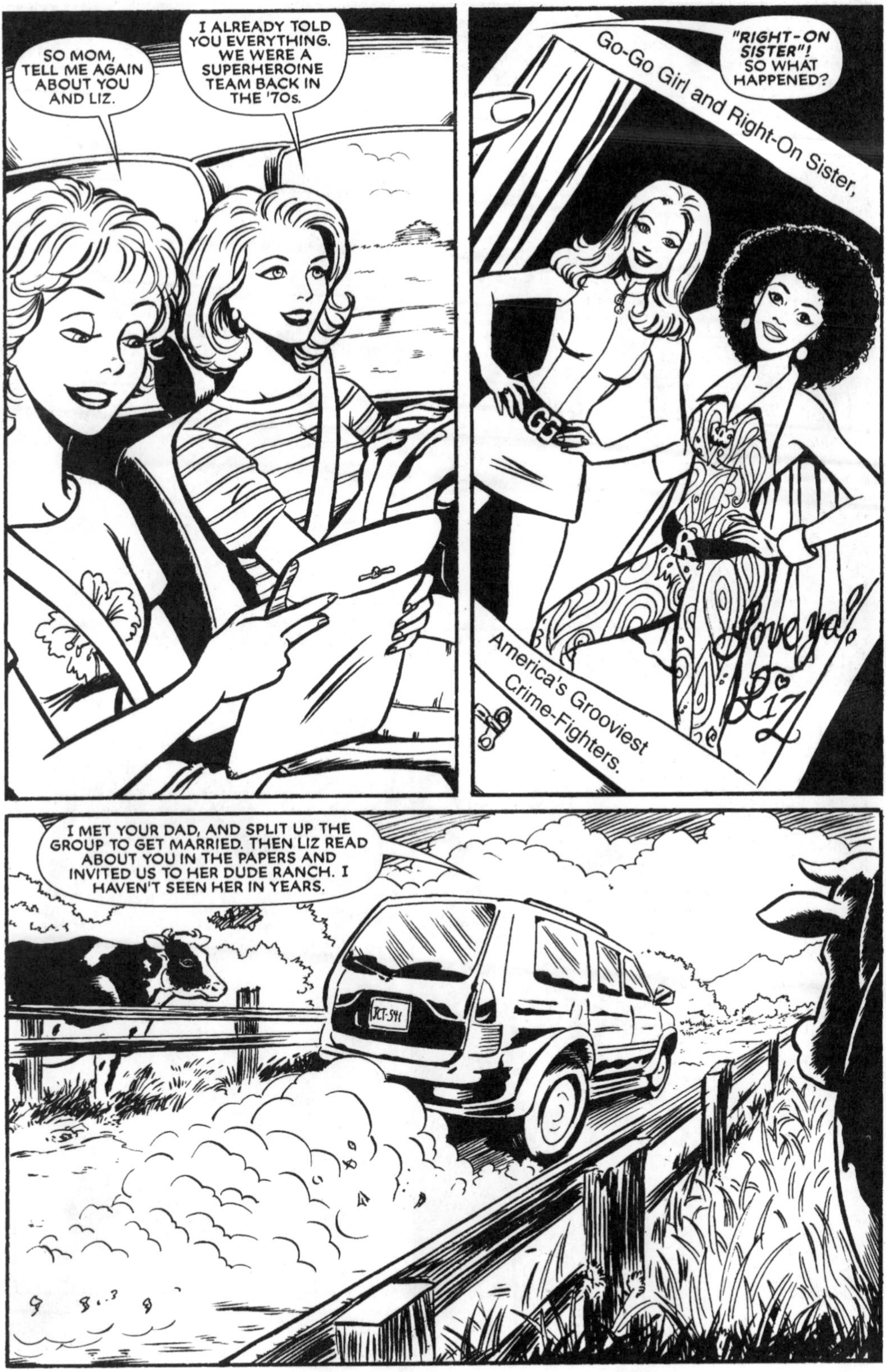
SO MOM, TELL ME AGAIN ABOUT YOU AND LIZ.
I ALREADY TOLD YOU EVERYTHING. WE WERE A SUPERHEROINE TEAM BACK IN THE '70s.
Go-Go Girl and Right-On Sister,
"RIGHT-ON SISTER"! SO WHAT HAPPENED?
America's Grooviest Crime-Fighters.
Love ya! Liz
I MET YOUR DAD, AND SPLIT UP THE GROUP TO GET MARRIED. THEN LIZ READ ABOUT YOU IN THE PAPERS AND INVITED US TO HER DUDE RANCH. I HAVEN'T SEEN HER IN YEARS.

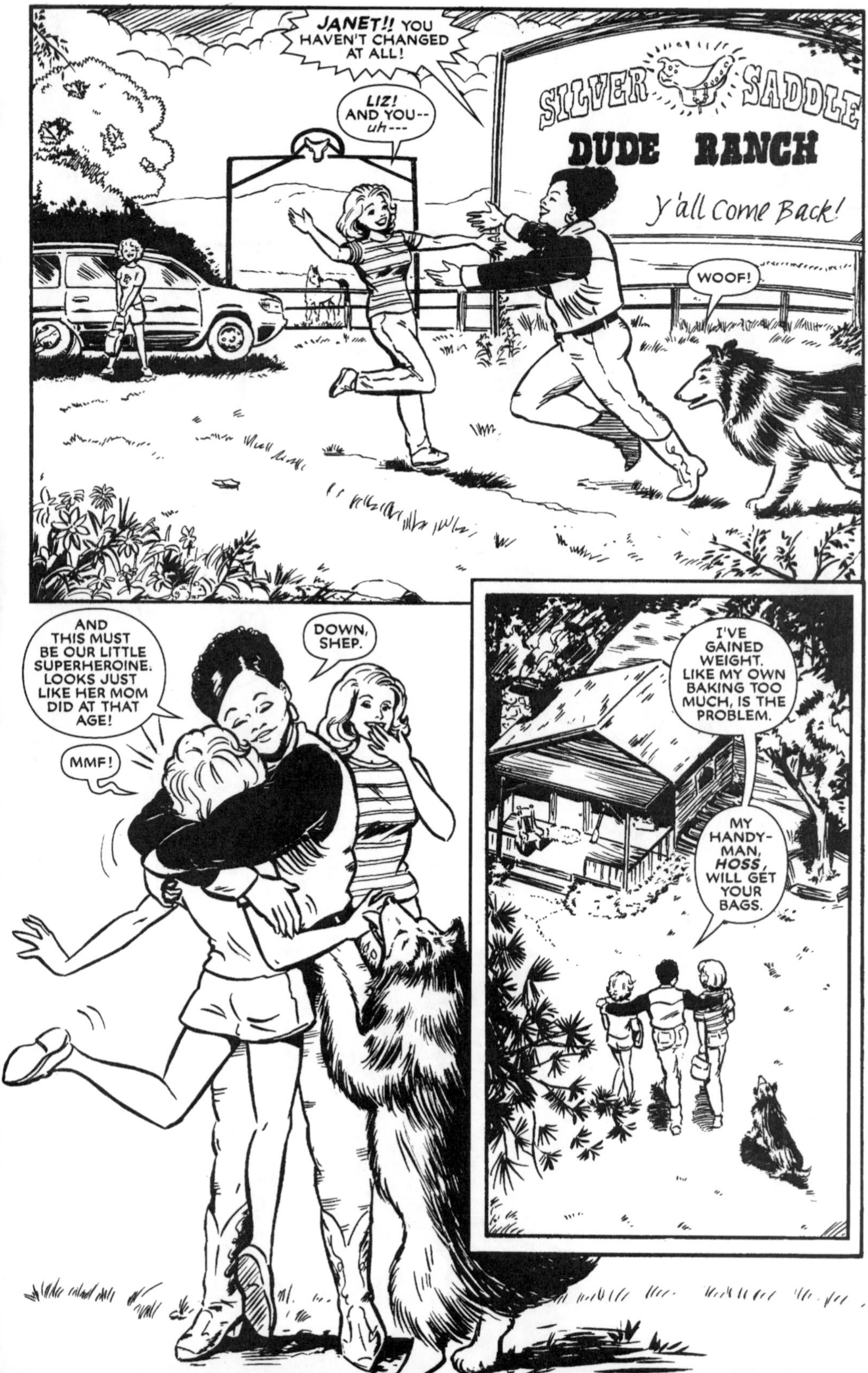
JANET!! YOU HAVEN'T CHANGED AT ALL!
LIZ! AND YOU-- uh---
SILVER SADDLE
DUDE RANCH
Y'all Come Back!
WOOF!
AND THIS MUST BE OUR LITTLE SUPERHEROINE. LOOKS JUST LIKE HER MOM DID AT THAT AGE!
DOWN, SHEP.
MMF!
I'VE GAINED WEIGHT. LIKE MY OWN BAKING TOO MUCH, IS THE PROBLEM.
MY HANDY-MAN, HOSS, WILL GET YOUR BAGS.

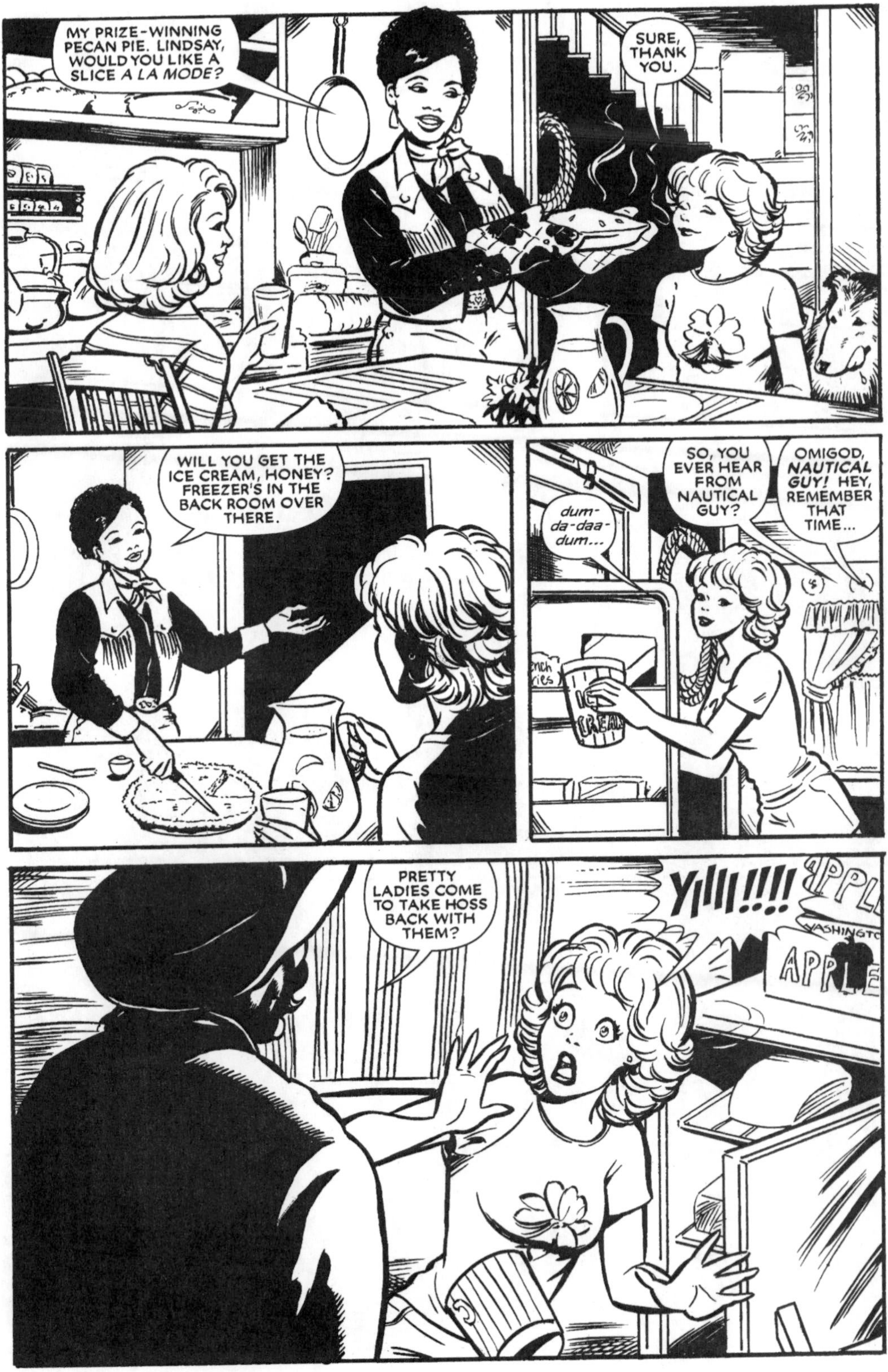

MY PRIZE-WINNING PECAN PIE. LINDSAY, WOULD YOU LIKE A SLICE *A LA MODE?*
SURE, THANK YOU.
WILL YOU GET THE ICE CREAM, HONEY? FREEZER'S IN THE BACK ROOM OVER THERE.
SO, YOU EVER HEAR FROM NAUTICAL GUY?
OMIGOD, ***NAUTICAL GUY!*** HEY, REMEMBER THAT TIME...
dum-da-daa-dum...
ICE CREAM
PRETTY LADIES COME TO TAKE HOSS BACK WITH THEM?
YIIII!!!!
APPLE

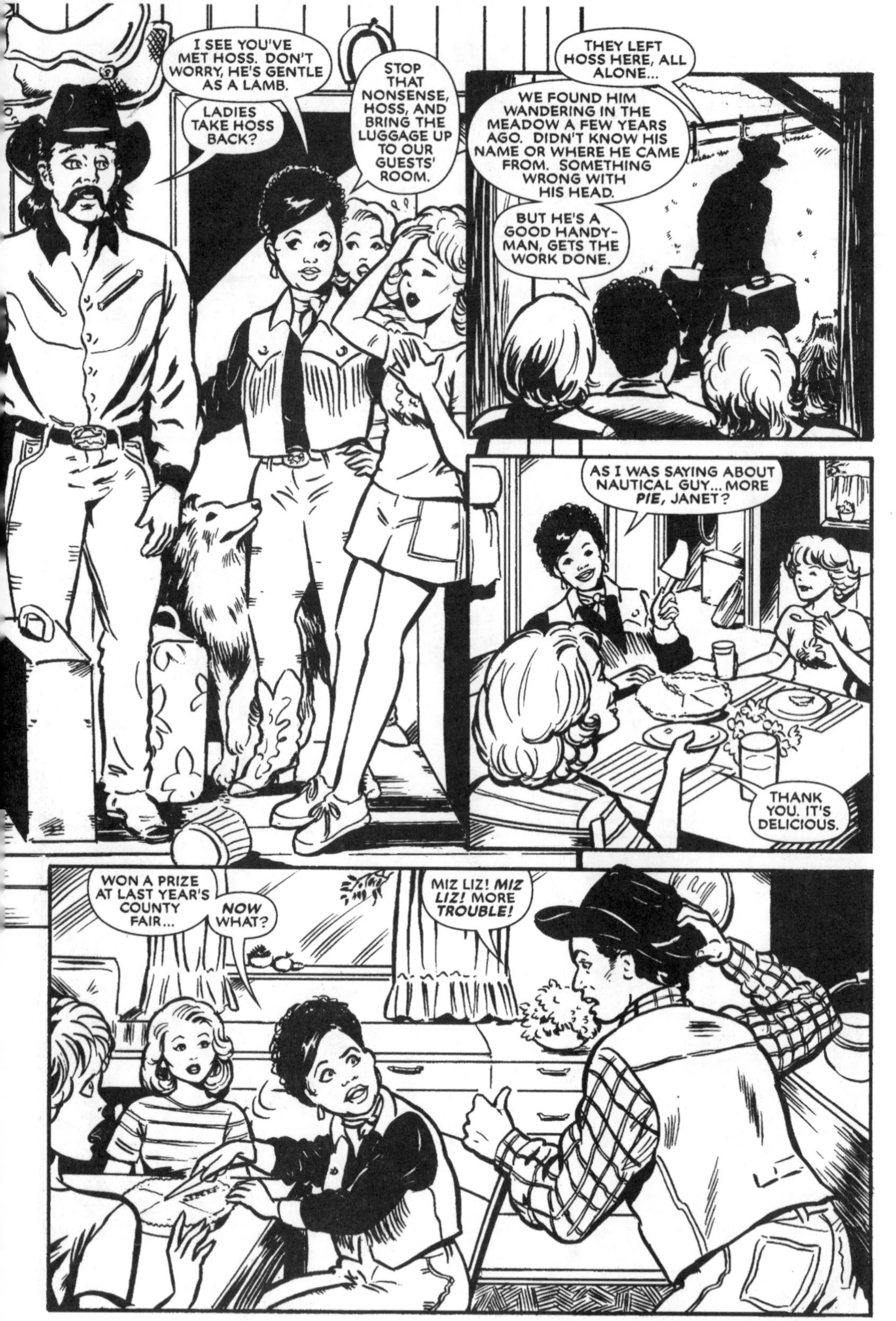

I SEE YOU'VE MET HOSS. DON'T WORRY, HE'S GENTLE AS A LAMB.
LADIES TAKE HOSS BACK?
STOP THAT NONSENSE, HOSS, AND BRING THE LUGGAGE UP TO OUR GUESTS' ROOM.
THEY LEFT HOSS HERE, ALL ALONE...
WE FOUND HIM WANDERING IN THE MEADOW A FEW YEARS AGO. DIDN'T KNOW HIS NAME OR WHERE HE CAME FROM. SOMETHING WRONG WITH HIS HEAD.
BUT HE'S A GOOD HANDY-MAN, GETS THE WORK DONE.
AS I WAS SAYING ABOUT NAUTICAL GUY... MORE *PIE*, JANET?
THANK YOU. IT'S DELICIOUS.
WON A PRIZE AT LAST YEAR'S COUNTY FAIR...
NOW WHAT?
MIZ LIZ! *MIZ LIZ!* MORE *TROUBLE!*

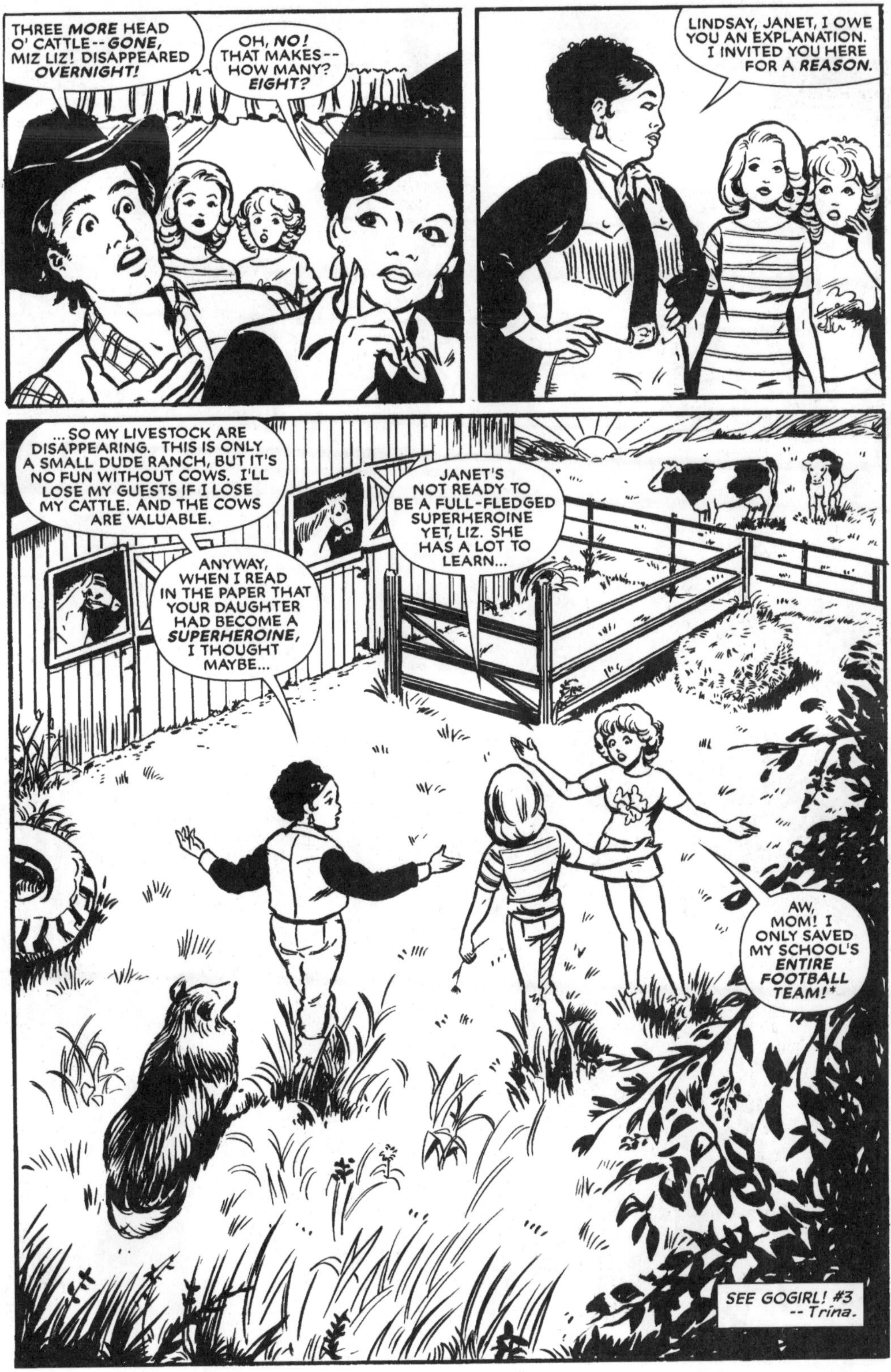
THREE MORE HEAD O' CATTLE--GONE, MIZ LIZ! DISAPPEARED OVERNIGHT!
OH, NO! THAT MAKES--HOW MANY? EIGHT?
LINDSAY, JANET, I OWE YOU AN EXPLANATION. I INVITED YOU HERE FOR A REASON.
... SO MY LIVESTOCK ARE DISAPPEARING. THIS IS ONLY A SMALL DUDE RANCH, BUT IT'S NO FUN WITHOUT COWS. I'LL LOSE MY GUESTS IF I LOSE MY CATTLE. AND THE COWS ARE VALUABLE.
ANYWAY, WHEN I READ IN THE PAPER THAT YOUR DAUGHTER HAD BECOME A SUPERHEROINE, I THOUGHT MAYBE...
JANET'S NOT READY TO BE A FULL-FLEDGED SUPERHEROINE YET, LIZ. SHE HAS A LOT TO LEARN...
AW, MOM! I ONLY SAVED MY SCHOOL'S ENTIRE FOOTBALL TEAM!*
SEE GOGIRL! #3 -- Trina.

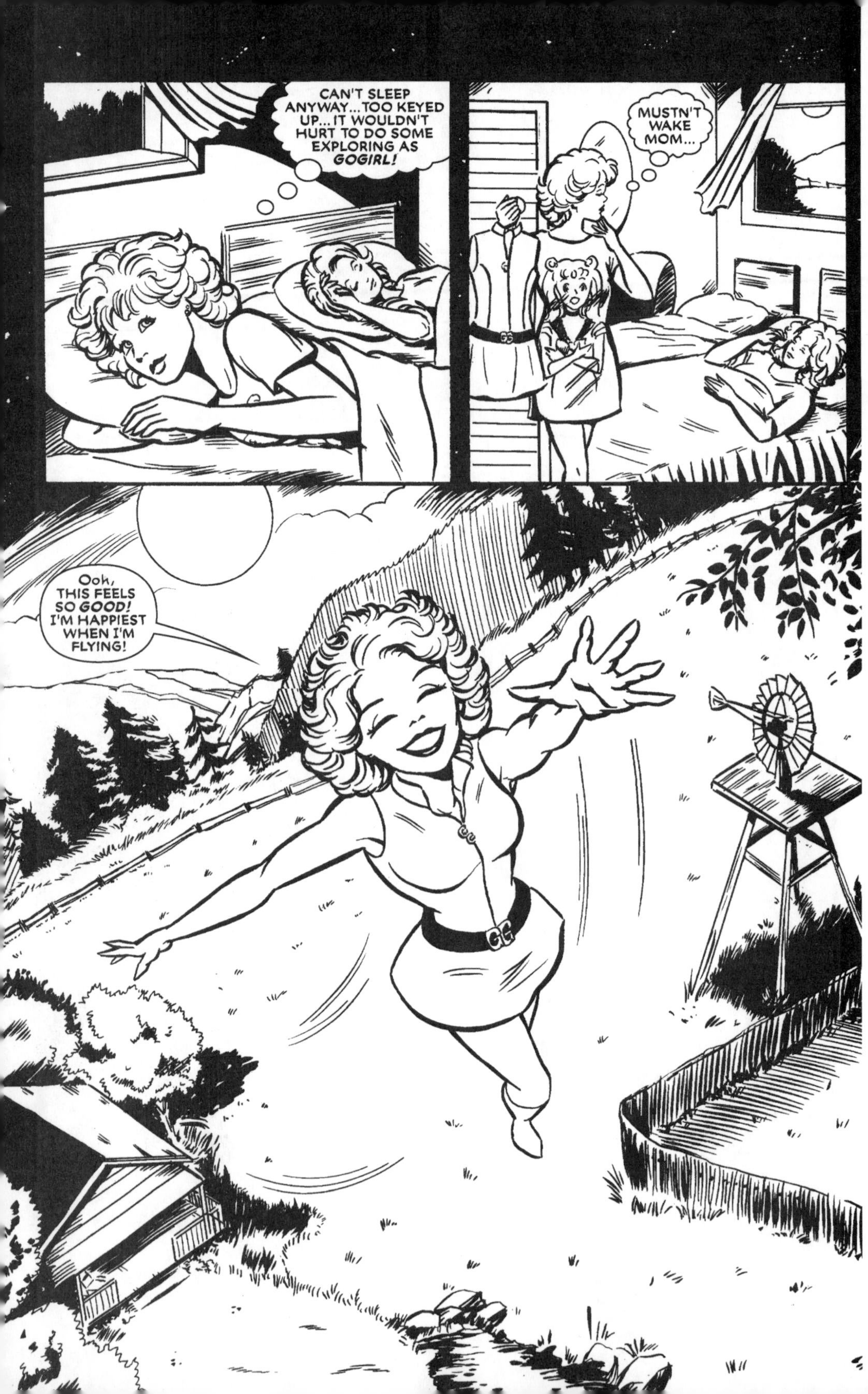
CAN'T SLEEP ANYWAY...TOO KEYED UP...IT WOULDN'T HURT TO DO SOME EXPLORING AS *GOGIRL!*
MUSTN'T WAKE MOM...
Ooh, THIS FEELS SO *GOOD!* I'M HAPPIEST WHEN I'M FLYING!

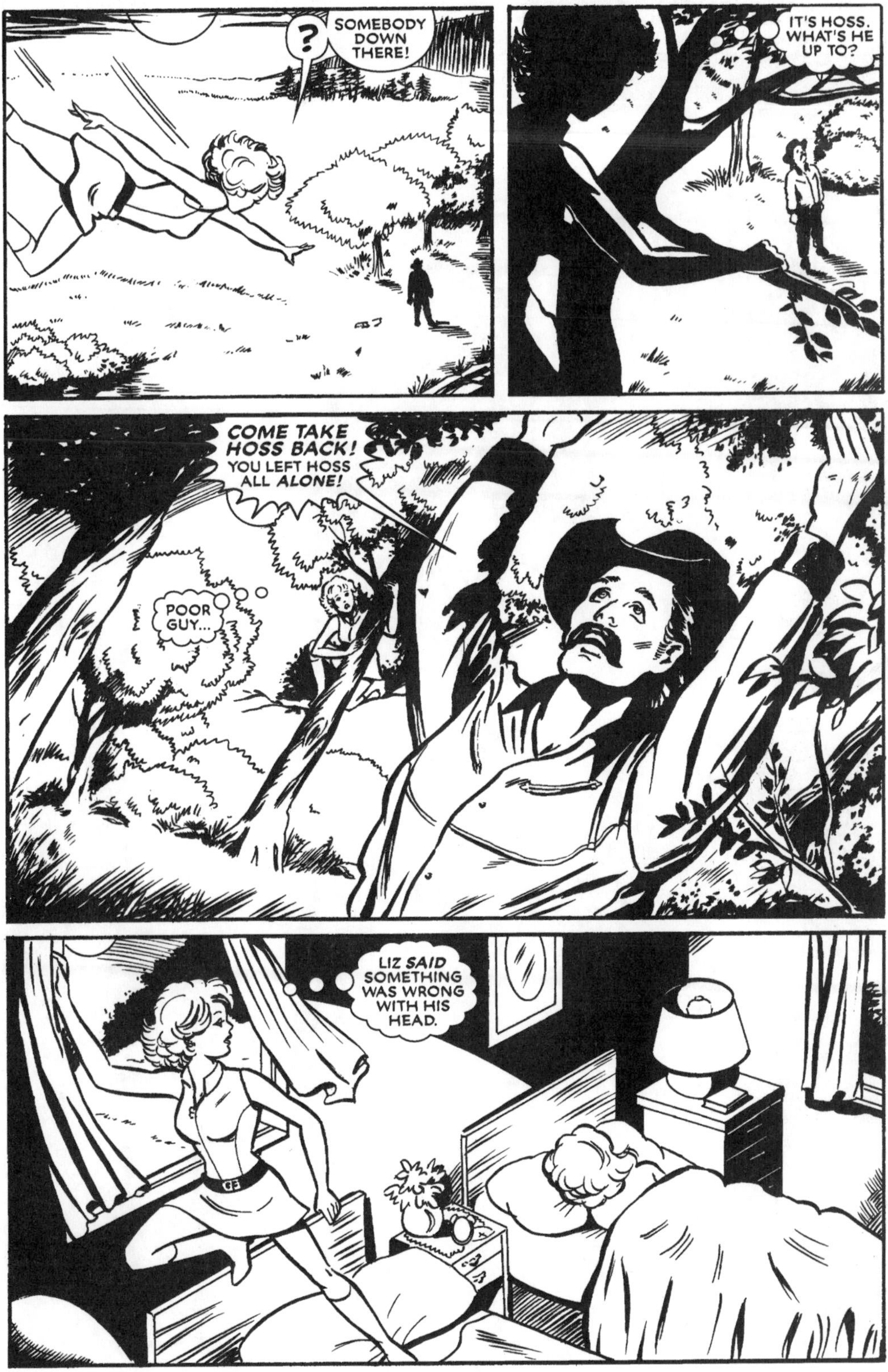
?
SOMEBODY DOWN THERE!
IT'S HOSS. WHAT'S HE UP TO?
COME TAKE HOSS BACK! YOU LEFT HOSS ALL ALONE!
POOR GUY...
LIZ SAID SOMETHING WAS WRONG WITH HIS HEAD.

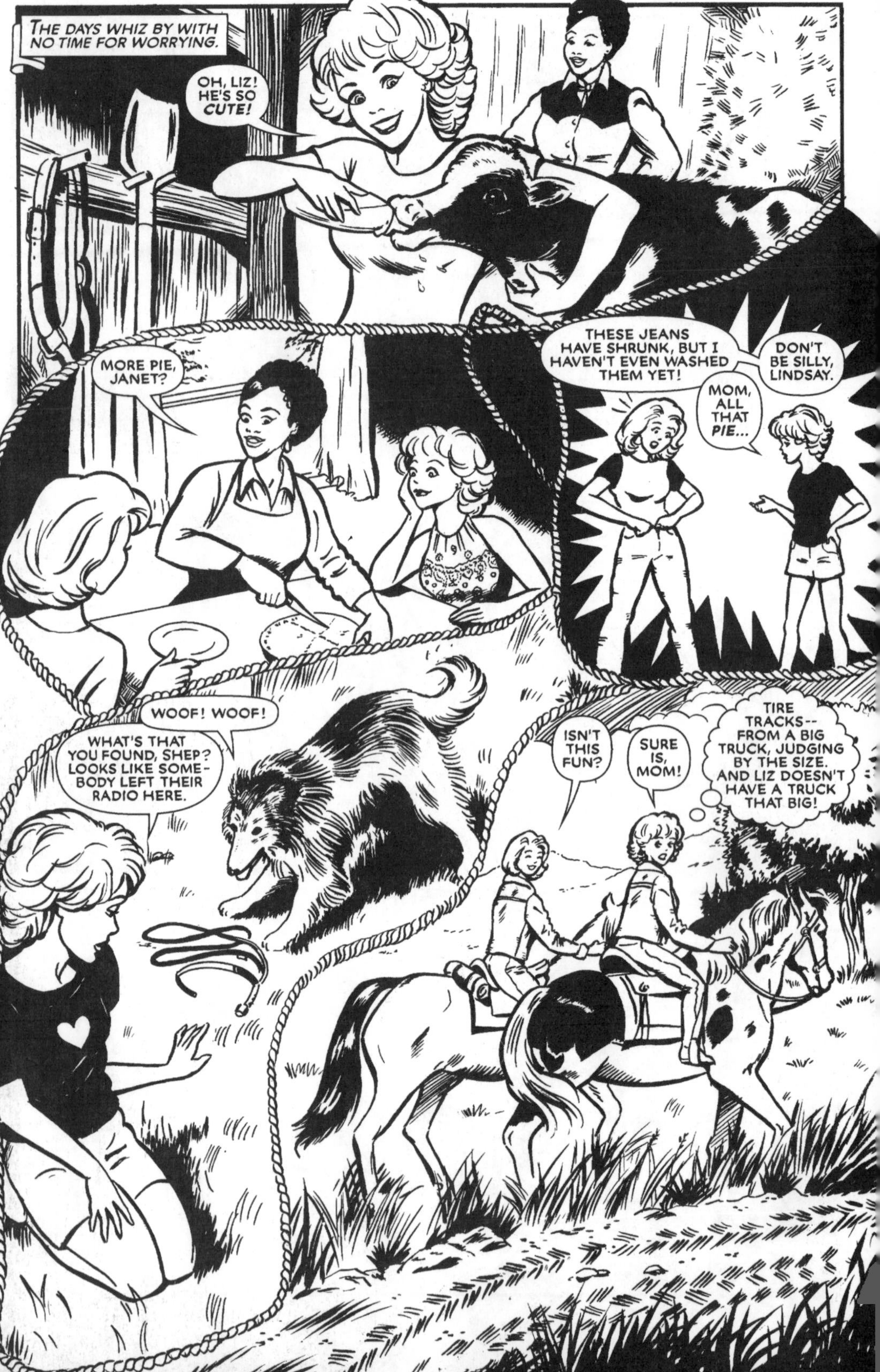
THE DAYS WHIZ BY WITH NO TIME FOR WORRYING.
OH, LIZ! HE'S SO CUTE!
MORE PIE, JANET?
THESE JEANS HAVE SHRUNK, BUT I HAVEN'T EVEN WASHED THEM YET!
DON'T BE SILLY, LINDSAY.
MOM, ALL THAT PIE...
WOOF! WOOF!
WHAT'S THAT YOU FOUND, SHEP? LOOKS LIKE SOME-BODY LEFT THEIR RADIO HERE.
ISN'T THIS FUN?
SURE IS, MOM!
TIRE TRACKS-- FROM A BIG TRUCK, JUDGING BY THE SIZE. AND LIZ DOESN'T HAVE A TRUCK THAT BIG!

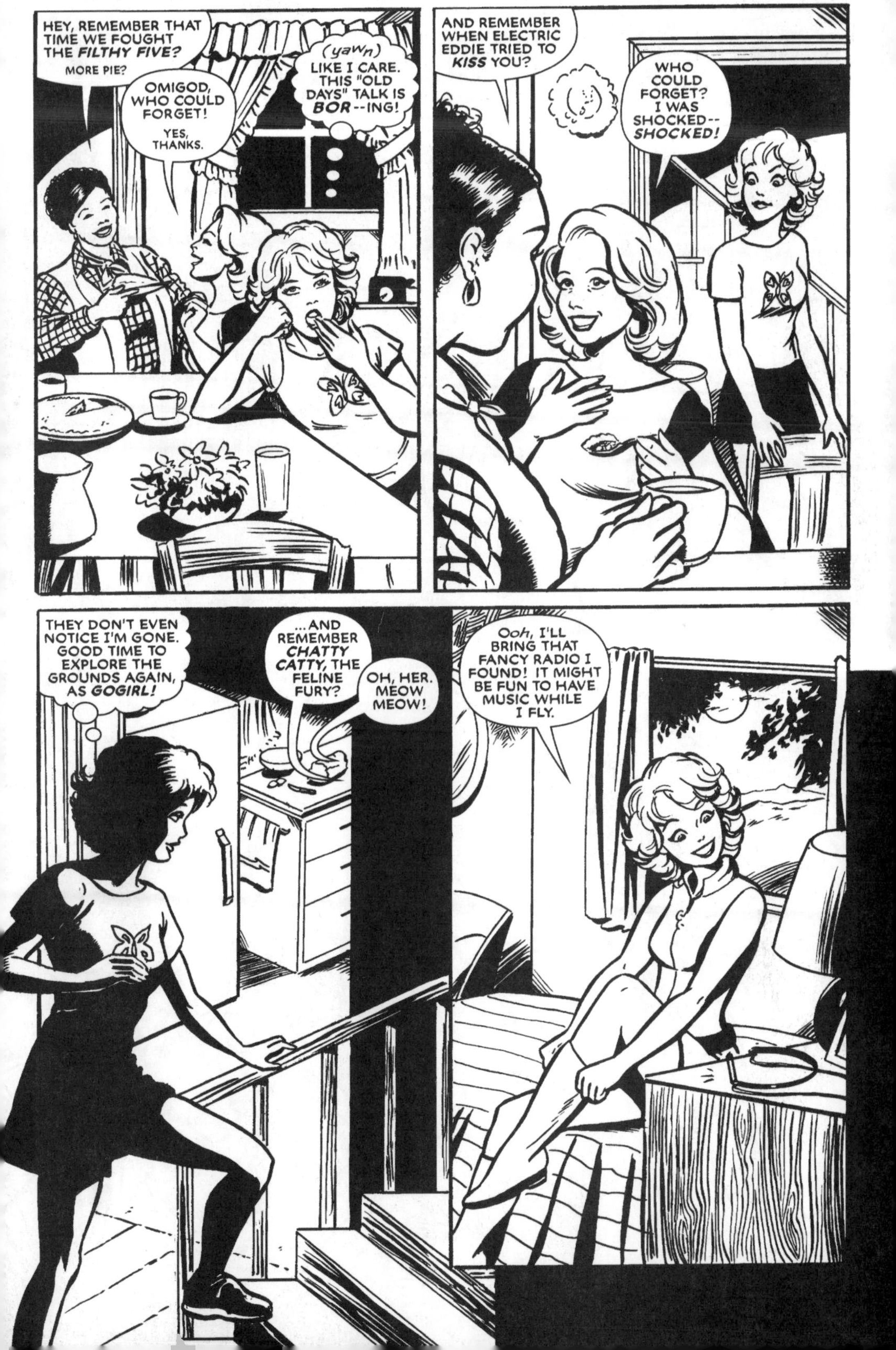
HEY, REMEMBER THAT TIME WE FOUGHT THE FILTHY FIVE?
MORE PIE?
OMIGOD, WHO COULD FORGET!
YES, THANKS.
(yawn) LIKE I CARE. THIS "OLD DAYS" TALK IS BOR--ING!
AND REMEMBER WHEN ELECTRIC EDDIE TRIED TO KISS YOU?
WHO COULD FORGET? I WAS SHOCKED-- SHOCKED!
THEY DON'T EVEN NOTICE I'M GONE. GOOD TIME TO EXPLORE THE GROUNDS AGAIN, AS GOGIRL!
...AND REMEMBER CHATTY CATTY, THE FELINE FURY?
OH, HER. MEOW MEOW!
Ooh, I'LL BRING THAT FANCY RADIO I FOUND! IT MIGHT BE FUN TO HAVE MUSIC WHILE I FLY.

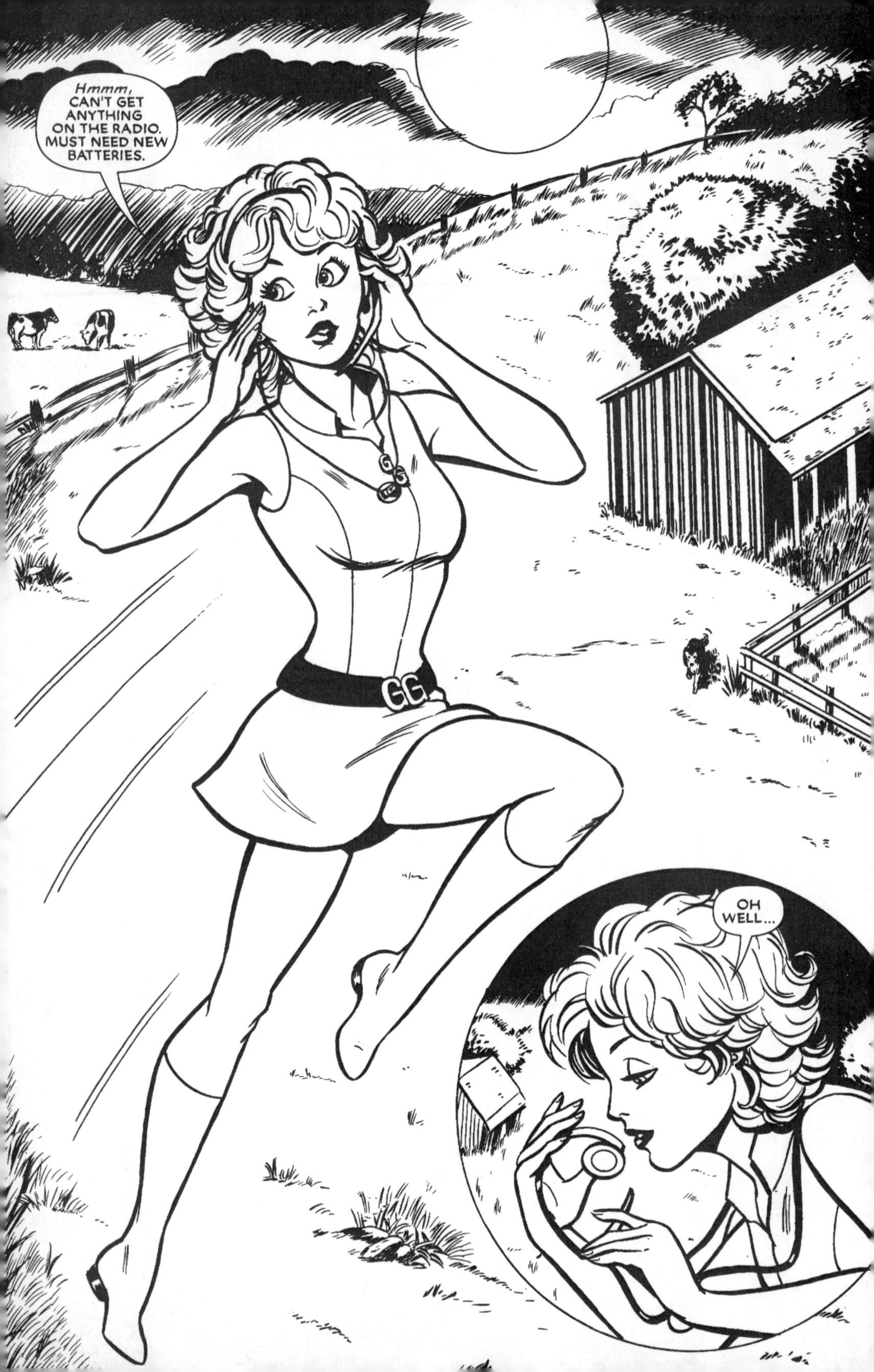
Hmmm, CAN'T GET ANYTHING ON THE RADIO. MUST NEED NEW BATTERIES.
OH WELL...

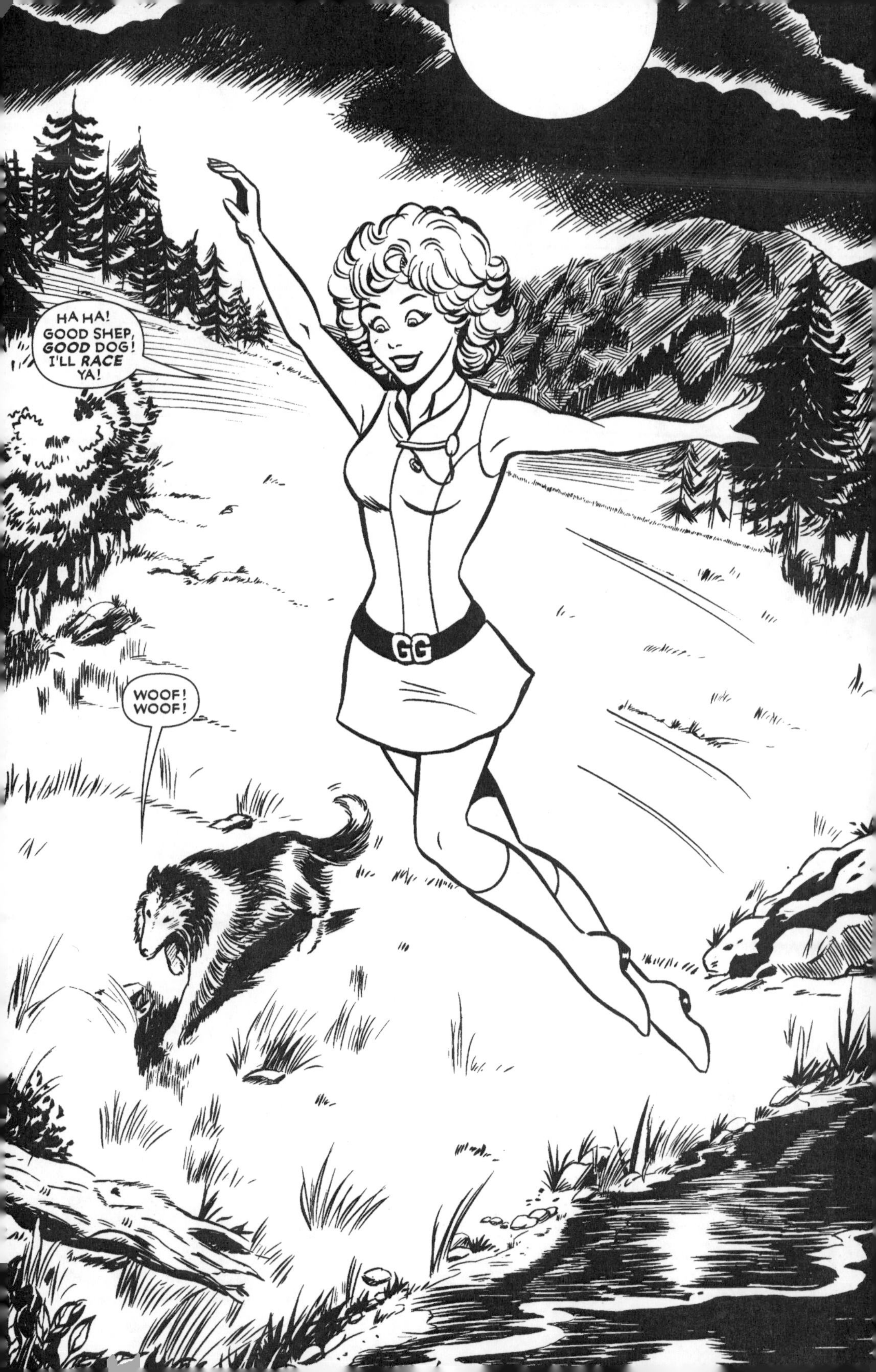
HA HA! GOOD SHEP, GOOD DOG! I'LL RACE YA!
WOOF! WOOF!

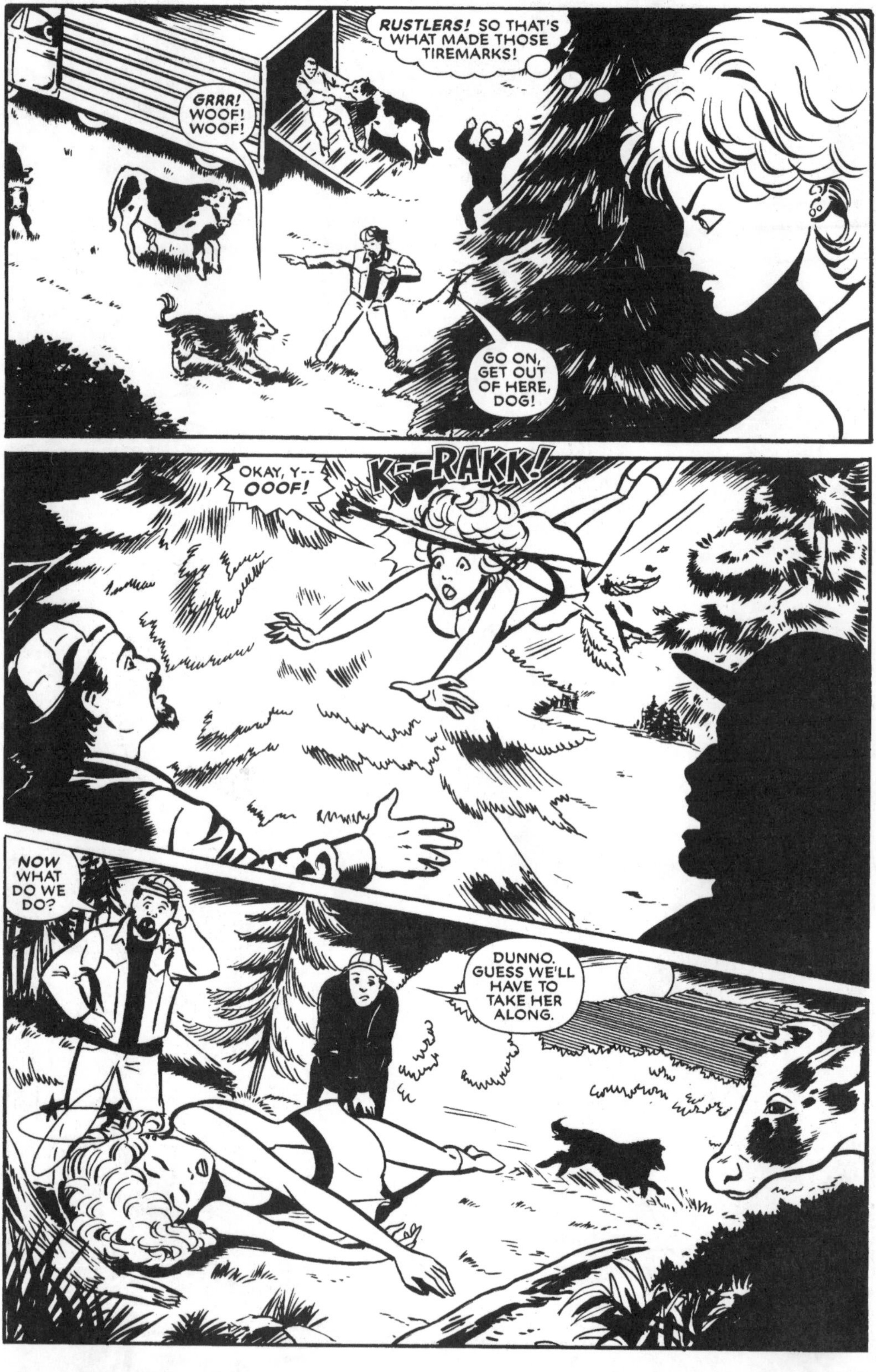
RUSTLERS! SO THAT'S WHAT MADE THOSE TIREMARKS!
GRRR! WOOF! WOOF!
GO ON, GET OUT OF HERE, DOG!
OKAY, Y-- OOOF!
K--RAKK!
NOW WHAT DO WE DO?
DUNNO. GUESS WE'LL HAVE TO TAKE HER ALONG.

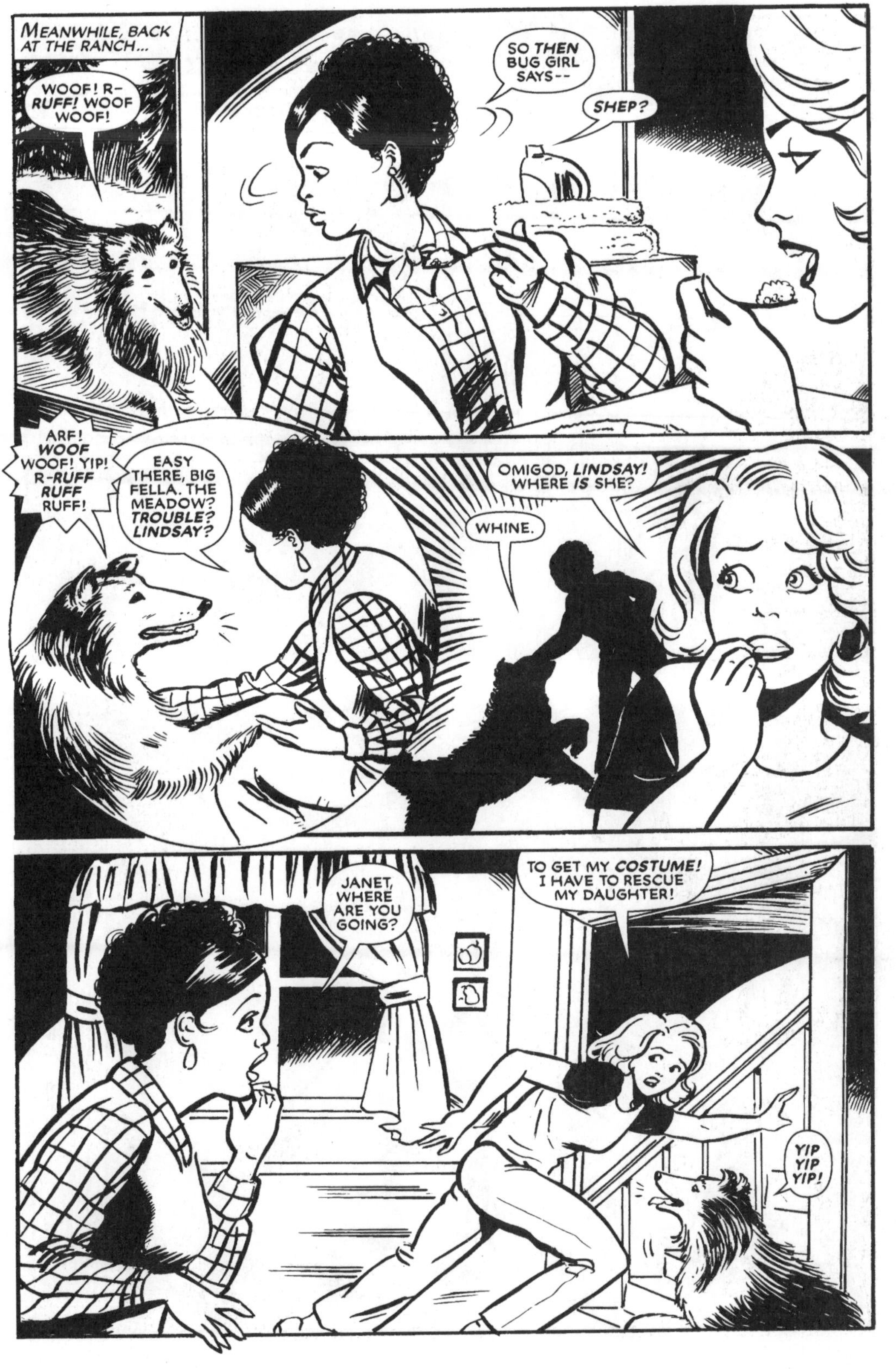
MEANWHILE, BACK AT THE RANCH...
WOOF! R-RUFF! WOOF WOOF!
SO THEN BUG GIRL SAYS--
SHEP?
ARF! WOOF WOOF! YIP! R-RUFF RUFF RUFF!
EASY THERE, BIG FELLA. THE MEADOW? TROUBLE? LINDSAY?
WHINE.
OMIGOD, LINDSAY! WHERE IS SHE?
JANET, WHERE ARE YOU GOING?
TO GET MY COSTUME! I HAVE TO RESCUE MY DAUGHTER!
YIP YIP YIP!

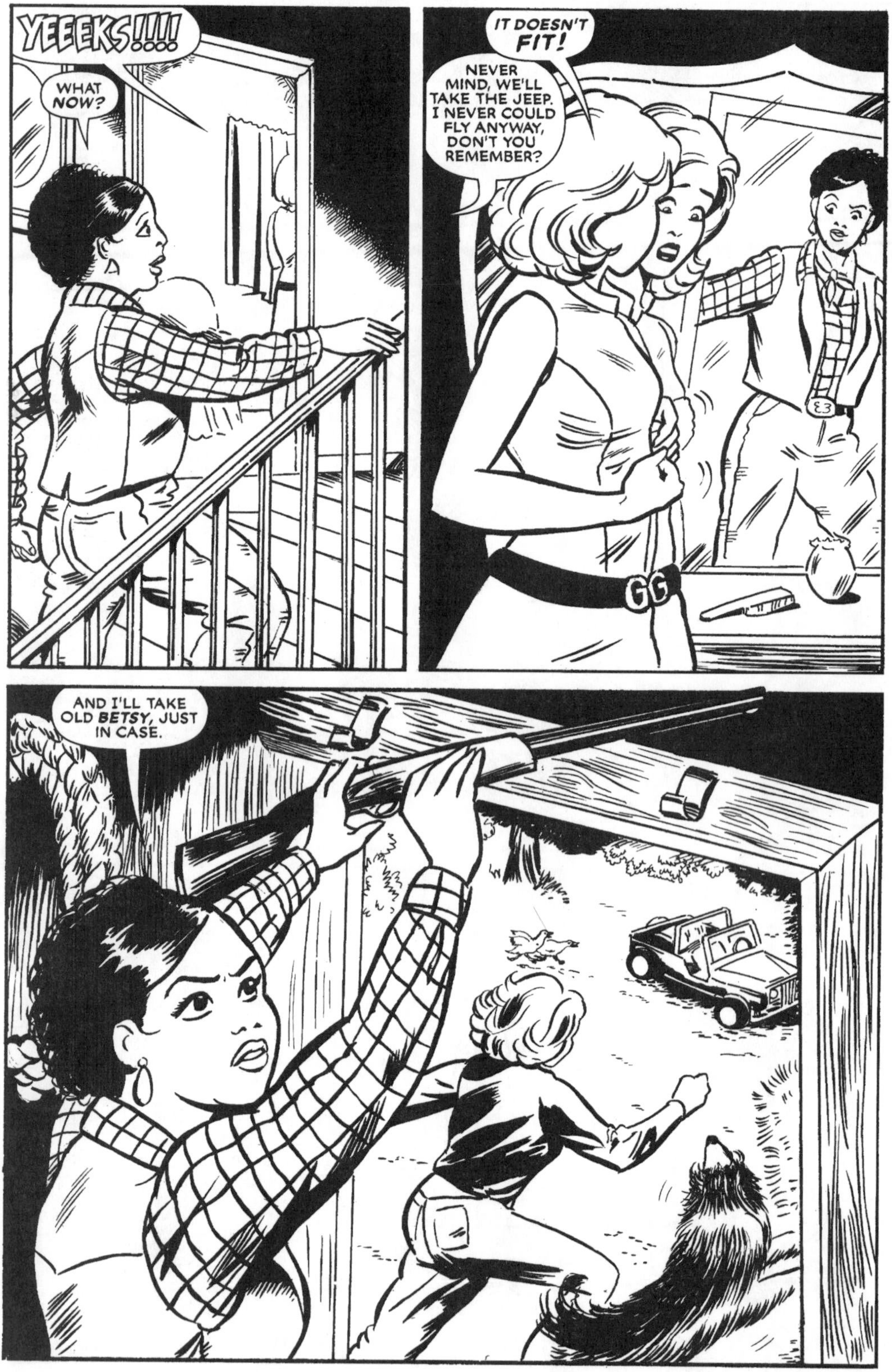
YEEEKS!!!!....
WHAT NOW?
IT DOESN'T FIT!
NEVER MIND, WE'LL TAKE THE JEEP. I NEVER COULD FLY ANYWAY, DON'T YOU REMEMBER?
AND I'LL TAKE OLD BETSY, JUST IN CASE.

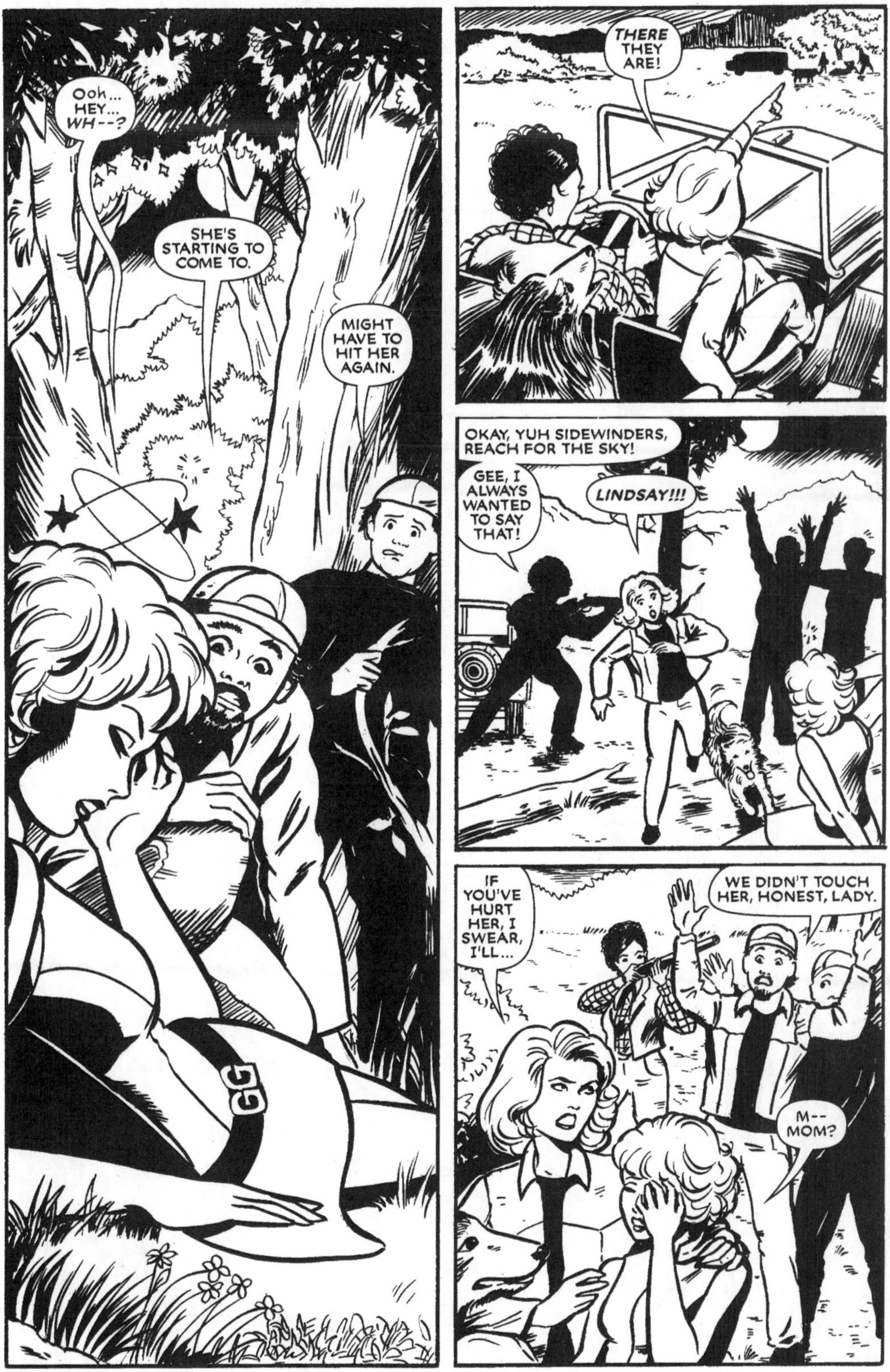
Ooh... HEY... WH--?
SHE'S STARTING TO COME TO.
MIGHT HAVE TO HIT HER AGAIN.
THERE THEY ARE!
OKAY, YUH SIDEWINDERS, REACH FOR THE SKY!
GEE, I ALWAYS WANTED TO SAY THAT!
LINDSAY!!!
IF YOU'VE HURT HER, I SWEAR, I'LL...
WE DIDN'T TOUCH HER, HONEST, LADY.
M-- MOM?

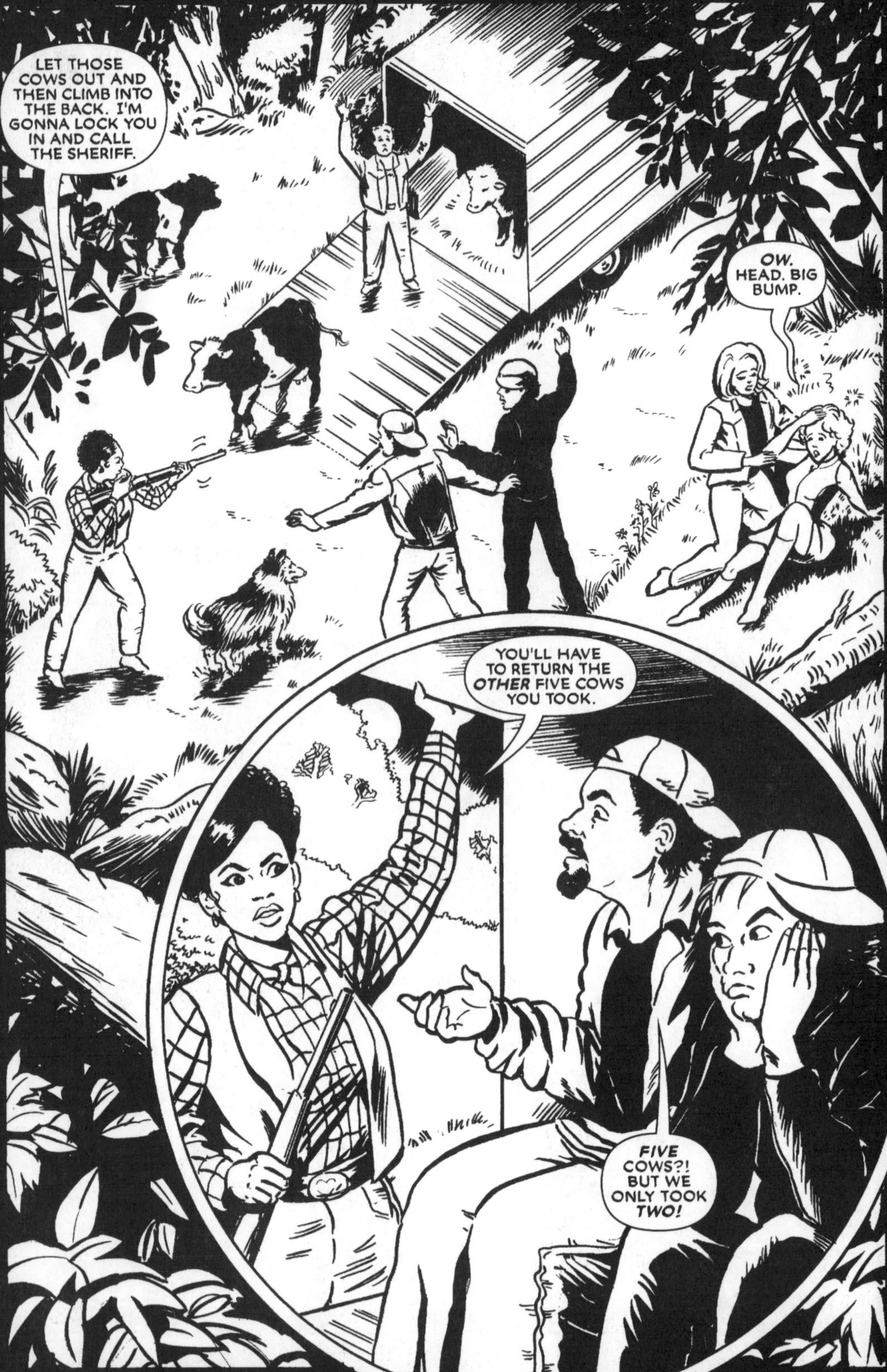
LET THOSE COWS OUT AND THEN CLIMB INTO THE BACK. I'M GONNA LOCK YOU IN AND CALL THE SHERIFF.
OW. HEAD. BIG BUMP.
YOU'LL HAVE TO RETURN THE OTHER FIVE COWS YOU TOOK.
FIVE COWS?! BUT WE ONLY TOOK TWO!

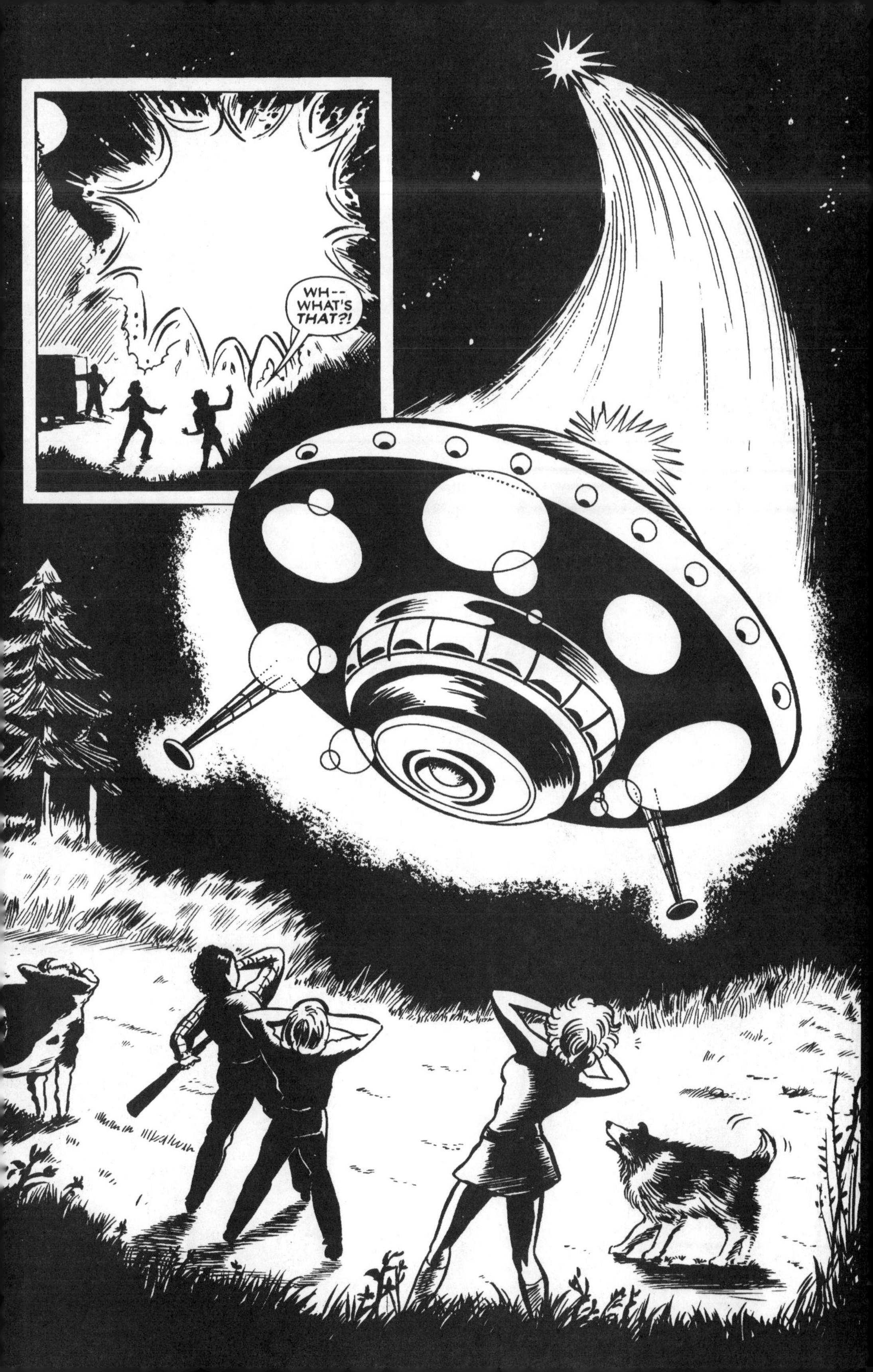
WH-- WHAT'S THAT?!

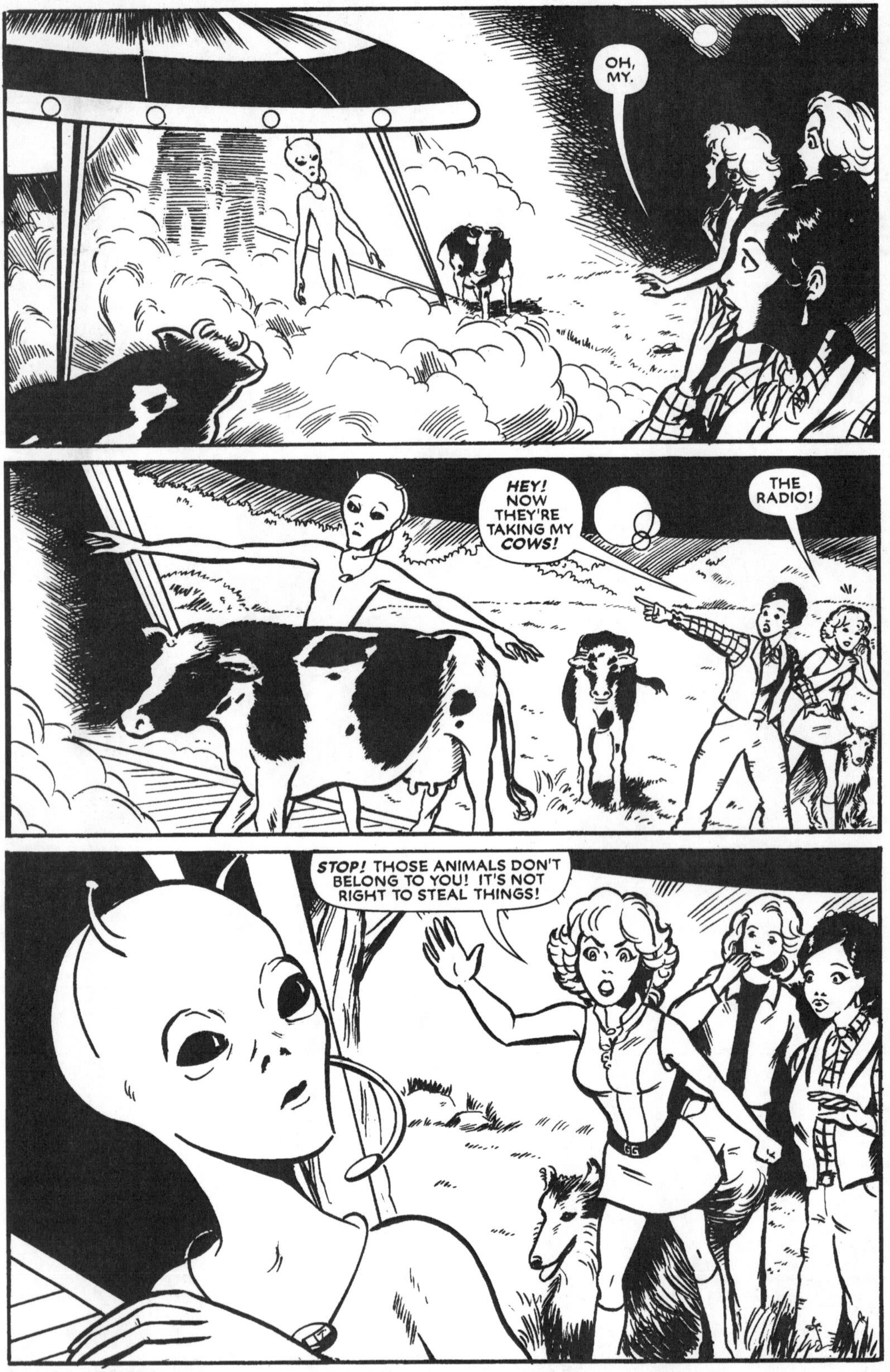
OH, MY.
HEY! NOW THEY'RE TAKING MY COWS!
THE RADIO!
STOP! THOSE ANIMALS DON'T BELONG TO YOU! IT'S NOT RIGHT TO STEAL THINGS!

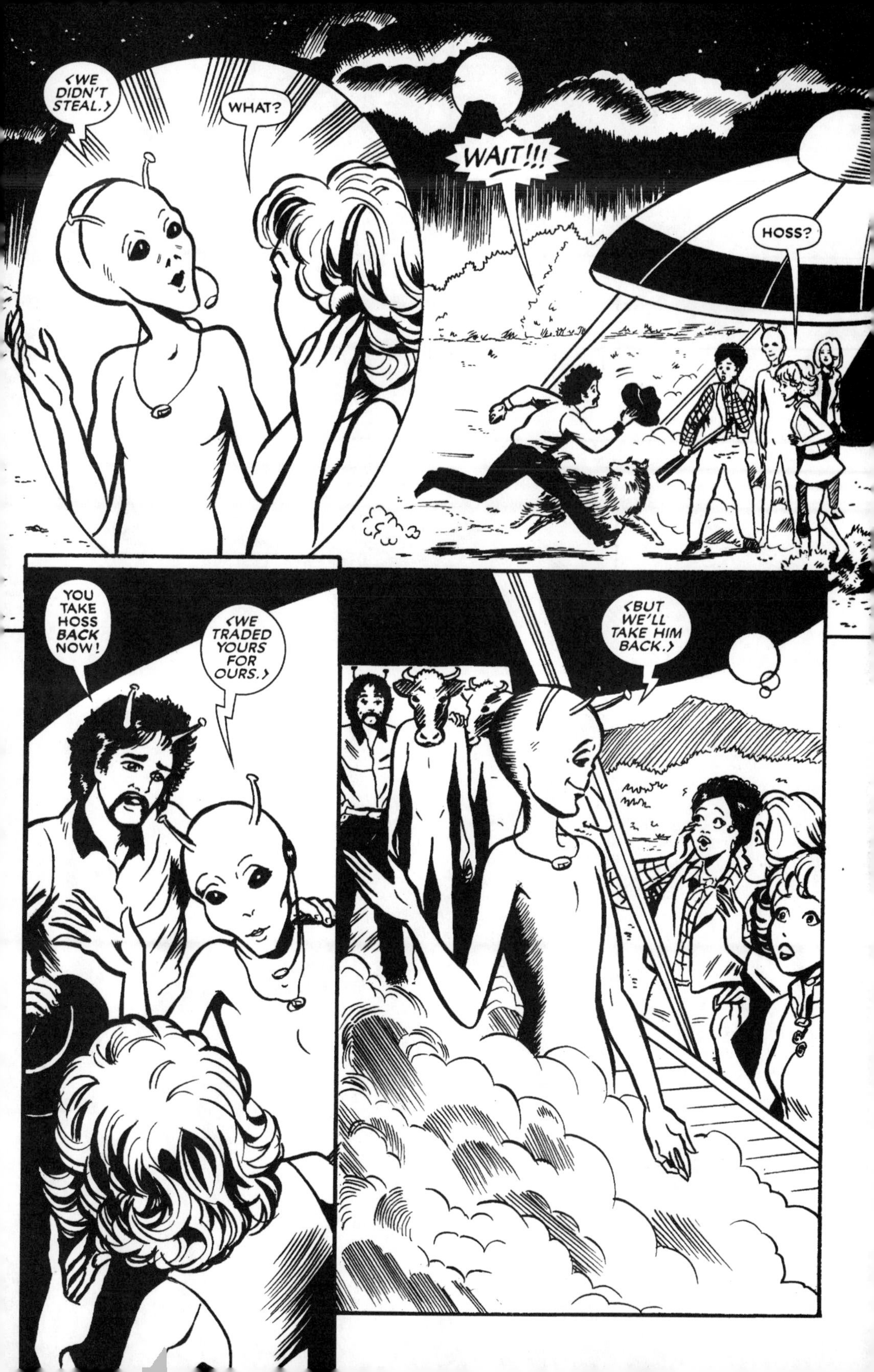

<WE DIDN'T STEAL.>
WHAT?
WAIT!!!
HOSS?
YOU TAKE HOSS BACK NOW!
<WE TRADED YOURS FOR OURS.>
<BUT WE'LL TAKE HIM BACK.>

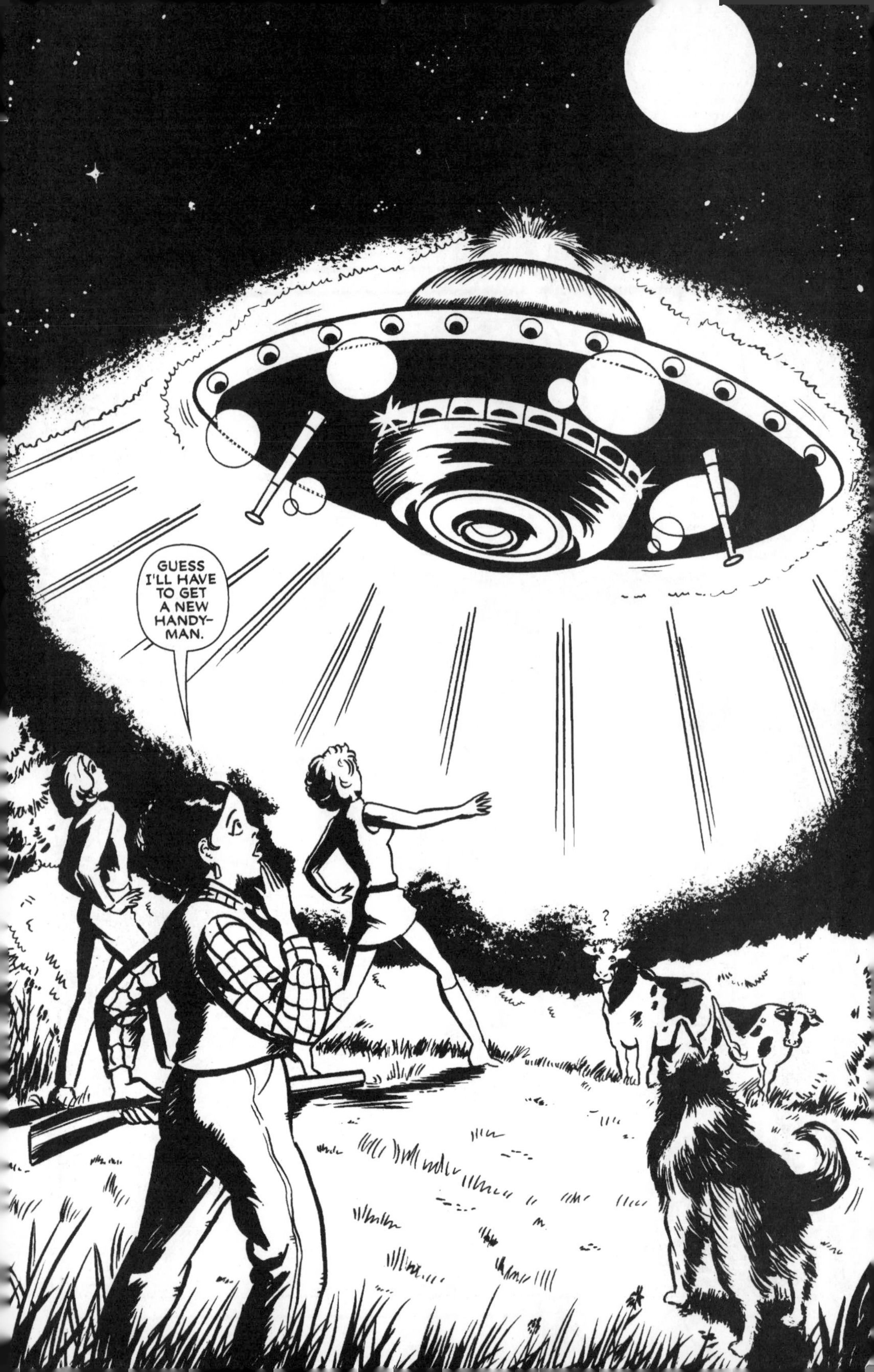
GUESS I'LL HAVE TO GET A NEW HANDY-MAN.

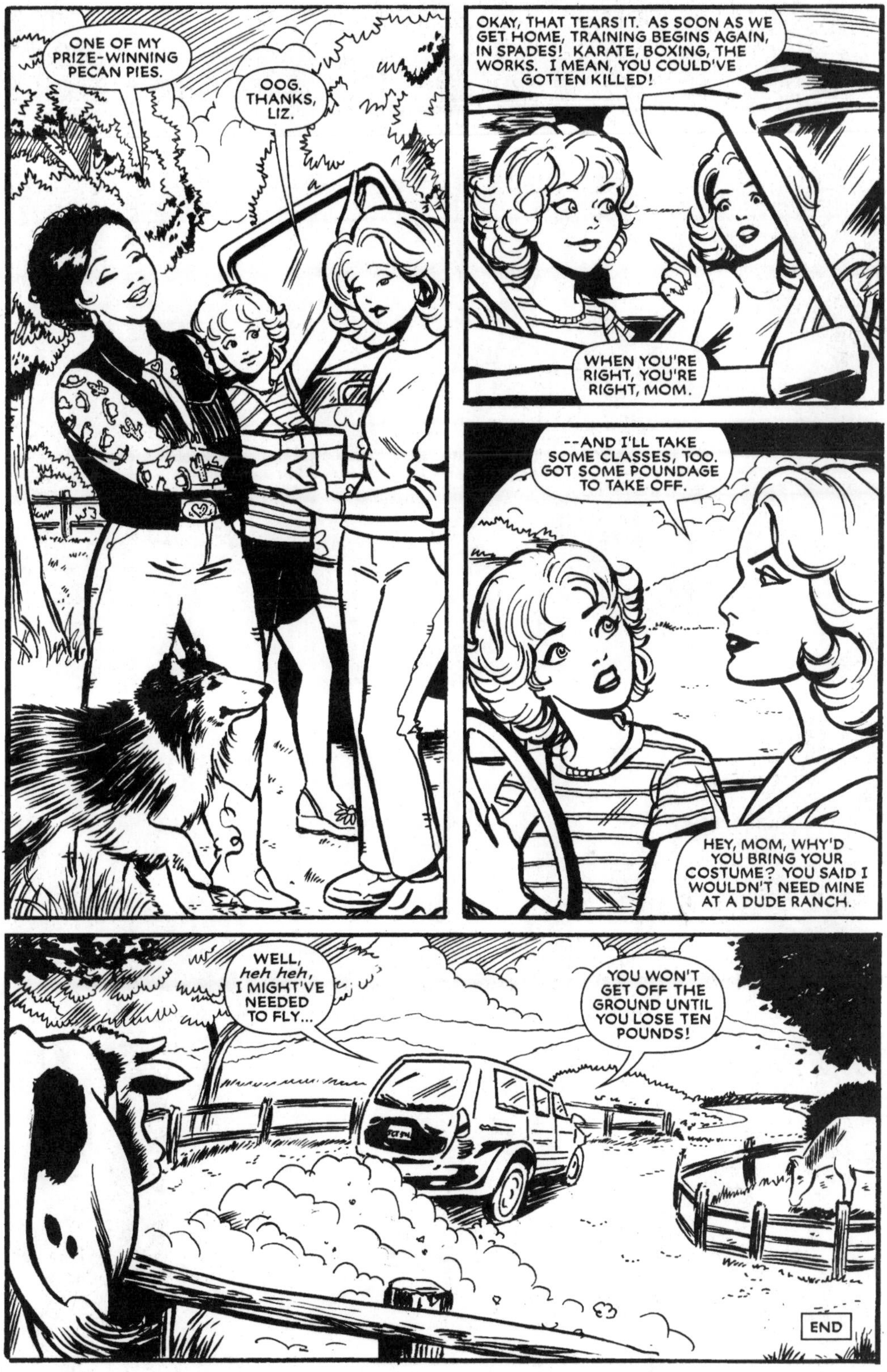
ONE OF MY PRIZE-WINNING PECAN PIES.
OOG. THANKS, LIZ.
OKAY, THAT TEARS IT. AS SOON AS WE GET HOME, TRAINING BEGINS AGAIN, IN SPADES! KARATE, BOXING, THE WORKS. I MEAN, YOU COULD'VE GOTTEN KILLED!
WHEN YOU'RE RIGHT, YOU'RE RIGHT, MOM.
--AND I'LL TAKE SOME CLASSES, TOO. GOT SOME POUNDAGE TO TAKE OFF.
HEY, MOM, WHY'D YOU BRING YOUR COSTUME? YOU SAID I WOULDN'T NEED MINE AT A DUDE RANCH.
WELL, *heh heh*, I MIGHT'VE NEEDED TO FLY...
YOU WON'T GET OFF THE GROUND UNTIL YOU LOSE TEN POUNDS!
END

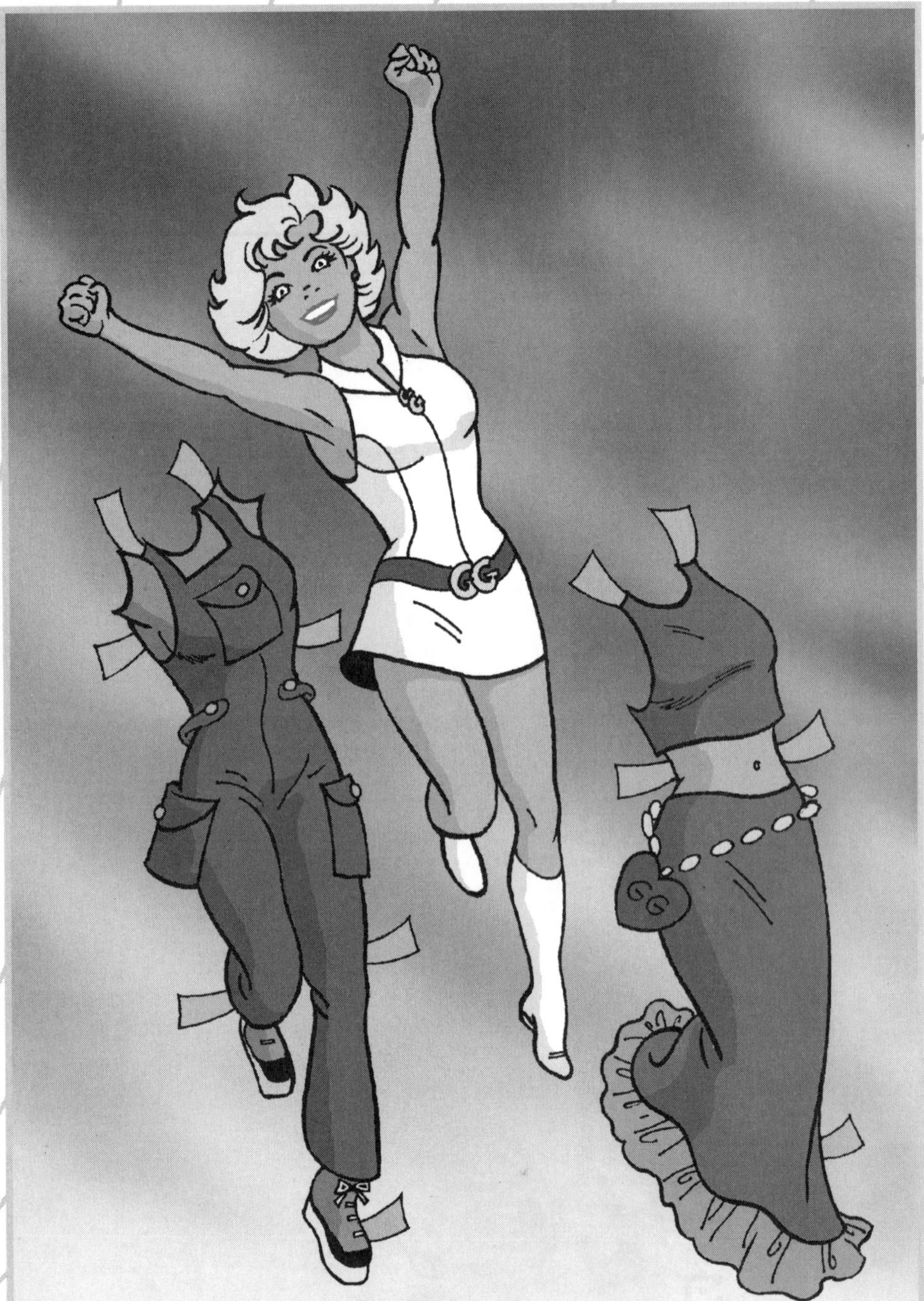
GG
GG
GG
Trina Robbins '01

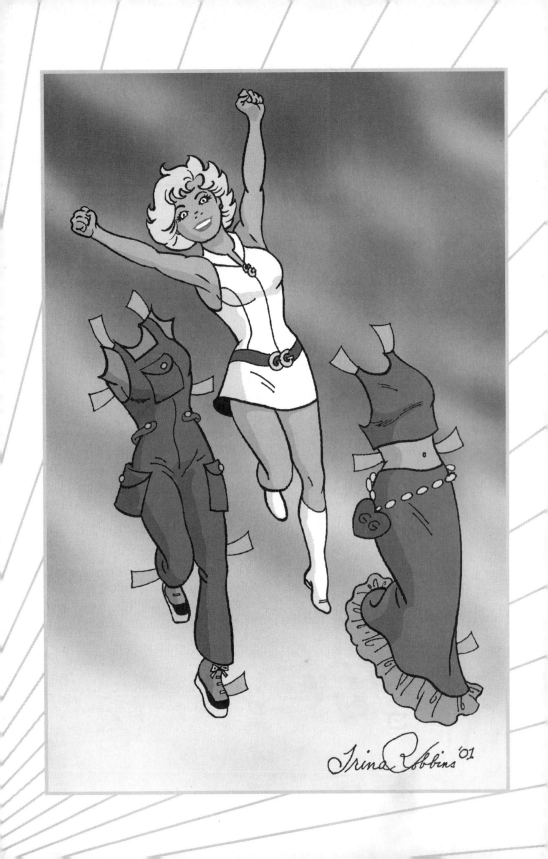

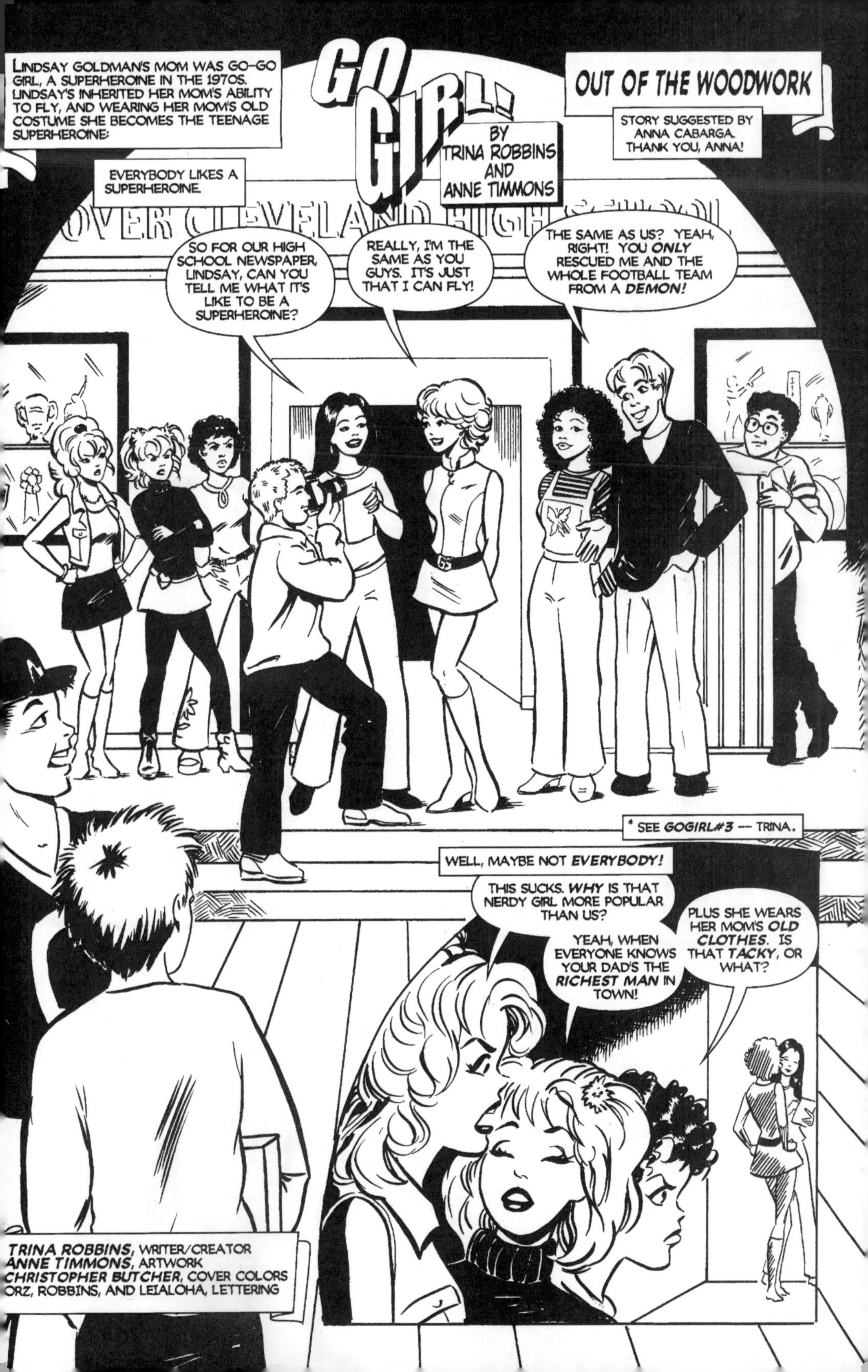
LINDSAY GOLDMAN'S MOM WAS GO-GO GIRL, A SUPERHEROINE IN THE 1970S. LINDSAY'S INHERITED HER MOM'S ABILITY TO FLY, AND WEARING HER MOM'S OLD COSTUME SHE BECOMES THE TEENAGE SUPERHEROINE:
GO GIRL!
BY TRINA ROBBINS AND ANNE TIMMONS
OUT OF THE WOODWORK
STORY SUGGESTED BY ANNA CABARGA. THANK YOU, ANNA!
EVERYBODY LIKES A SUPERHEROINE.
OVER CLEVELAND HIGH SCHOOL
SO FOR OUR HIGH SCHOOL NEWSPAPER, LINDSAY, CAN YOU TELL ME WHAT IT'S LIKE TO BE A SUPERHEROINE?
REALLY, I'M THE SAME AS YOU GUYS. IT'S JUST THAT I CAN FLY!
THE SAME AS US? YEAH, RIGHT! YOU *ONLY* RESCUED ME AND THE WHOLE FOOTBALL TEAM FROM A ***DEMON!***
* SEE *GOGIRL#3* — TRINA.
WELL, MAYBE NOT ***EVERYBODY!***
THIS SUCKS. ***WHY*** IS THAT NERDY GIRL MORE POPULAR THAN US?
YEAH, WHEN EVERYONE KNOWS YOUR DAD'S THE ***RICHEST MAN*** IN TOWN!
PLUS SHE WEARS HER MOM'S ***OLD CLOTHES***. IS THAT ***TACKY***, OR WHAT?
TRINA ROBBINS, WRITER/CREATOR
ANNE TIMMONS, ARTWORK
CHRISTOPHER BUTCHER, COVER COLORS
ORZ, ROBBINS, AND LEIALOHA, LETTERING

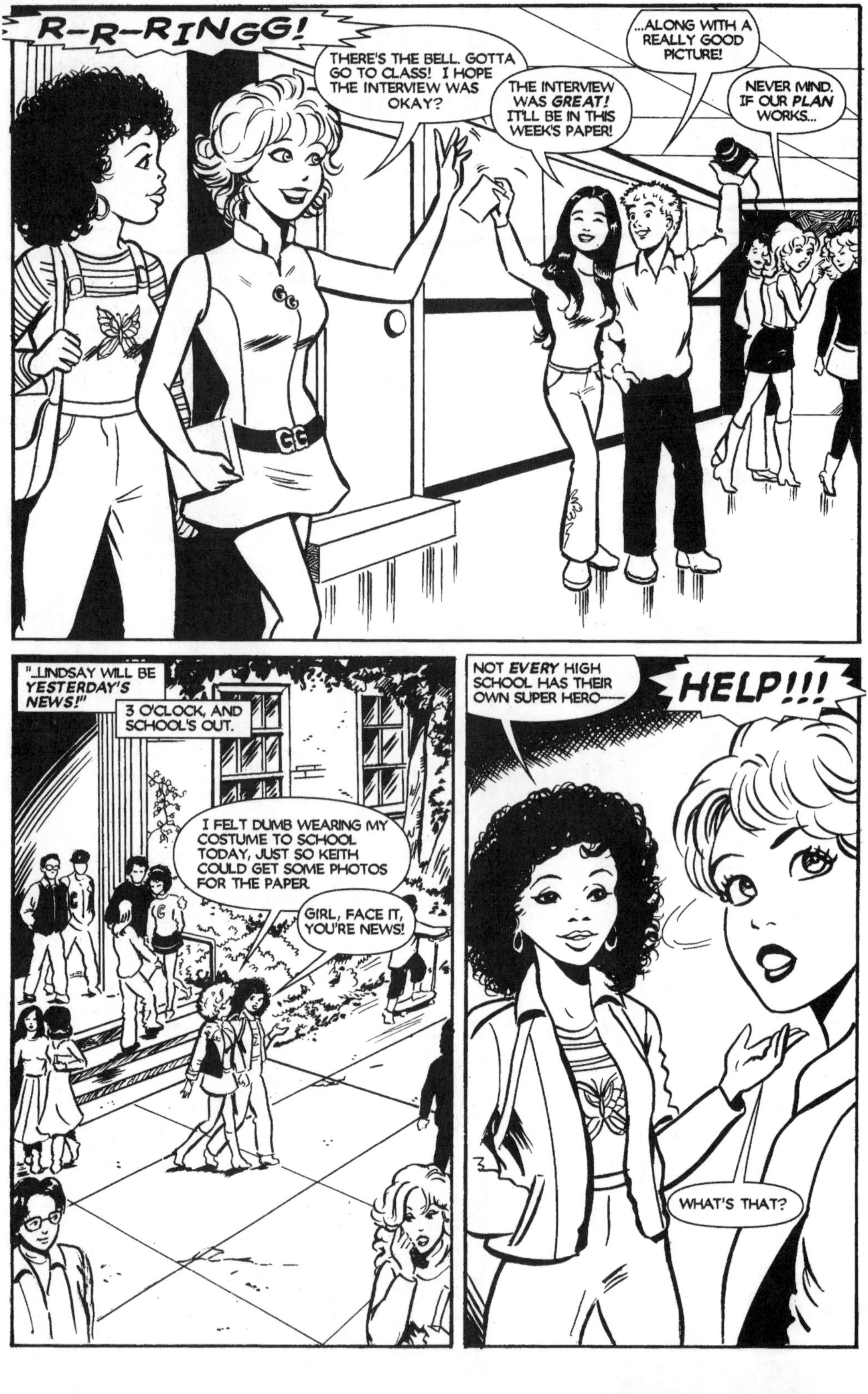
R-R-RINGG!
THERE'S THE BELL. GOTTA GO TO CLASS! I HOPE THE INTERVIEW WAS OKAY?
THE INTERVIEW WAS *GREAT!* IT'LL BE IN THIS WEEK'S PAPER!
...ALONG WITH A REALLY GOOD PICTURE!
NEVER MIND. IF OUR *PLAN* WORKS...
"...LINDSAY WILL BE *YESTERDAY'S NEWS!*"
3 O'CLOCK, AND SCHOOL'S OUT.
I FELT DUMB WEARING MY COSTUME TO SCHOOL TODAY, JUST SO KEITH COULD GET SOME PHOTOS FOR THE PAPER.
GIRL, FACE IT, YOU'RE NEWS!
NOT *EVERY* HIGH SCHOOL HAS THEIR OWN SUPER HERO----
HELP!!!
WHAT'S THAT?

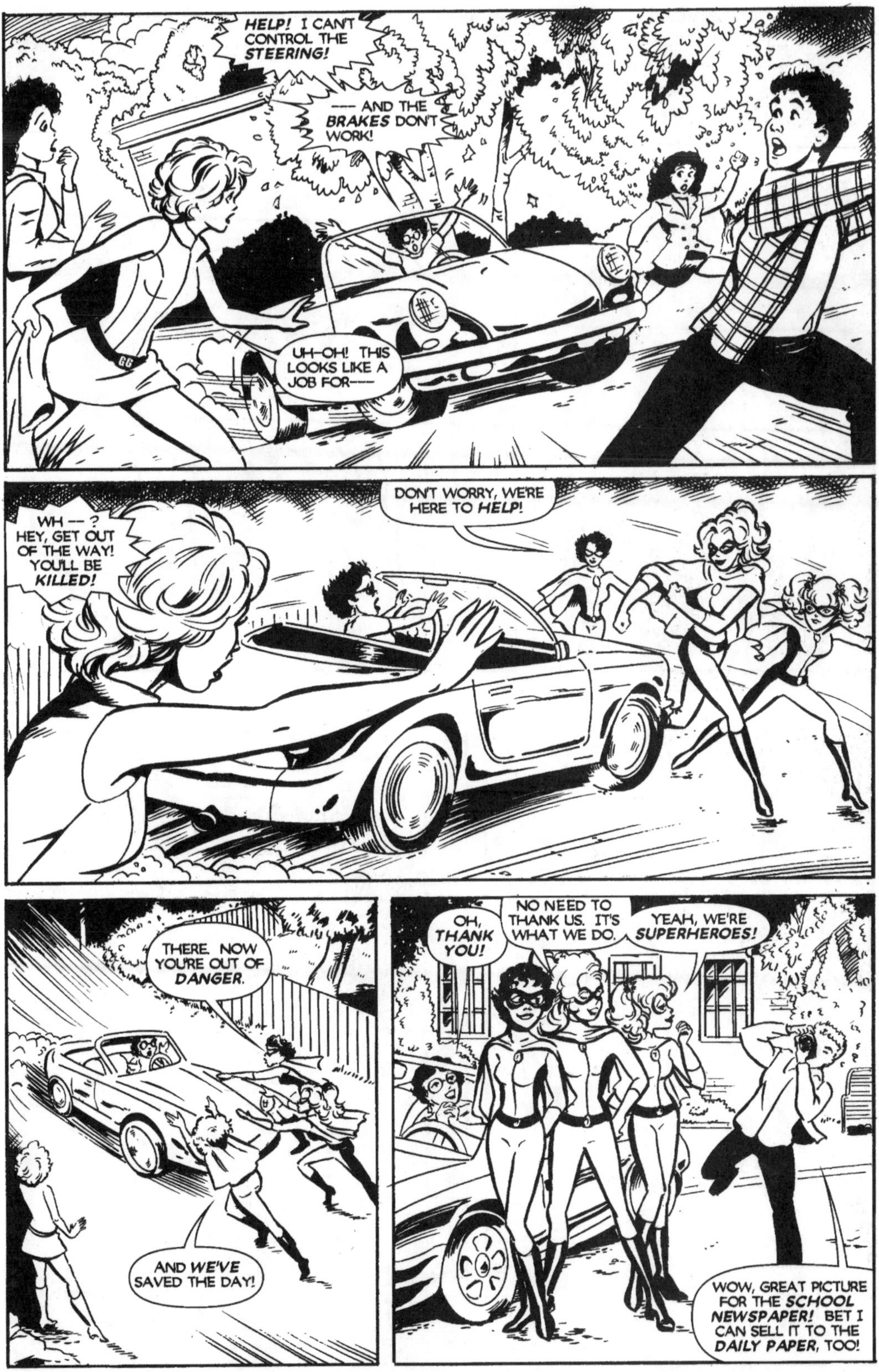
HELP! I CAN'T CONTROL THE STEERING!
--- AND THE BRAKES DON'T WORK!
UH-OH! THIS LOOKS LIKE A JOB FOR---
WH --? HEY, GET OUT OF THE WAY! YOU'LL BE KILLED!
DON'T WORRY, WE'RE HERE TO HELP!
THERE. NOW YOU'RE OUT OF DANGER.
AND WE'VE SAVED THE DAY!
OH, THANK YOU!
NO NEED TO THANK US. IT'S WHAT WE DO.
YEAH, WE'RE SUPERHEROES!
WOW, GREAT PICTURE FOR THE SCHOOL NEWSPAPER! BET I CAN SELL IT TO THE DAILY PAPER, TOO!

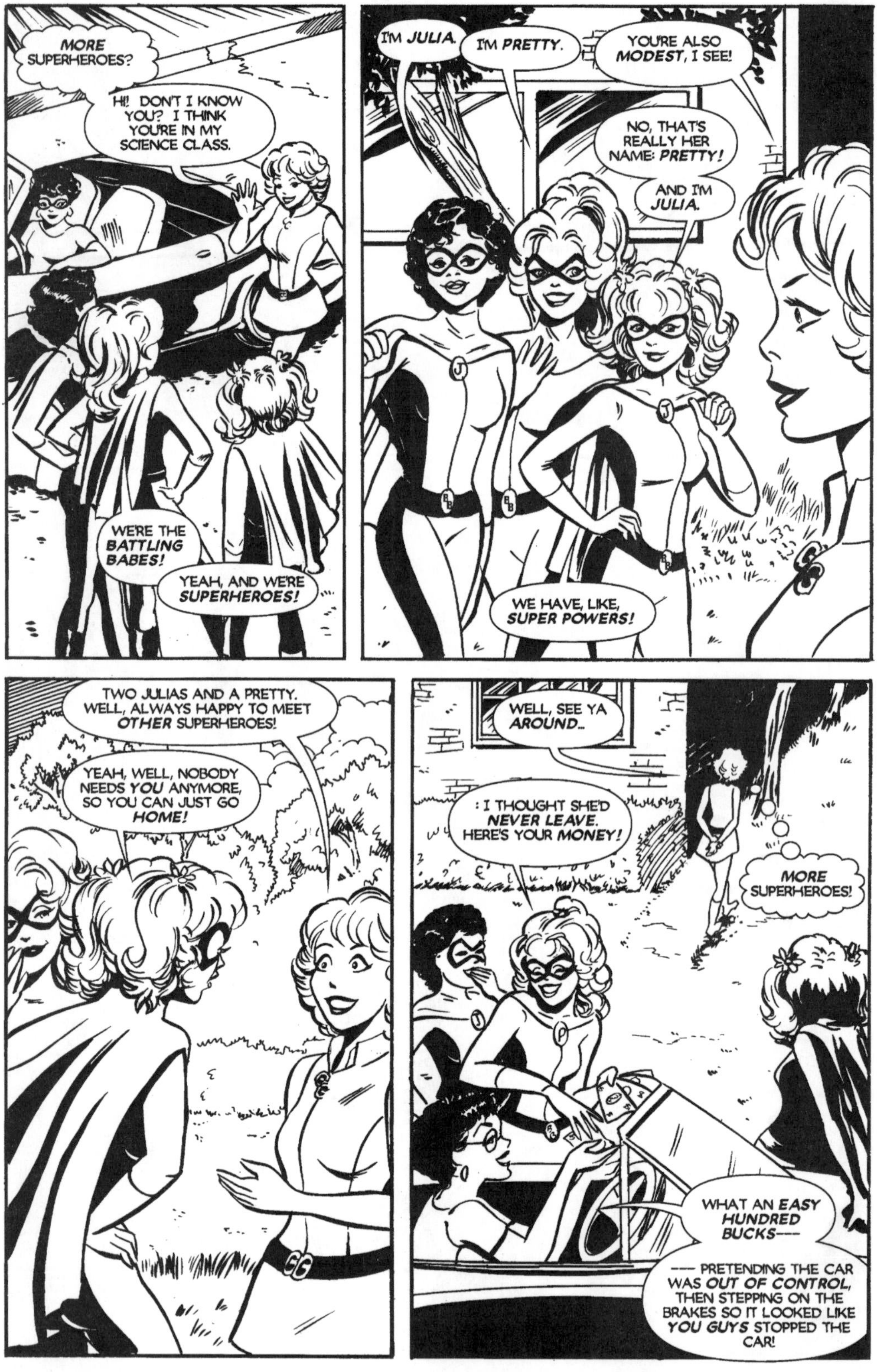
MORE SUPERHEROES?
HI! DON'T I KNOW YOU? I THINK YOU'RE IN MY SCIENCE CLASS.
WE'RE THE BATTLING BABES!
YEAH, AND WE'RE SUPERHEROES!
I'M JULIA.
I'M PRETTY.
YOU'RE ALSO MODEST, I SEE!
NO, THAT'S REALLY HER NAME: PRETTY!
AND I'M JULIA.
WE HAVE, LIKE, SUPER POWERS!
TWO JULIAS AND A PRETTY. WELL, ALWAYS HAPPY TO MEET OTHER SUPERHEROES!
YEAH, WELL, NOBODY NEEDS YOU ANYMORE, SO YOU CAN JUST GO HOME!
WELL, SEE YA AROUND...
MORE SUPERHEROES!
I THOUGHT SHE'D NEVER LEAVE. HERE'S YOUR MONEY!
WHAT AN EASY HUNDRED BUCKS---
--- PRETENDING THE CAR WAS OUT OF CONTROL, THEN STEPPING ON THE BRAKES SO IT LOOKED LIKE YOU GUYS STOPPED THE CAR!

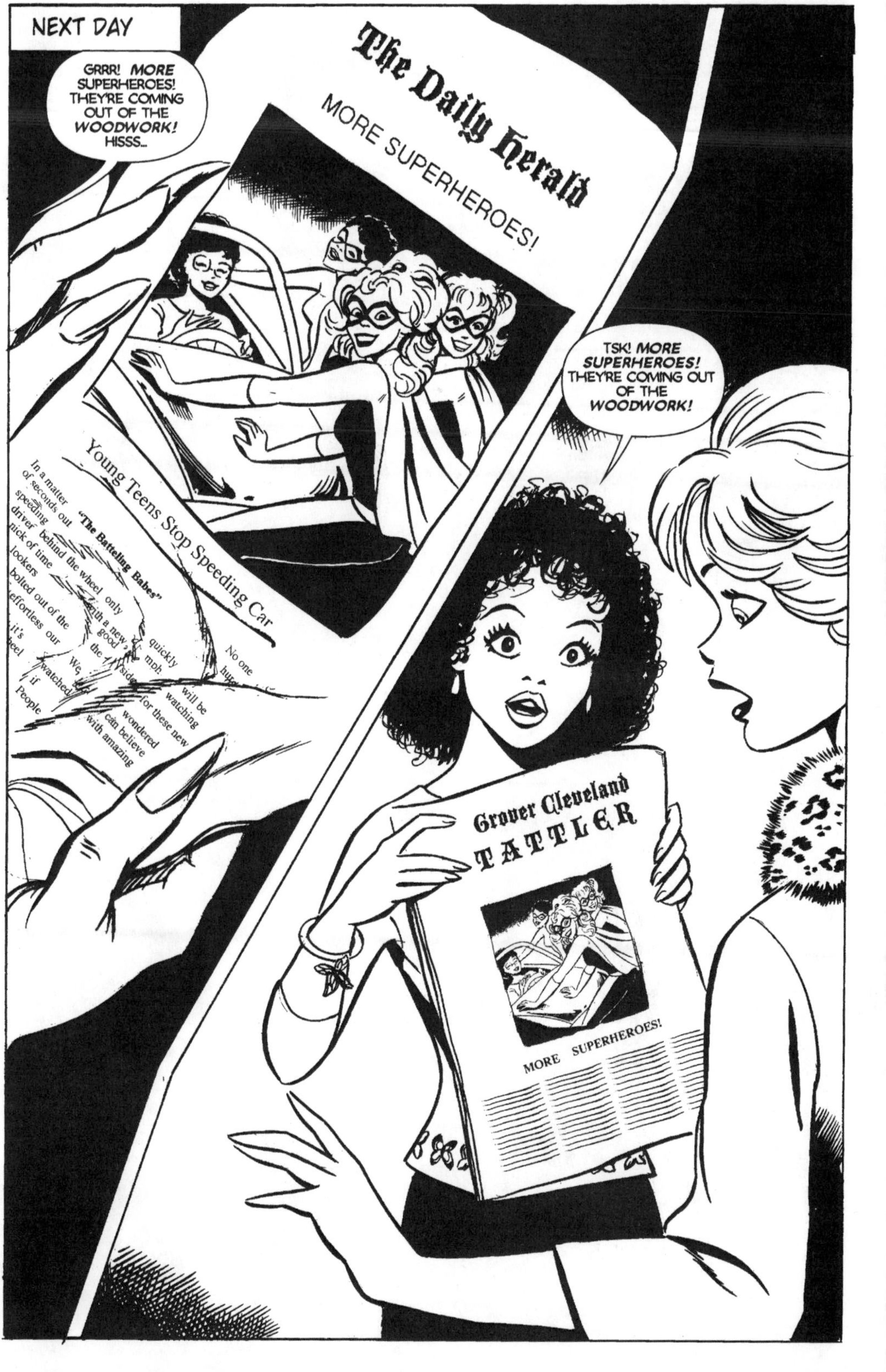
NEXT DAY
GRRR! MORE SUPERHEROES! THEY'RE COMING OUT OF THE WOODWORK! HISSS...
The Daily Herald
MORE SUPERHEROES!
Young Teens Stop Speeding Car
"The Batteling Babes"
TSK! MORE SUPERHEROES! THEY'RE COMING OUT OF THE WOODWORK!
Grover Cleveland
TATTLER
MORE SUPERHEROES!

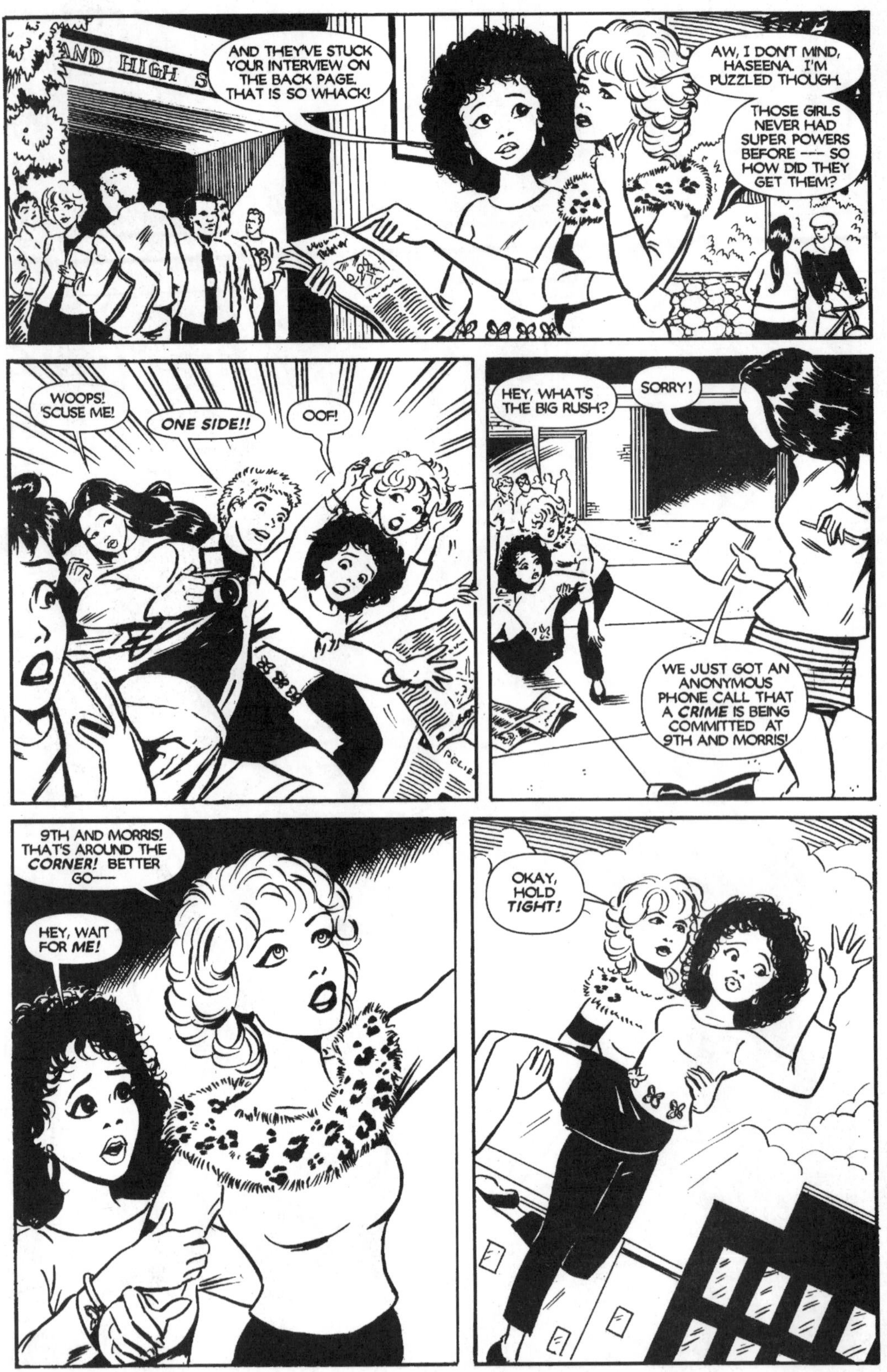
AND HIGH S
AND THEY'VE STUCK YOUR INTERVIEW ON THE BACK PAGE. THAT IS SO WHACK!
AW, I DON'T MIND, HASEENA. I'M PUZZLED THOUGH.
THOSE GIRLS NEVER HAD SUPER POWERS BEFORE --- SO HOW DID THEY GET THEM?
WOOPS! 'SCUSE ME!
ONE SIDE!!
OOF!
HEY, WHAT'S THE BIG RUSH?
SORRY!
WE JUST GOT AN ANONYMOUS PHONE CALL THAT A CRIME IS BEING COMMITTED AT 9TH AND MORRIS!
9TH AND MORRIS! THAT'S AROUND THE CORNER! BETTER GO----
HEY, WAIT FOR ME!
OKAY, HOLD TIGHT!

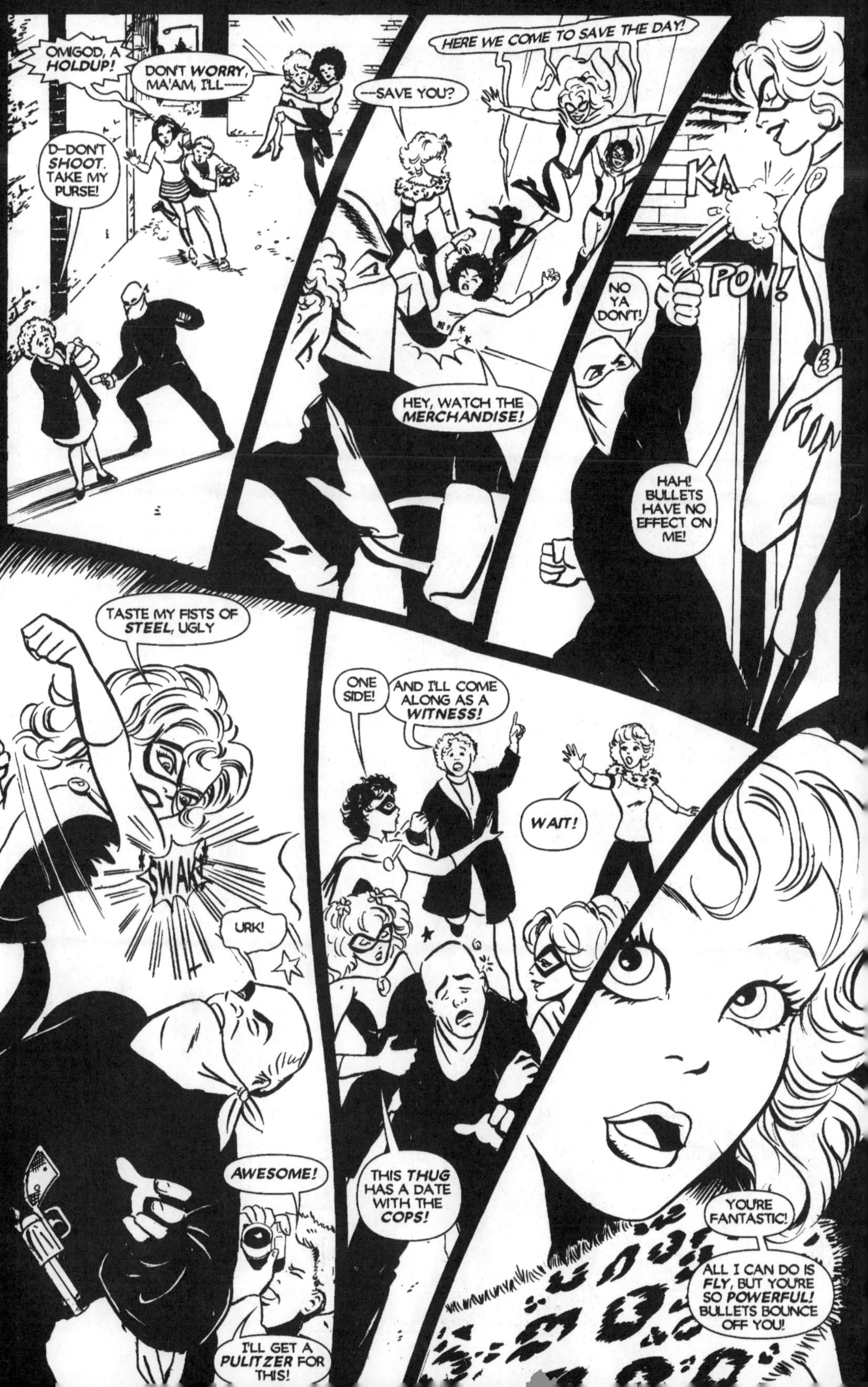
OMIGOD, A HOLDUP!
DON'T WORRY, MA'AM, I'LL---
D-DON'T SHOOT. TAKE MY PURSE!
HERE WE COME TO SAVE THE DAY!
--SAVE YOU?
HEY, WATCH THE MERCHANDISE!
KA
POW!
NO YA DON'T!
HAH! BULLETS HAVE NO EFFECT ON ME!
TASTE MY FISTS OF STEEL, UGLY
SWAK!
URK!
AWESOME!
I'LL GET A PULITZER FOR THIS!
ONE SIDE!
AND I'LL COME ALONG AS A WITNESS!
WAIT!
THIS THUG HAS A DATE WITH THE COPS!
YOU'RE FANTASTIC!
ALL I CAN DO IS FLY, BUT YOU'RE SO POWERFUL! BULLETS BOUNCE OFF YOU!

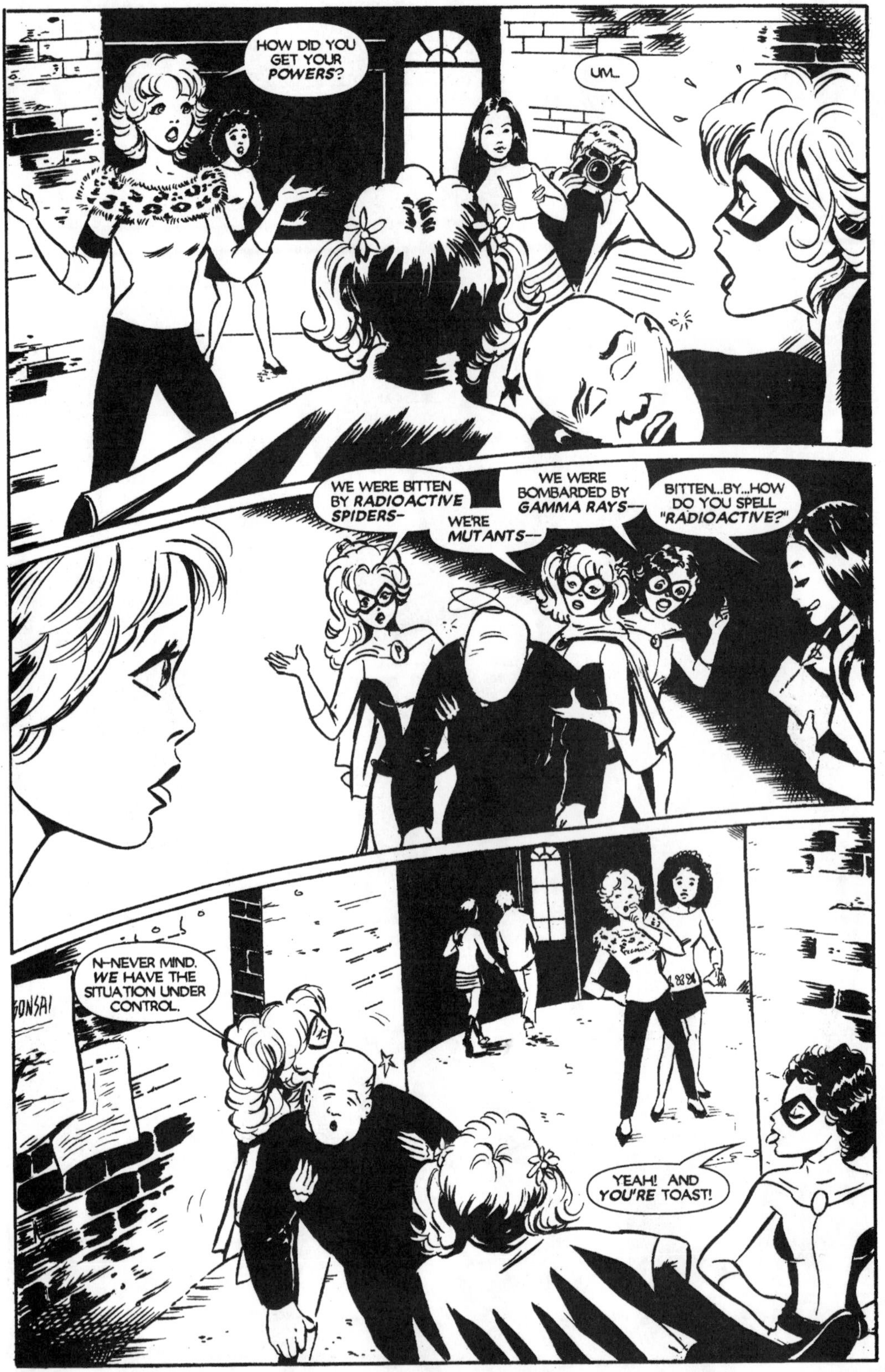
HOW DID YOU GET YOUR POWERS?
UM..
WE WERE BITTEN BY RADIOACTIVE SPIDERS-
WE'RE MUTANTS--
WE WERE BOMBARDED BY GAMMA RAYS--
BITTEN...BY...HOW DO YOU SPELL "RADIOACTIVE?"
N-NEVER MIND. WE HAVE THE SITUATION UNDER CONTROL.
YEAH! AND YOU'RE TOAST!

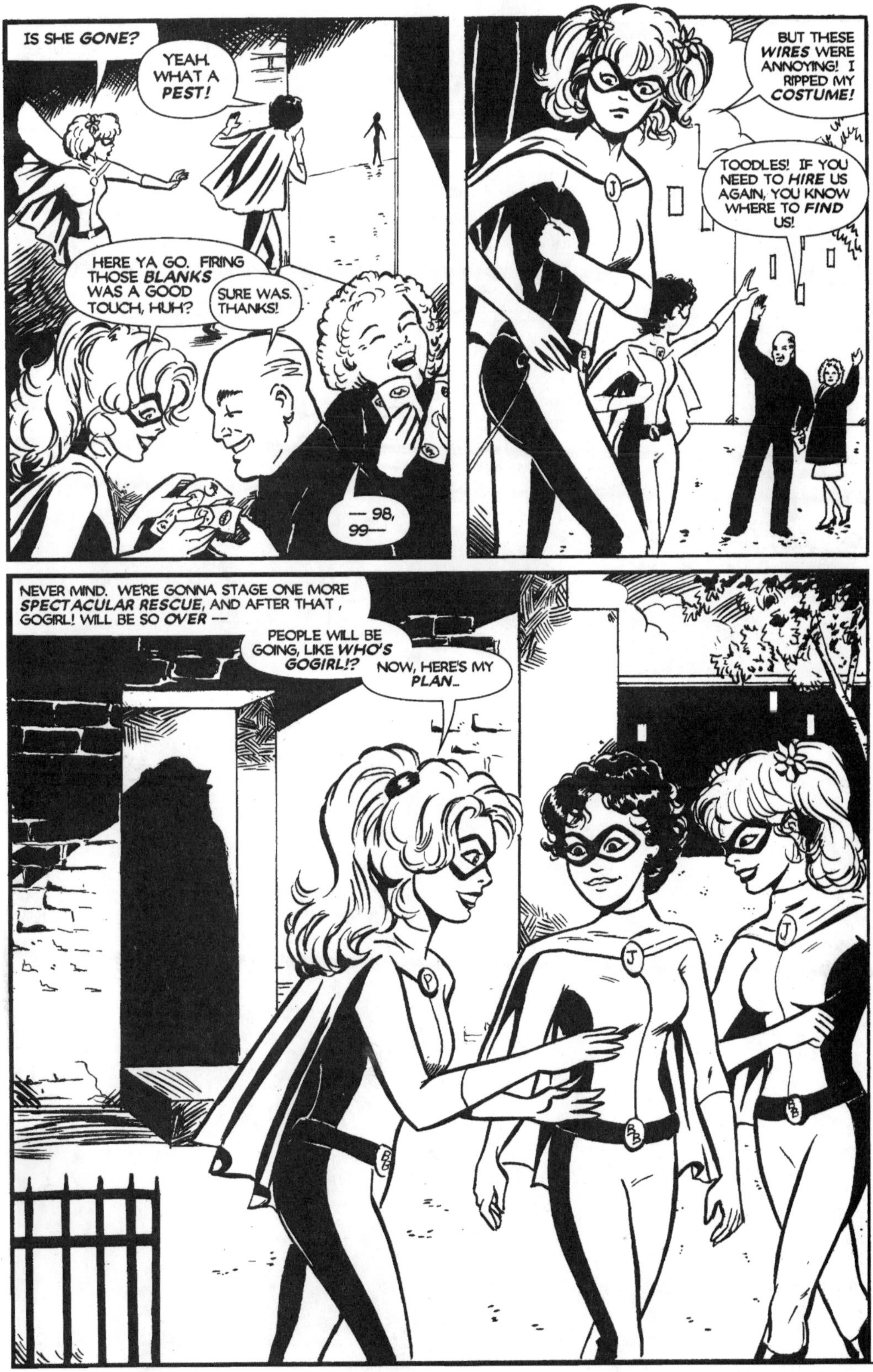
IS SHE *GONE?*
YEAH. WHAT A *PEST!*
HERE YA GO. FIRING THOSE *BLANKS* WAS A GOOD TOUCH, HUH?
SURE WAS. THANKS!
— 98, 99—
BUT THESE *WIRES* WERE ANNOYING! I RIPPED MY *COSTUME!*
TOODLES! IF YOU NEED TO *HIRE* US AGAIN, YOU KNOW WHERE TO *FIND* US!
NEVER MIND. WE'RE GONNA STAGE ONE MORE *SPECTACULAR RESCUE*, AND AFTER THAT, GOGIRL! WILL BE SO *OVER* —
PEOPLE WILL BE GOING, LIKE *WHO'S GOGIRL!?*
NOW, HERE'S MY *PLAN*..

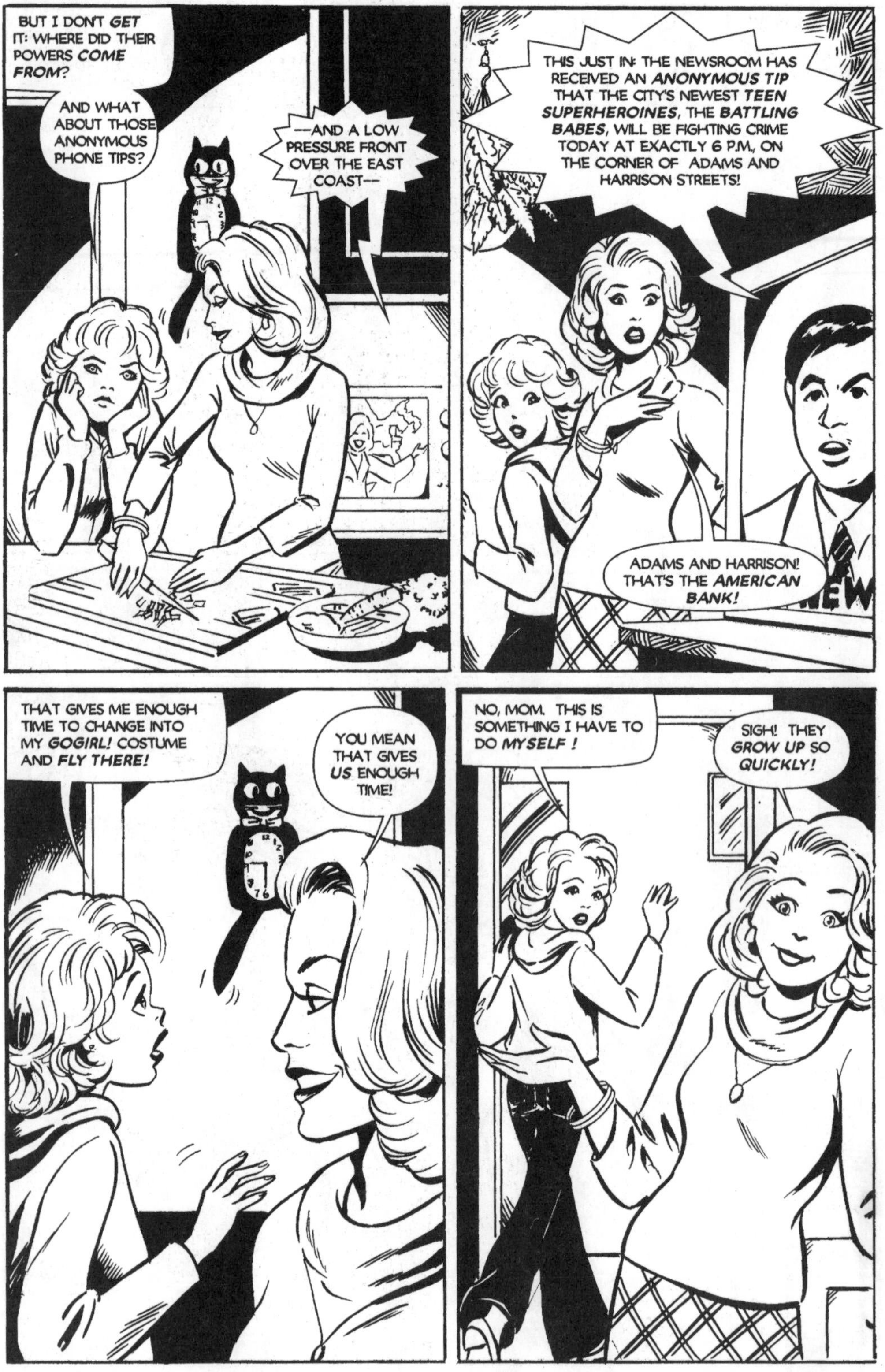
BUT I DON'T *GET* IT: WHERE DID THEIR POWERS *COME FROM*?
AND WHAT ABOUT THOSE ANONYMOUS PHONE TIPS?
--AND A LOW PRESSURE FRONT OVER THE EAST COAST--
THIS JUST IN: THE NEWSROOM HAS RECEIVED AN *ANONYMOUS TIP* THAT THE CITY'S NEWEST *TEEN SUPERHEROINES*, THE *BATTLING BABES*, WILL BE FIGHTING CRIME TODAY AT EXACTLY 6 P.M., ON THE CORNER OF ADAMS AND HARRISON STREETS!
ADAMS AND HARRISON! THAT'S THE *AMERICAN BANK!*
THAT GIVES ME ENOUGH TIME TO CHANGE INTO MY *GOGIRL!* COSTUME AND *FLY THERE!*
YOU MEAN THAT GIVES *US* ENOUGH TIME!
NO, MOM. THIS IS SOMETHING I HAVE TO DO *MYSELF* !
SIGH! THEY *GROW UP* SO *QUICKLY!*

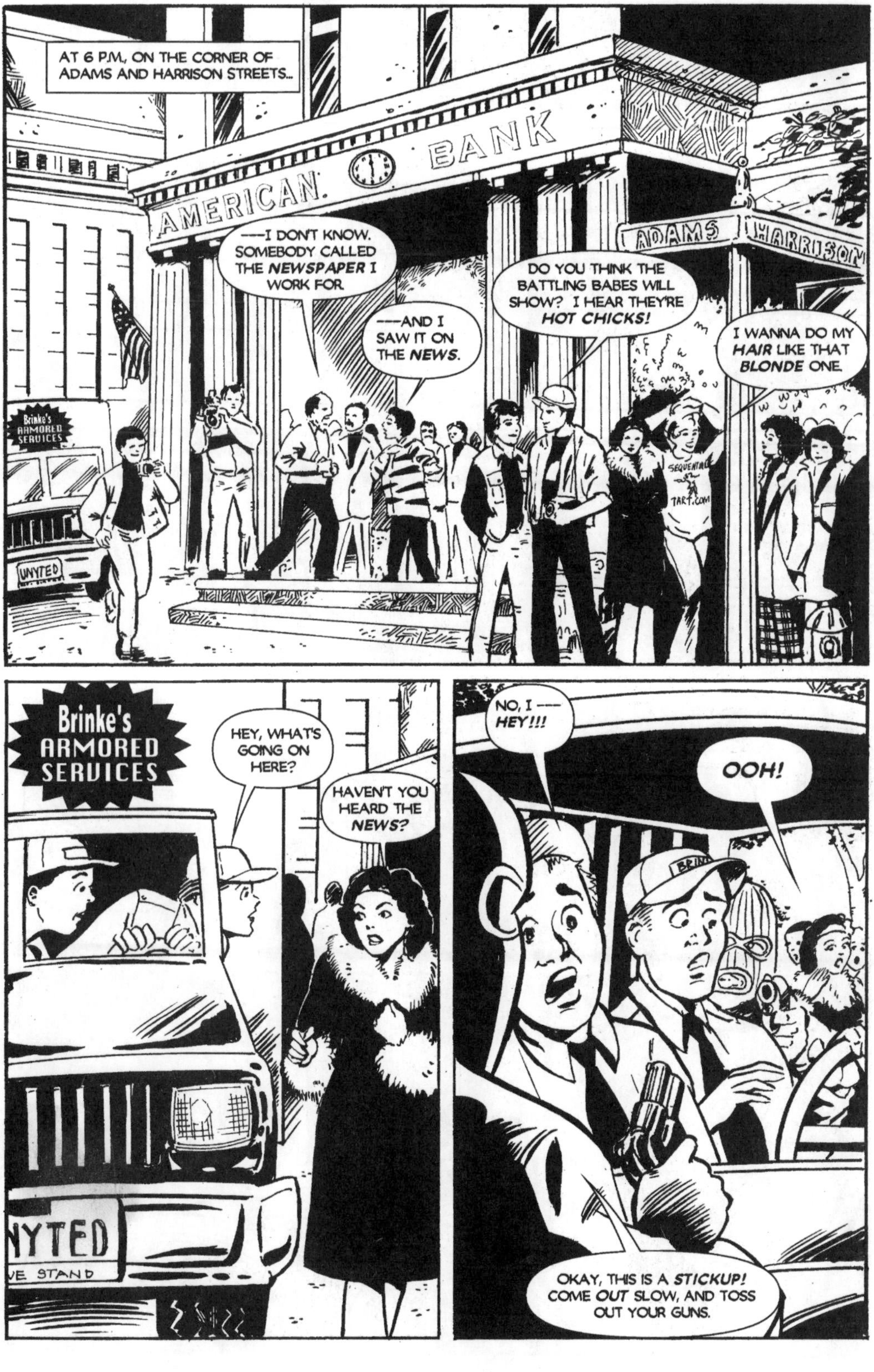
AT 6 P.M., ON THE CORNER OF ADAMS AND HARRISON STREETS...
AMERICAN BANK
ADAMS
HARRISON
---I DON'T KNOW. SOMEBODY CALLED THE NEWSPAPER I WORK FOR.
---AND I SAW IT ON THE NEWS.
DO YOU THINK THE BATTLING BABES WILL SHOW? I HEAR THEY'RE HOT CHICKS!
I WANNA DO MY HAIR LIKE THAT BLONDE ONE.
Brinke's ARMORED SERVICES
UNYTED
SEQUENTIAL TART.COM
Brinke's ARMORED SERVICES
HEY, WHAT'S GOING ON HERE?
HAVEN'T YOU HEARD THE NEWS?
NYTED
VE STAND
NO, I --- HEY!!!
OOH!
OKAY, THIS IS A STICKUP! COME OUT SLOW, AND TOSS OUT YOUR GUNS.

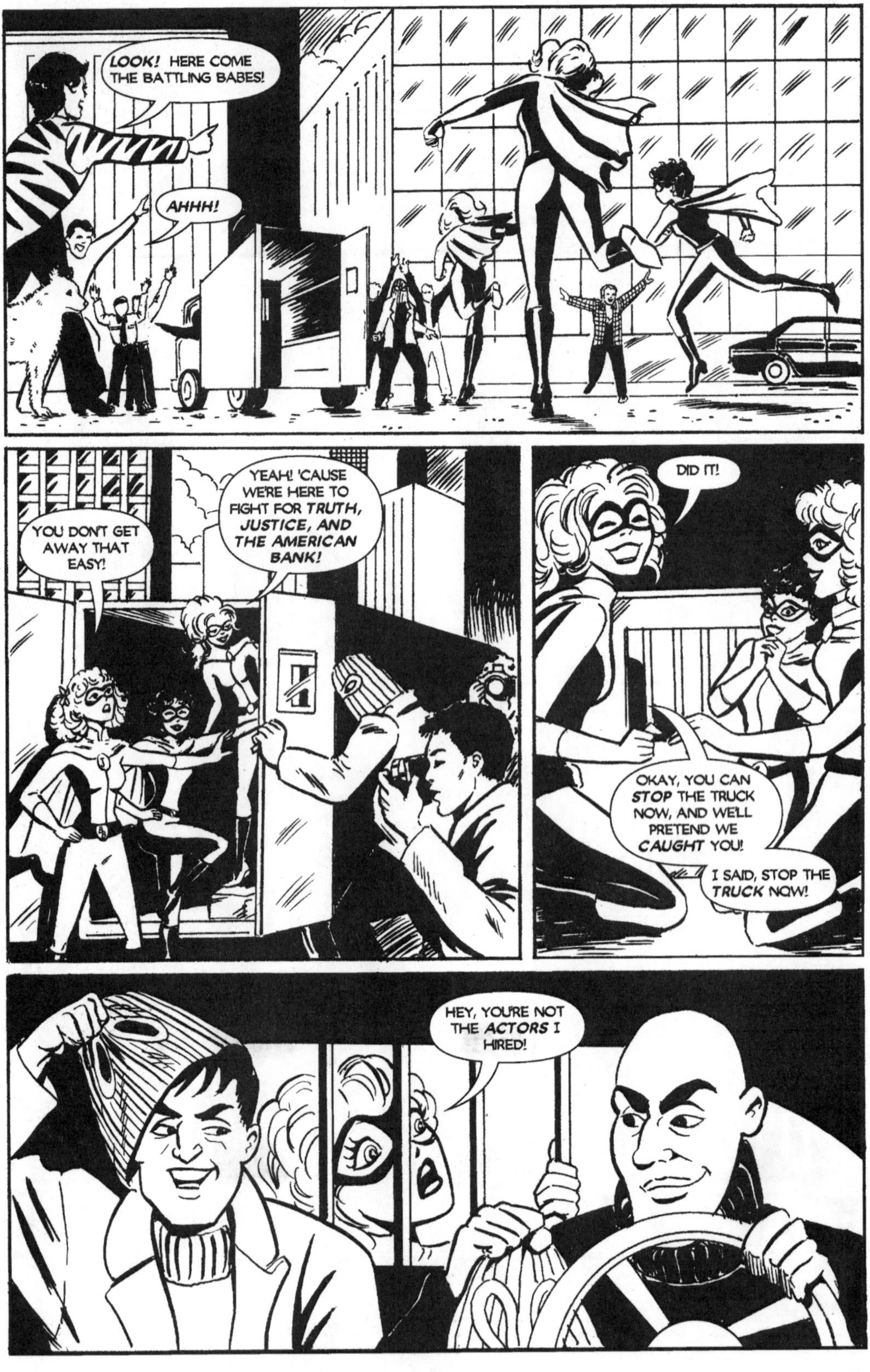
LOOK! HERE COME THE BATTLING BABES!
AHHH!
YOU DON'T GET AWAY THAT EASY!
YEAH! 'CAUSE WE'RE HERE TO FIGHT FOR TRUTH, JUSTICE, AND THE AMERICAN BANK!
DID IT!
OKAY, YOU CAN STOP THE TRUCK NOW, AND WE'LL PRETEND WE CAUGHT YOU!
I SAID, STOP THE TRUCK NOW!
HEY, YOU'RE NOT THE ACTORS I HIRED!

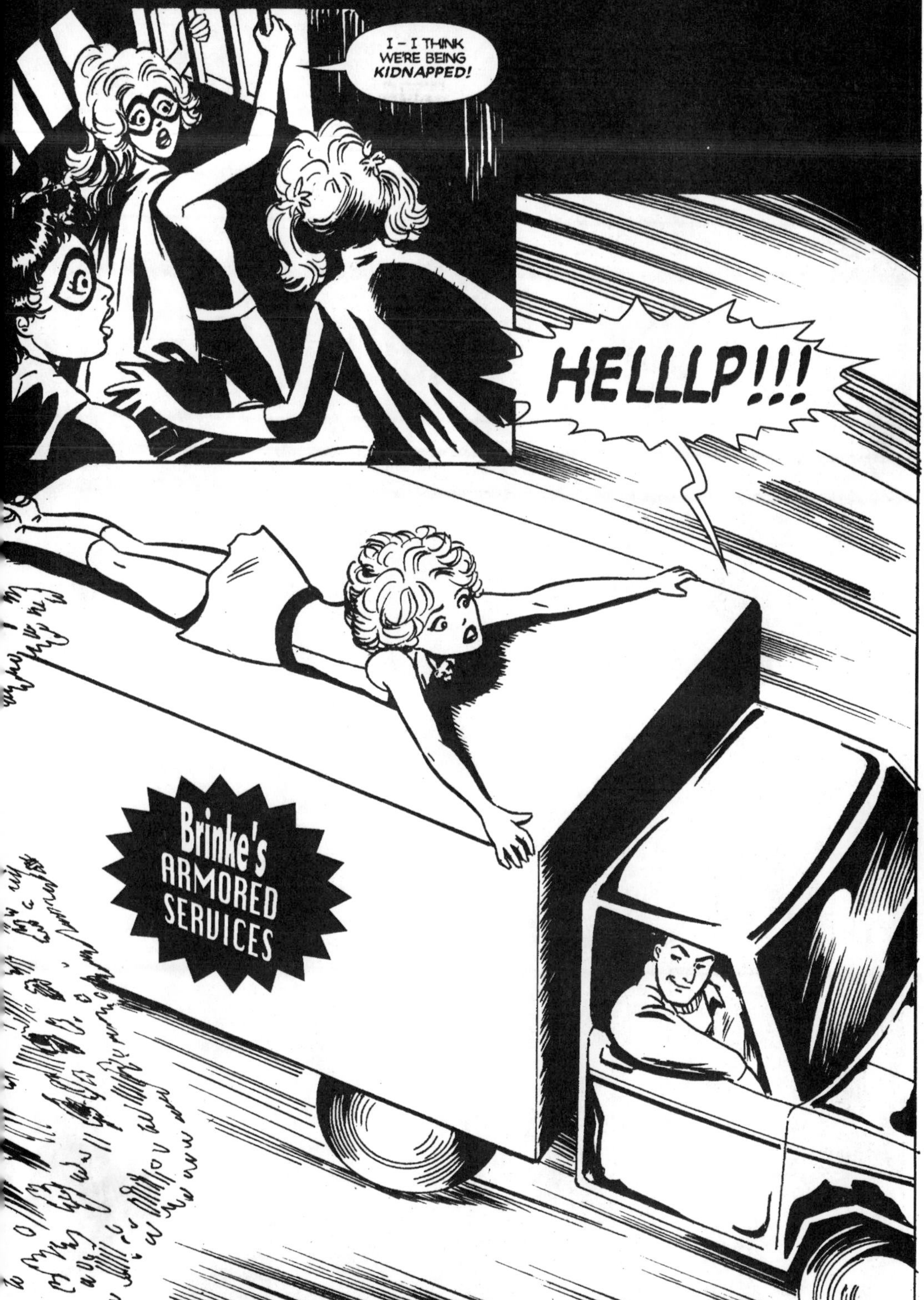
I – I THINK WE'RE BEING KIDNAPPED!
HELLLP!!!
Brinke's ARMORED SERVICES

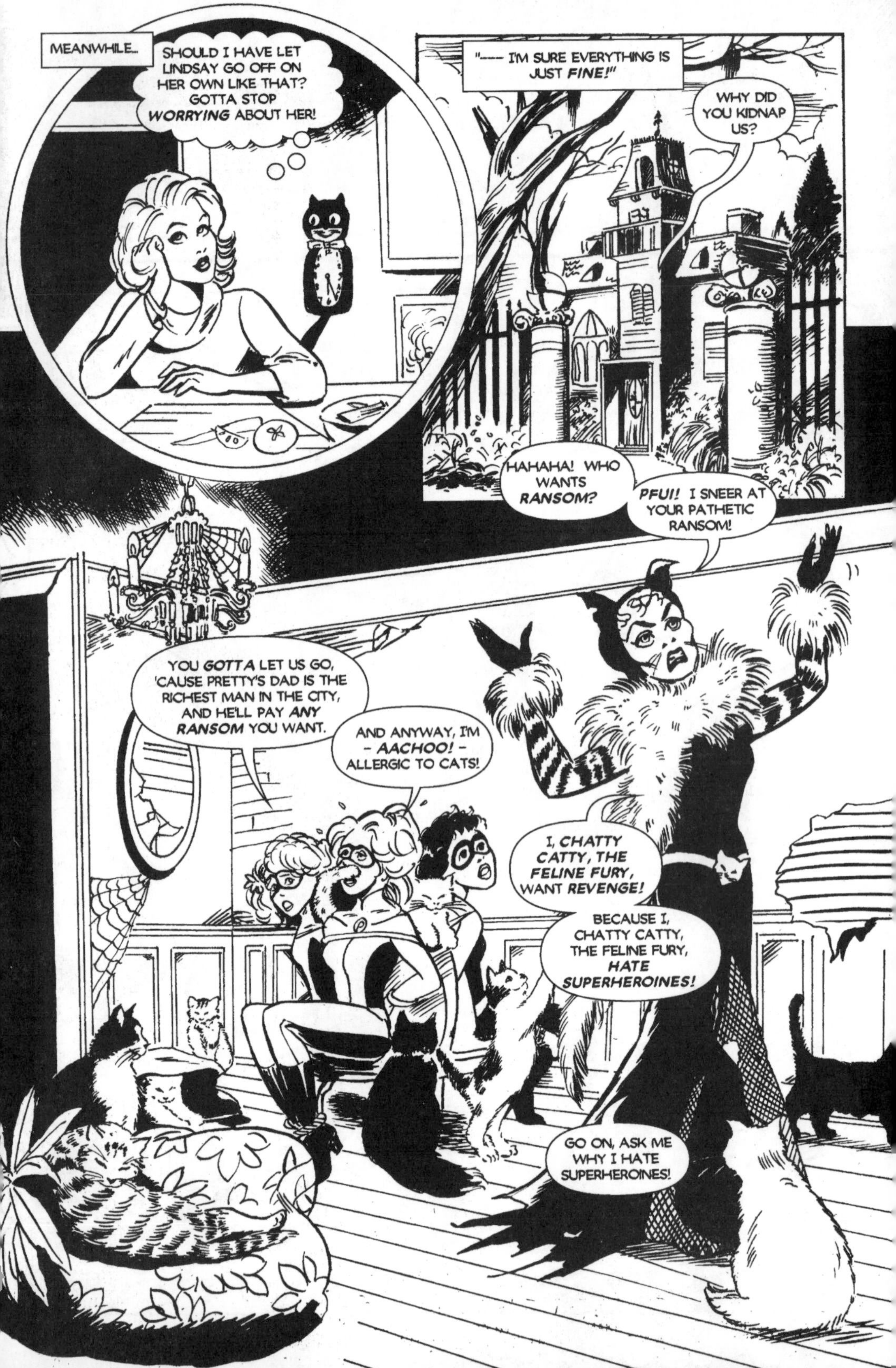
MEANWHILE...
SHOULD I HAVE LET LINDSAY GO OFF ON HER OWN LIKE THAT? GOTTA STOP WORRYING ABOUT HER!
"---- I'M SURE EVERYTHING IS JUST FINE!"
WHY DID YOU KIDNAP US?
HAHAHA! WHO WANTS RANSOM?
PFUI! I SNEER AT YOUR PATHETIC RANSOM!
YOU GOTTA LET US GO, 'CAUSE PRETTY'S DAD IS THE RICHEST MAN IN THE CITY, AND HE'LL PAY ANY RANSOM YOU WANT.
AND ANYWAY, I'M - AACHOO! - ALLERGIC TO CATS!
I, CHATTY CATTY, THE FELINE FURY, WANT REVENGE!
BECAUSE I, CHATTY CATTY, THE FELINE FURY, HATE SUPERHEROINES!
GO ON, ASK ME WHY I HATE SUPERHEROINES!

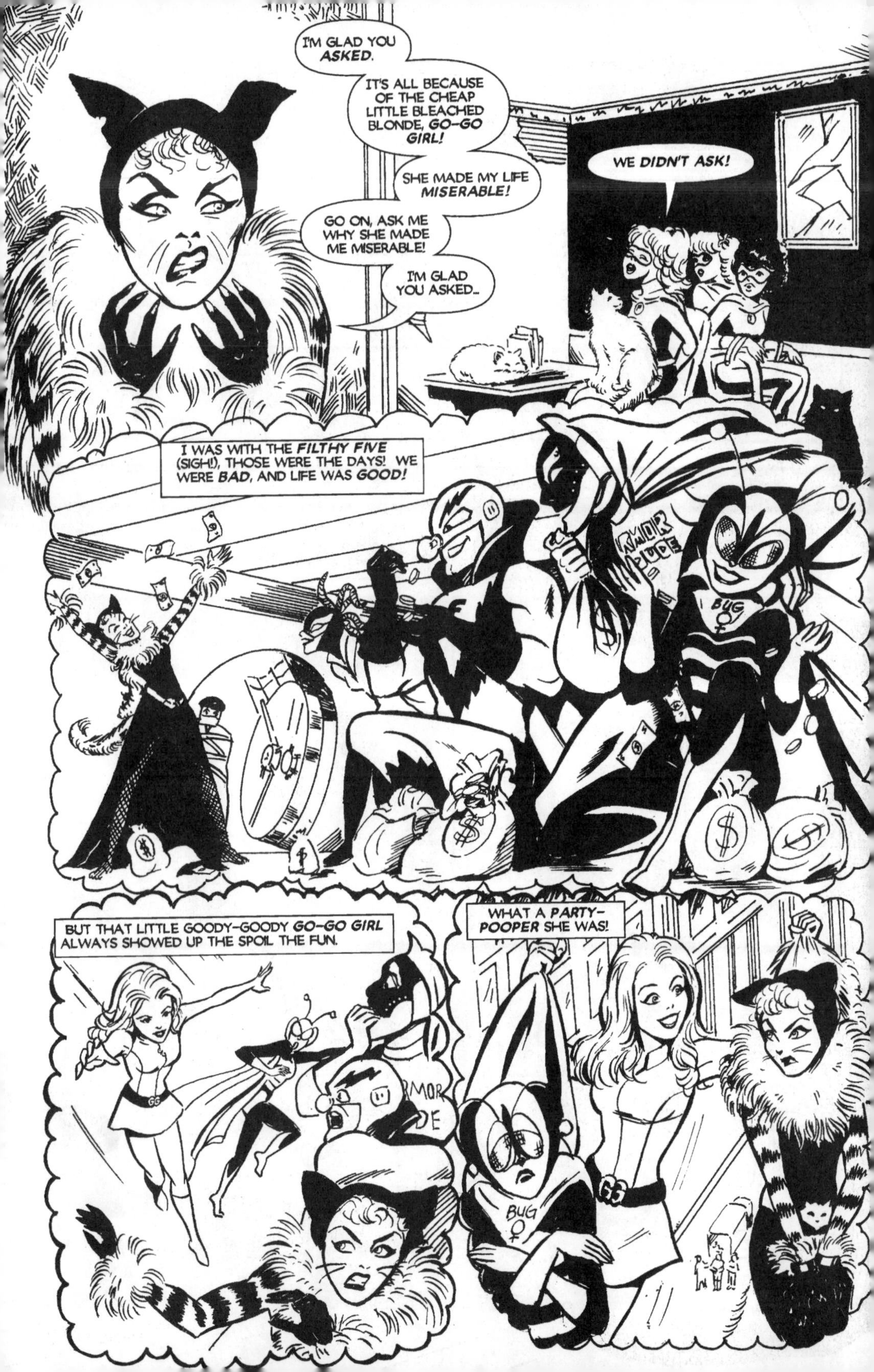
I'M GLAD YOU ASKED.
IT'S ALL BECAUSE OF THE CHEAP LITTLE BLEACHED BLONDE, GO-GO GIRL!
SHE MADE MY LIFE MISERABLE!
GO ON, ASK ME WHY SHE MADE ME MISERABLE!
I'M GLAD YOU ASKED...
WE DIDN'T ASK!
I WAS WITH THE FILTHY FIVE (SIGH!), THOSE WERE THE DAYS! WE WERE BAD, AND LIFE WAS GOOD!
BUG
BUT THAT LITTLE GOODY-GOODY GO-GO GIRL ALWAYS SHOWED UP THE SPOIL THE FUN.
WHAT A PARTY-POOPER SHE WAS!
GG
BUG

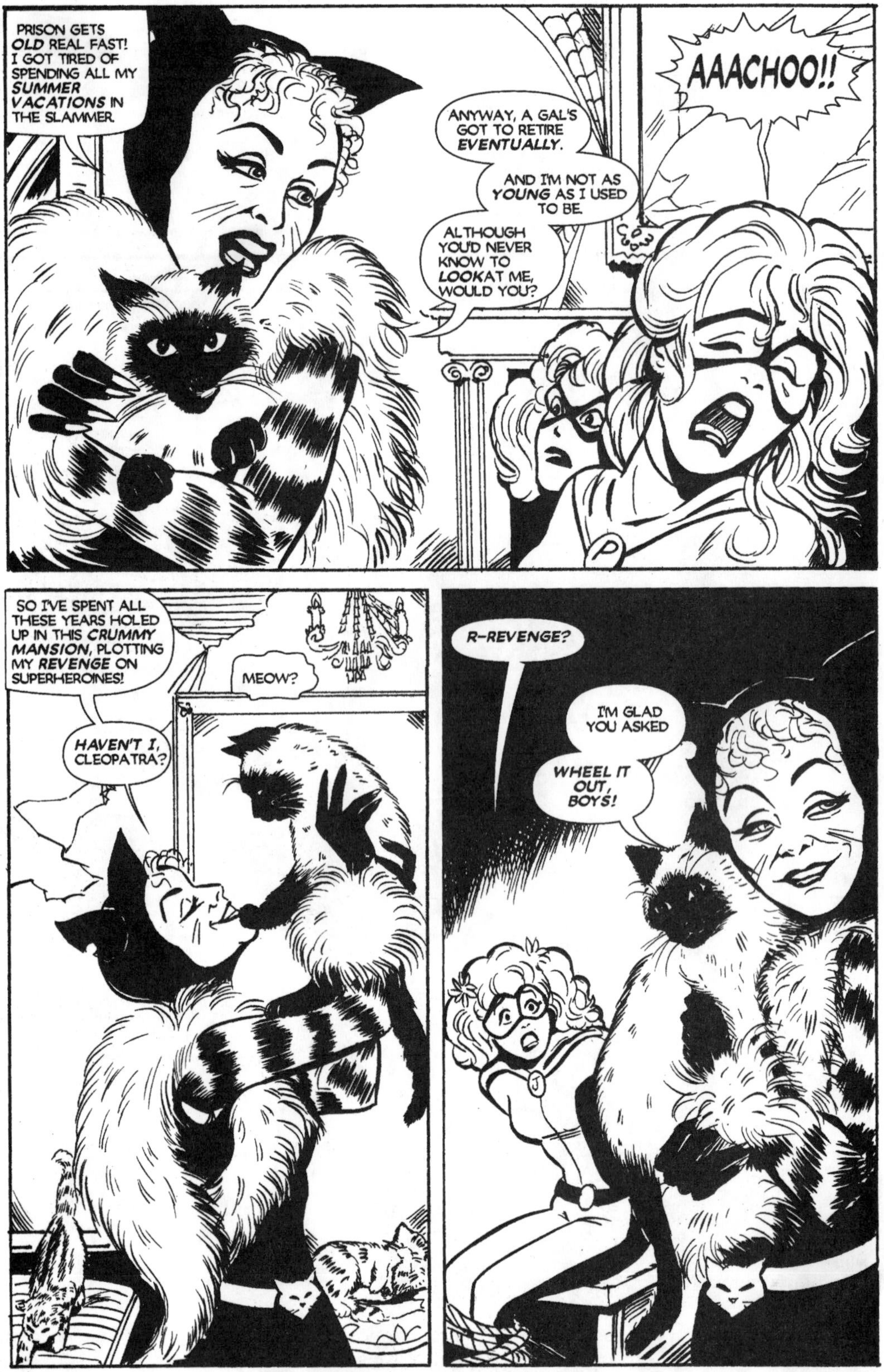
PRISON GETS OLD REAL FAST! I GOT TIRED OF SPENDING ALL MY SUMMER VACATIONS IN THE SLAMMER.
ANYWAY, A GAL'S GOT TO RETIRE EVENTUALLY.
AND I'M NOT AS YOUNG AS I USED TO BE.
ALTHOUGH YOU'D NEVER KNOW TO LOOKAT ME, WOULD YOU?
AAACHOO!!
SO I'VE SPENT ALL THESE YEARS HOLED UP IN THIS CRUMMY MANSION, PLOTTING MY REVENGE ON SUPERHEROINES!
MEOW?
HAVEN'T I, CLEOPATRA?
R-REVENGE?
I'M GLAD YOU ASKED
WHEEL IT OUT, BOYS!

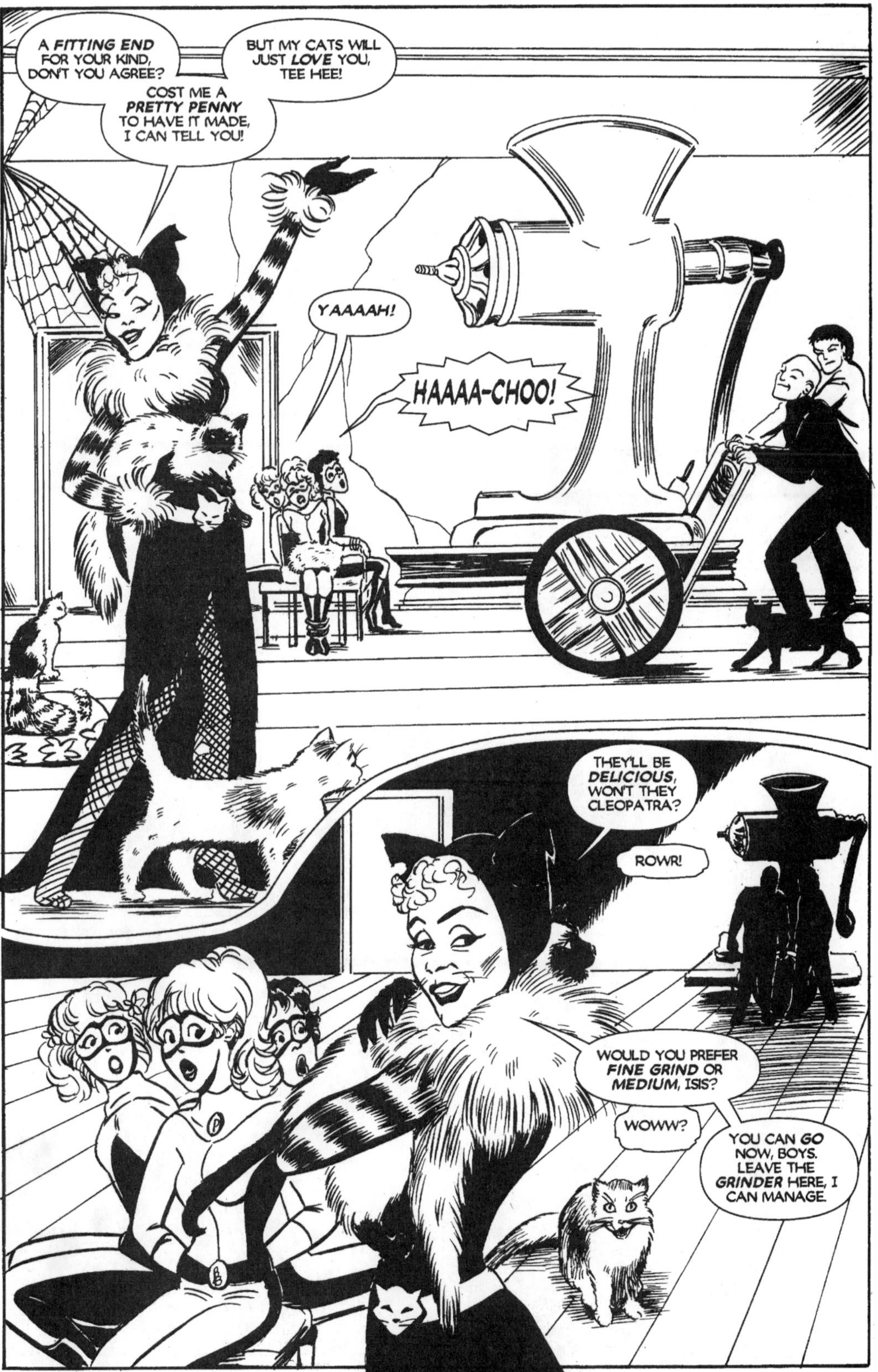
A FITTING END FOR YOUR KIND, DON'T YOU AGREE?
BUT MY CATS WILL JUST LOVE YOU, TEE HEE!
COST ME A PRETTY PENNY TO HAVE IT MADE, I CAN TELL YOU!
YAAAAH!
HAAAA-CHOO!
THEY'LL BE DELICIOUS, WON'T THEY CLEOPATRA?
ROWR!
WOULD YOU PREFER FINE GRIND OR MEDIUM, ISIS?
WOWW?
YOU CAN GO NOW, BOYS. LEAVE THE GRINDER HERE, I CAN MANAGE.

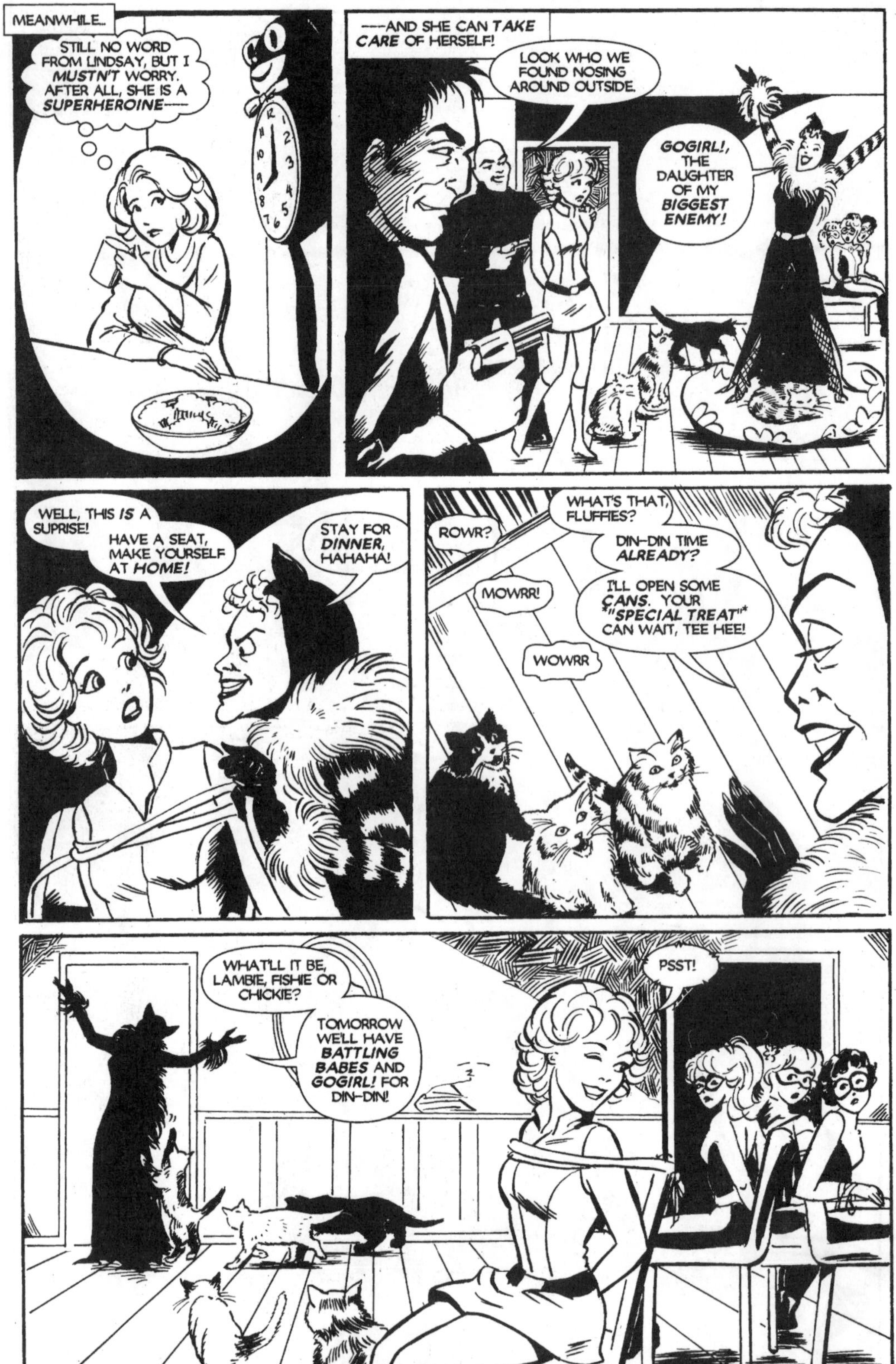
MEANWHILE...
STILL NO WORD FROM LINDSAY, BUT I MUSTN'T WORRY. AFTER ALL, SHE IS A SUPERHEROINE----
---AND SHE CAN TAKE CARE OF HERSELF!
LOOK WHO WE FOUND NOSING AROUND OUTSIDE.
GOGIRL!, THE DAUGHTER OF MY BIGGEST ENEMY!
WELL, THIS IS A SUPRISE!
HAVE A SEAT, MAKE YOURSELF AT HOME!
STAY FOR DINNER, HAHAHA!
ROWR?
WHAT'S THAT, FLUFFIES?
DIN-DIN TIME ALREADY?
MOWRR!
I'LL OPEN SOME CANS. YOUR "SPECIAL TREAT" CAN WAIT, TEE HEE!
WOWRR
WHAT'LL IT BE, LAMBIE, FISHIE OR CHICKIE?
TOMORROW WE'LL HAVE BATTLING BABES AND GOGIRL! FOR DIN-DIN!
PSST!

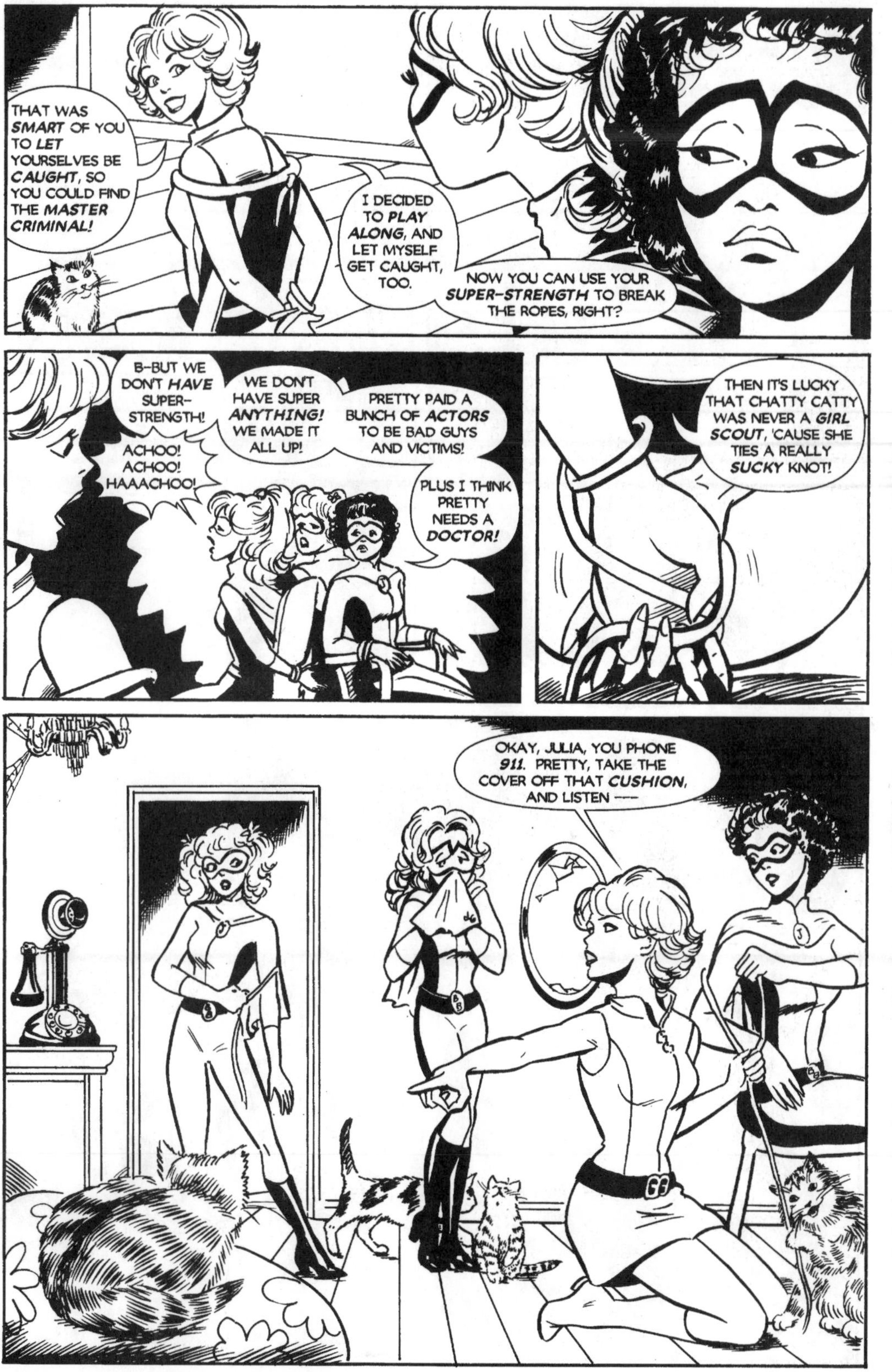
THAT WAS SMART OF YOU TO LET YOURSELVES BE CAUGHT, SO YOU COULD FIND THE MASTER CRIMINAL!
I DECIDED TO PLAY ALONG, AND LET MYSELF GET CAUGHT, TOO.
NOW YOU CAN USE YOUR SUPER-STRENGTH TO BREAK THE ROPES, RIGHT?
B-BUT WE DON'T HAVE SUPER-STRENGTH!
ACHOO! ACHOO! HAAACHOO!
WE DON'T HAVE SUPER ANYTHING! WE MADE IT ALL UP!
PRETTY PAID A BUNCH OF ACTORS TO BE BAD GUYS AND VICTIMS!
PLUS I THINK PRETTY NEEDS A DOCTOR!
THEN IT'S LUCKY THAT CHATTY CATTY WAS NEVER A GIRL SCOUT, 'CAUSE SHE TIES A REALLY SUCKY KNOT!
OKAY, JULIA, YOU PHONE 911. PRETTY, TAKE THE COVER OFF THAT CUSHION, AND LISTEN ---

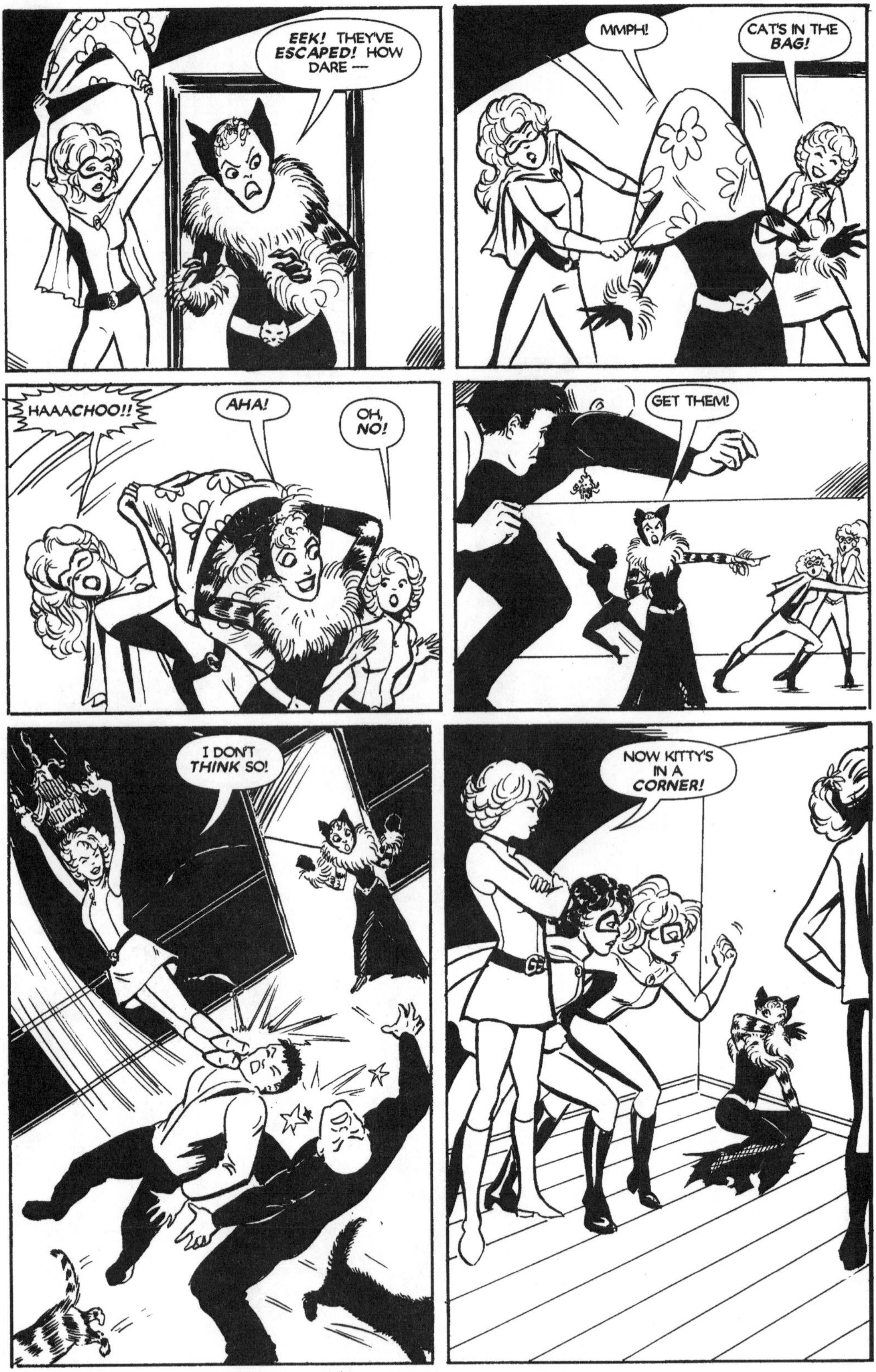
EEK! THEY'VE ESCAPED! HOW DARE ---
MMPH!
CAT'S IN THE BAG!
HAAACHOO!!
AHA!
OH, NO!
GET THEM!
I DON'T THINK SO!
NOW KITTY'S IN A CORNER!

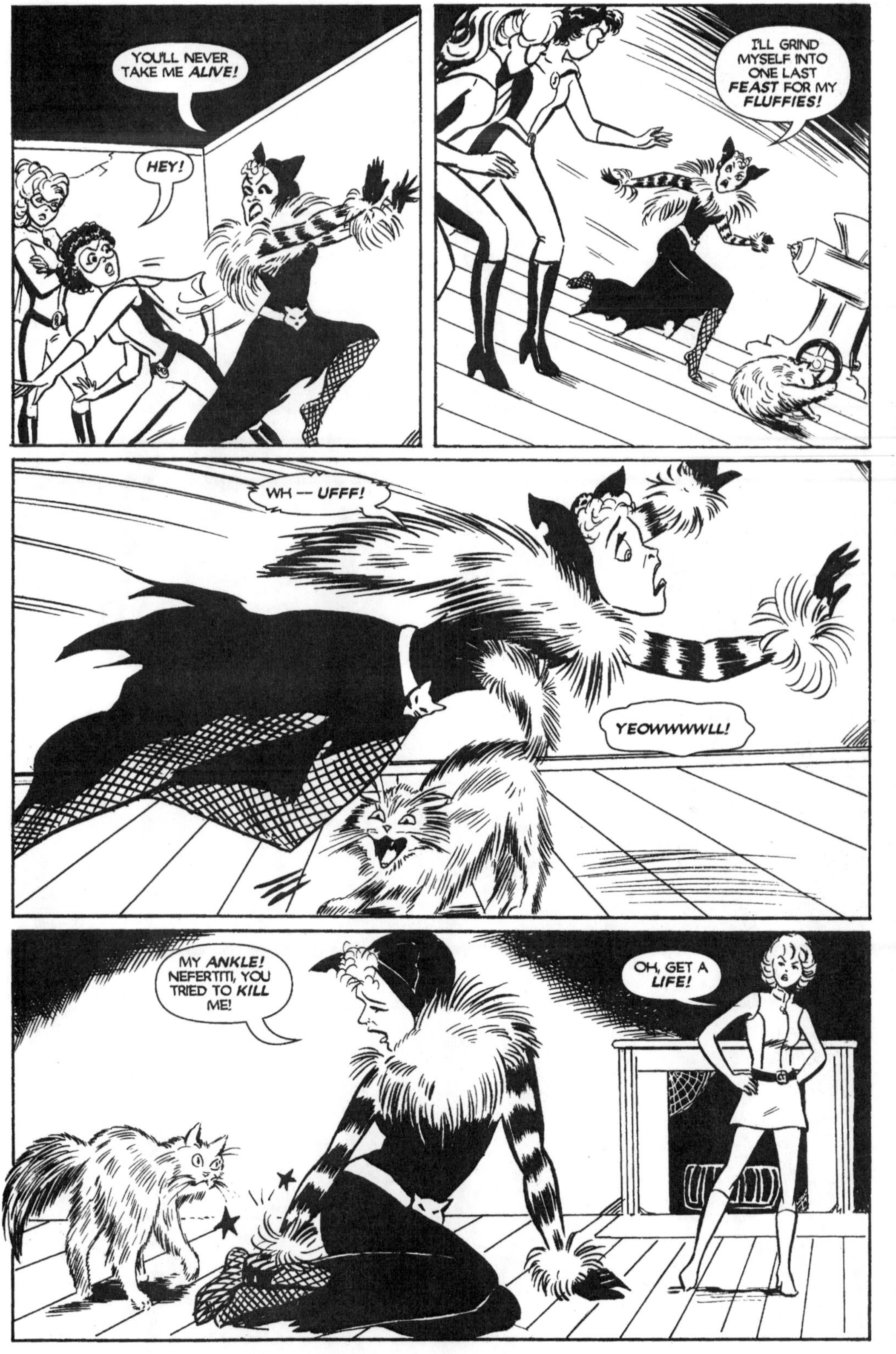
YOU'LL NEVER TAKE ME ALIVE!
HEY!
I'LL GRIND MYSELF INTO ONE LAST FEAST FOR MY FLUFFIES!
WH -- UFFF!
YEOWWWWLL!
MY ANKLE! NEFERTITI, YOU TRIED TO KILL ME!
OH, GET A LIFE!

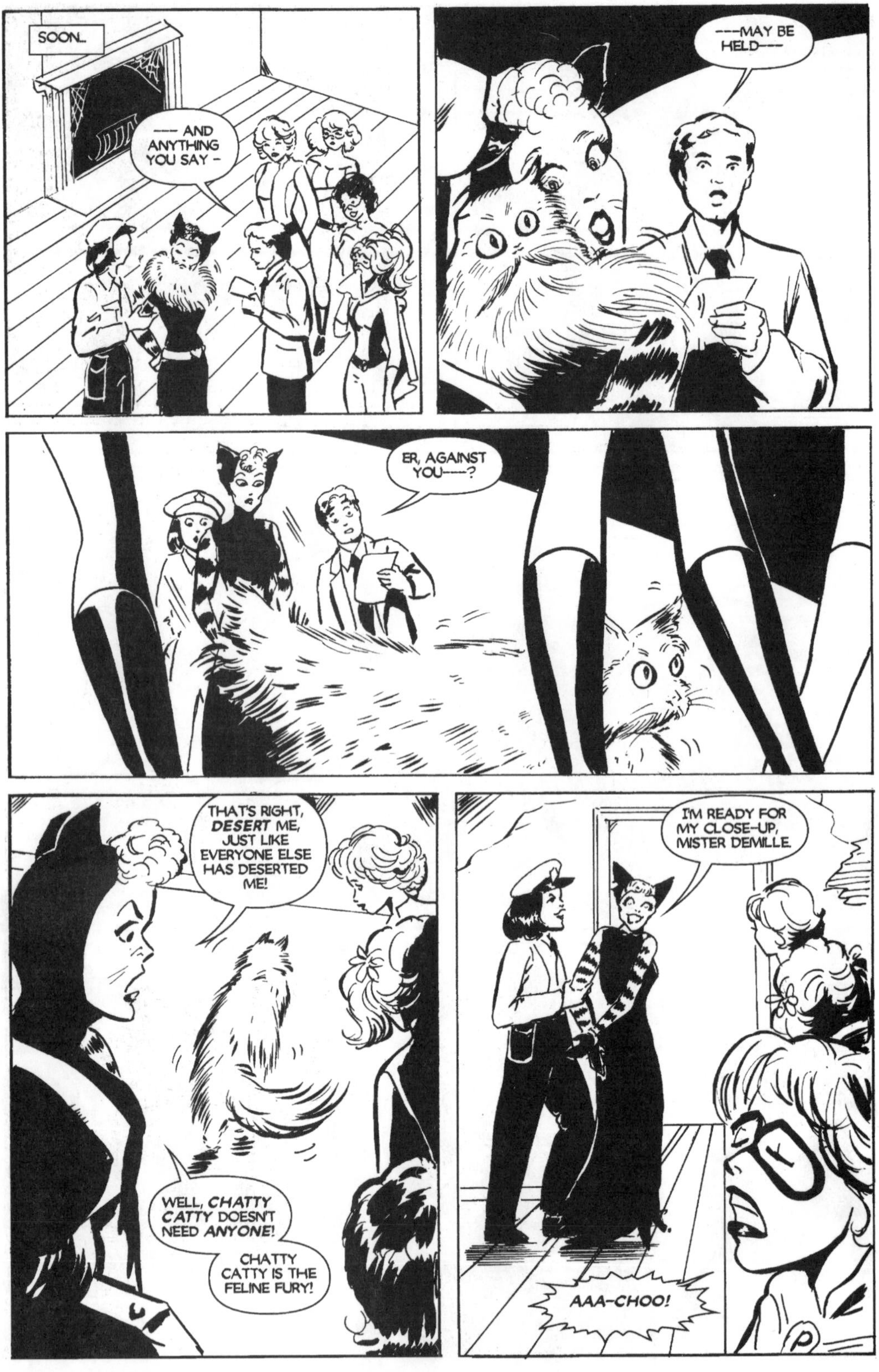
SOON...
--- AND ANYTHING YOU SAY -
---MAY BE HELD---
ER, AGAINST YOU---?
THAT'S RIGHT, *DESERT* ME, JUST LIKE EVERYONE ELSE HAS DESERTED ME!
WELL, *CHATTY CATTY* DOESN'T NEED *ANYONE*!
CHATTY CATTY IS THE FELINE FURY!
I'M READY FOR MY CLOSE-UP, MISTER DEMILLE.
AAA-CHOO!

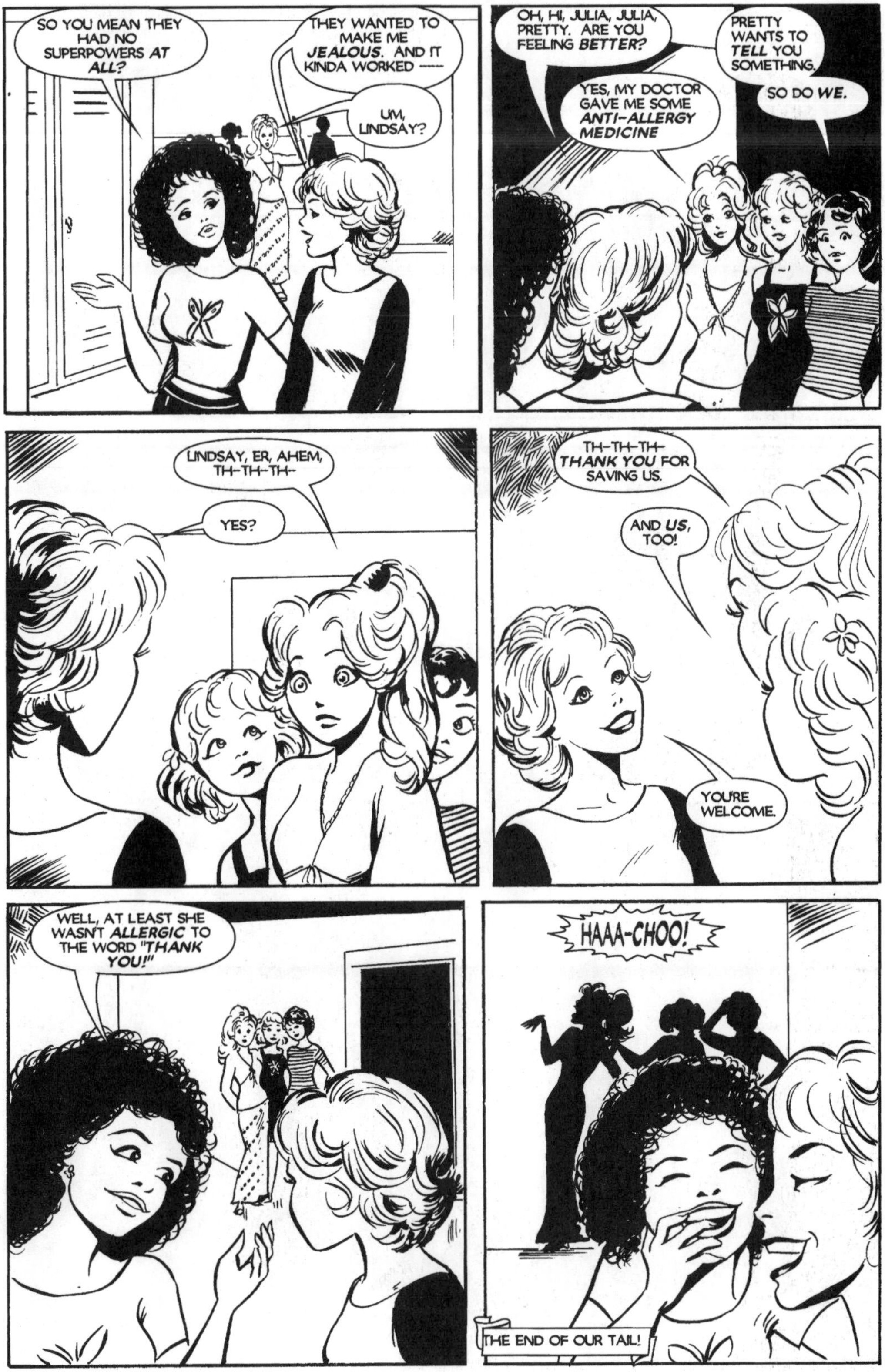

SO YOU MEAN THEY HAD NO SUPERPOWERS AT ALL?
THEY WANTED TO MAKE ME JEALOUS. AND IT KINDA WORKED -----
UM, LINDSAY?
OH, HI, JULIA, JULIA, PRETTY. ARE YOU FEELING BETTER?
YES, MY DOCTOR GAVE ME SOME ANTI-ALLERGY MEDICINE
PRETTY WANTS TO TELL YOU SOMETHING.
SO DO WE.
LINDSAY, ER, AHEM, TH-TH-TH-
YES?
TH-TH-TH- THANK YOU FOR SAVING US.
AND US, TOO!
YOU'RE WELCOME.
WELL, AT LEAST SHE WASN'T ALLERGIC TO THE WORD "THANK YOU!"
HAAA-CHOO!
THE END OF OUR TAIL!

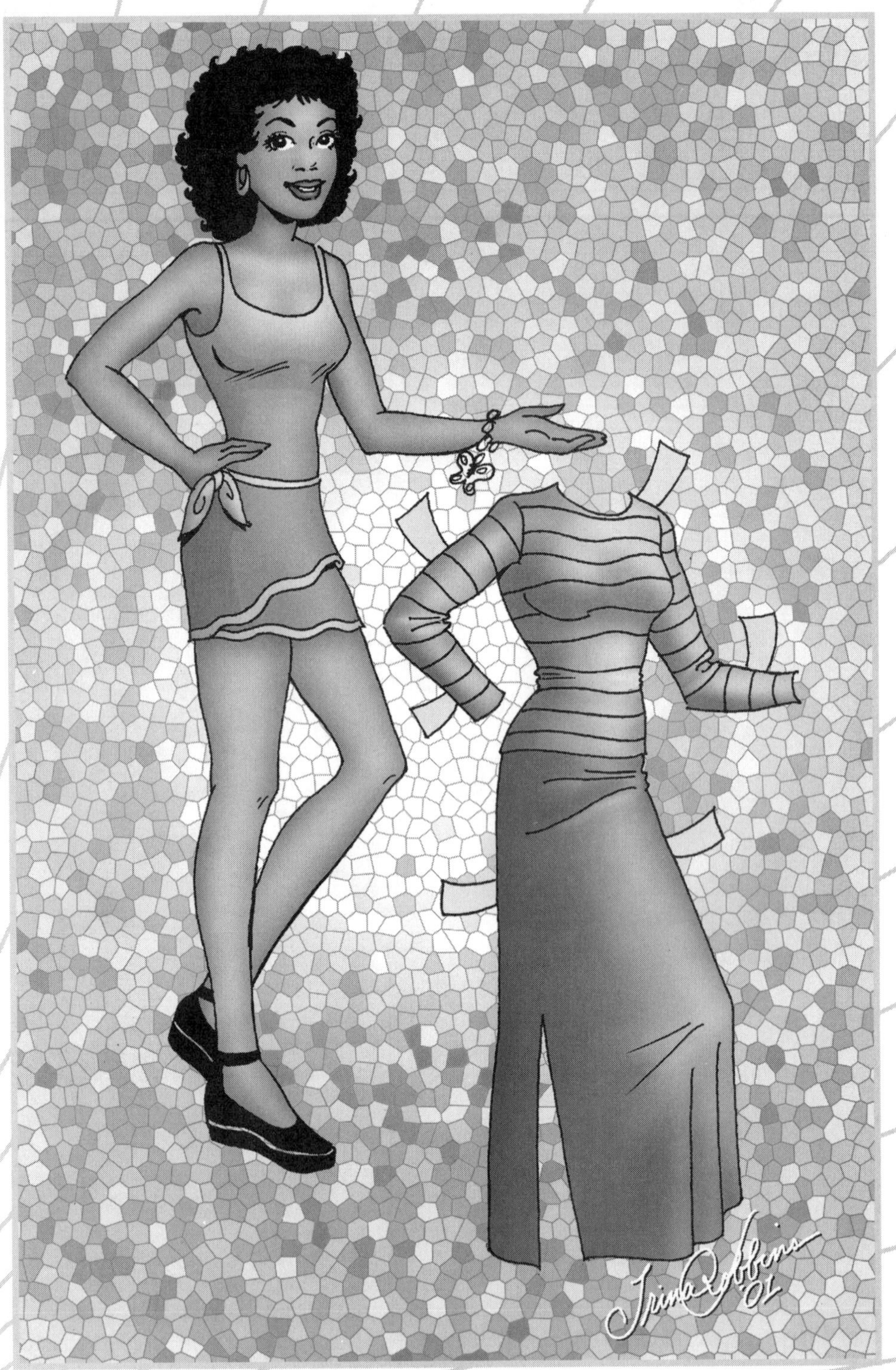
Trina Robbins '01

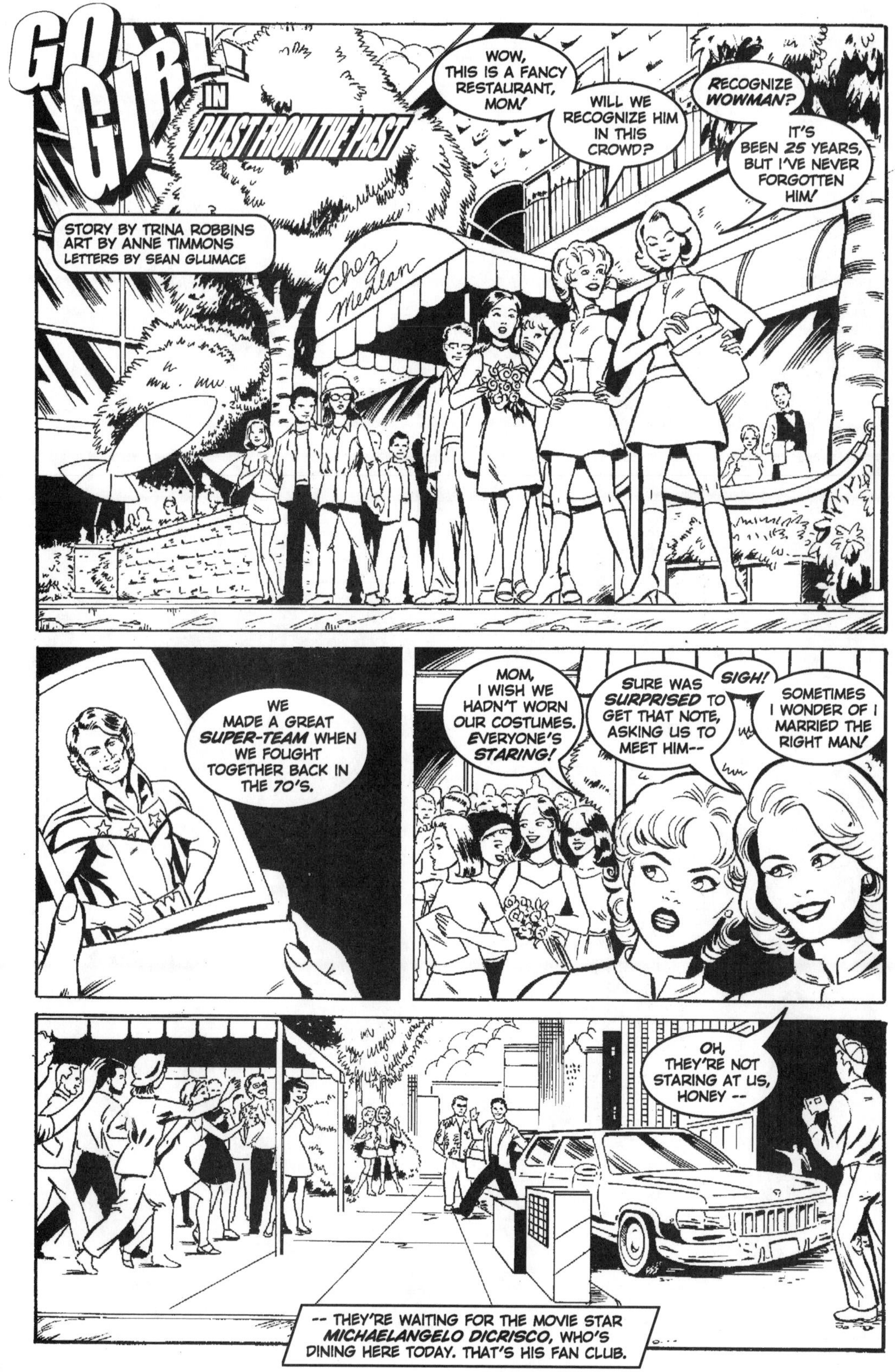
GO GIRL! IN BLAST FROM THE PAST
STORY BY TRINA ROBBINS
ART BY ANNE TIMMONS
LETTERS BY SEAN GLUMACE
Chez Medlan
WOW, THIS IS A FANCY RESTAURANT, MOM!
WILL WE RECOGNIZE HIM IN THIS CROWD?
RECOGNIZE WOWMAN?
IT'S BEEN 25 YEARS, BUT I'VE NEVER FORGOTTEN HIM!
WE MADE A GREAT SUPER-TEAM WHEN WE FOUGHT TOGETHER BACK IN THE 70'S.
MOM, I WISH WE HADN'T WORN OUR COSTUMES. EVERYONE'S STARING!
SURE WAS SURPRISED TO GET THAT NOTE, ASKING US TO MEET HIM--
SIGH!
SOMETIMES I WONDER OF I MARRIED THE RIGHT MAN!
OH, THEY'RE NOT STARING AT US, HONEY --
-- THEY'RE WAITING FOR THE MOVIE STAR MICHAELANGELO DICRISCO, WHO'S DINING HERE TODAY. THAT'S HIS FAN CLUB.

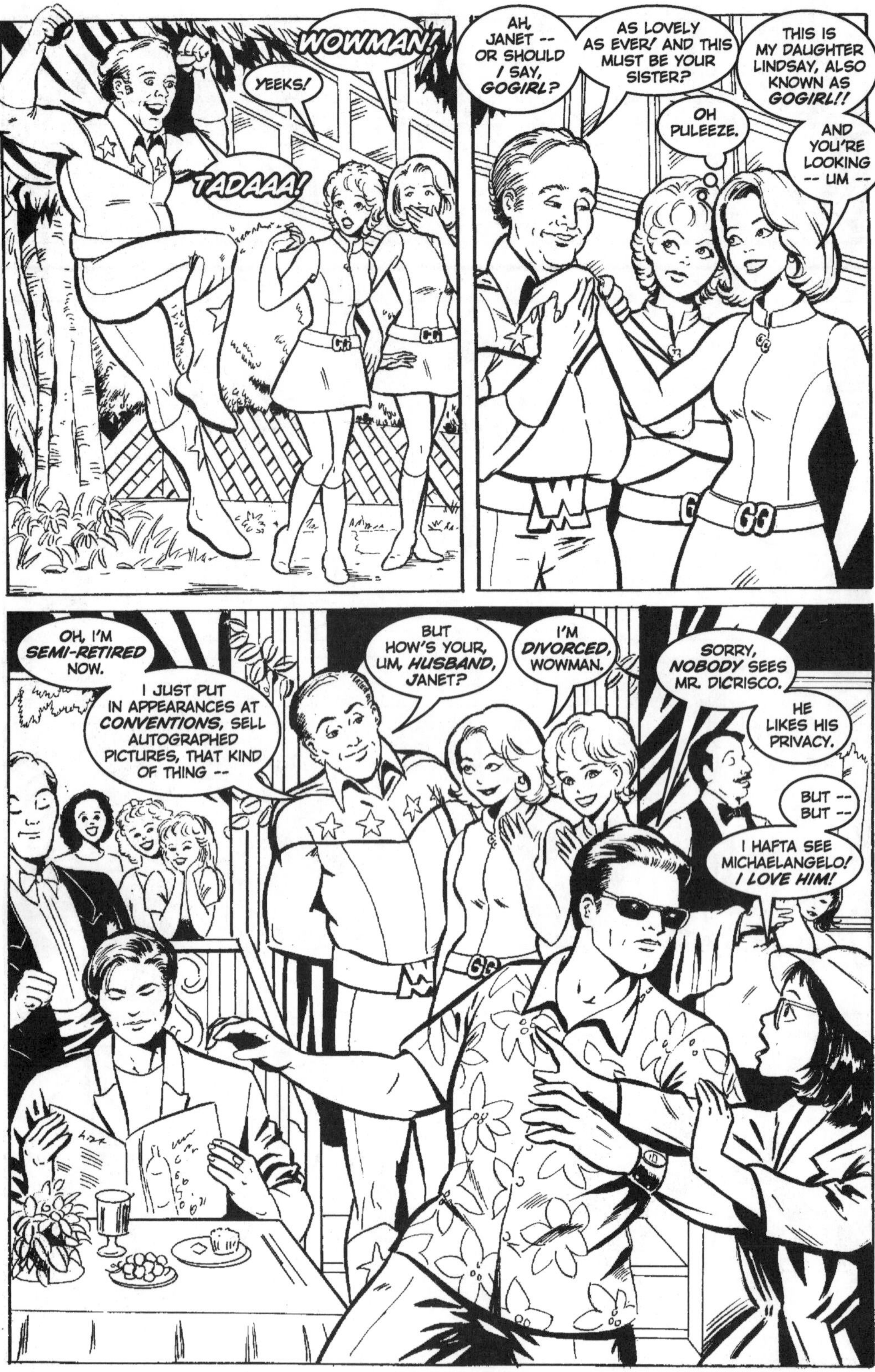
WOWMAN!
YEEKS!
TADAAA!
AH, JANET -- OR SHOULD I SAY, GOGIRL?
AS LOVELY AS EVER! AND THIS MUST BE YOUR SISTER?
OH PULEEZE.
THIS IS MY DAUGHTER LINDSAY, ALSO KNOWN AS GOGIRL!!
AND YOU'RE LOOKING -- UM --
OH, I'M SEMI-RETIRED NOW.
I JUST PUT IN APPEARANCES AT CONVENTIONS, SELL AUTOGRAPHED PICTURES, THAT KIND OF THING --
BUT HOW'S YOUR, UM, HUSBAND, JANET?
I'M DIVORCED, WOWMAN.
SORRY, NOBODY SEES MR. DICRISCO.
HE LIKES HIS PRIVACY.
BUT -- BUT --
I HAFTA SEE MICHAELANGELO! I LOVE HIM!

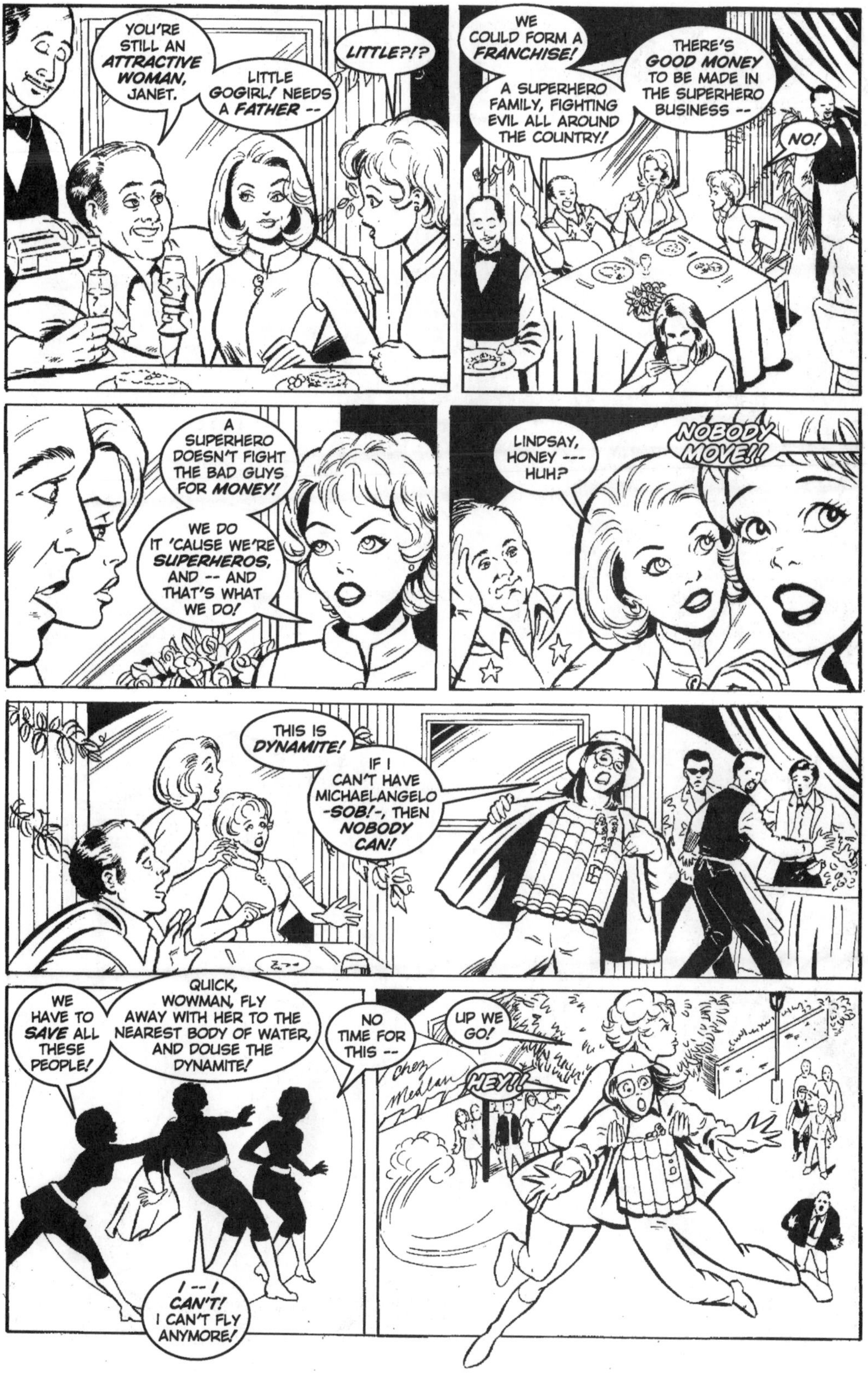
YOU'RE STILL AN ATTRACTIVE WOMAN, JANET.
LITTLE GOGIRL! NEEDS A FATHER --
LITTLE?!?
WE COULD FORM A FRANCHISE!
A SUPERHERO FAMILY, FIGHTING EVIL ALL AROUND THE COUNTRY!
THERE'S GOOD MONEY TO BE MADE IN THE SUPERHERO BUSINESS --
NO!
A SUPERHERO DOESN'T FIGHT THE BAD GUYS FOR MONEY!
WE DO IT 'CAUSE WE'RE SUPERHEROS, AND -- AND THAT'S WHAT WE DO!
LINDSAY, HONEY --- HUH?
NOBODY MOVE!!
THIS IS DYNAMITE!
IF I CAN'T HAVE MICHAELANGELO -SOB!-, THEN NOBODY CAN!
WE HAVE TO SAVE ALL THESE PEOPLE!
QUICK, WOWMAN, FLY AWAY WITH HER TO THE NEAREST BODY OF WATER, AND DOUSE THE DYNAMITE!
I -- I CAN'T! I CAN'T FLY ANYMORE!
NO TIME FOR THIS --
UP WE GO!
HEY!!
Chez Medlan

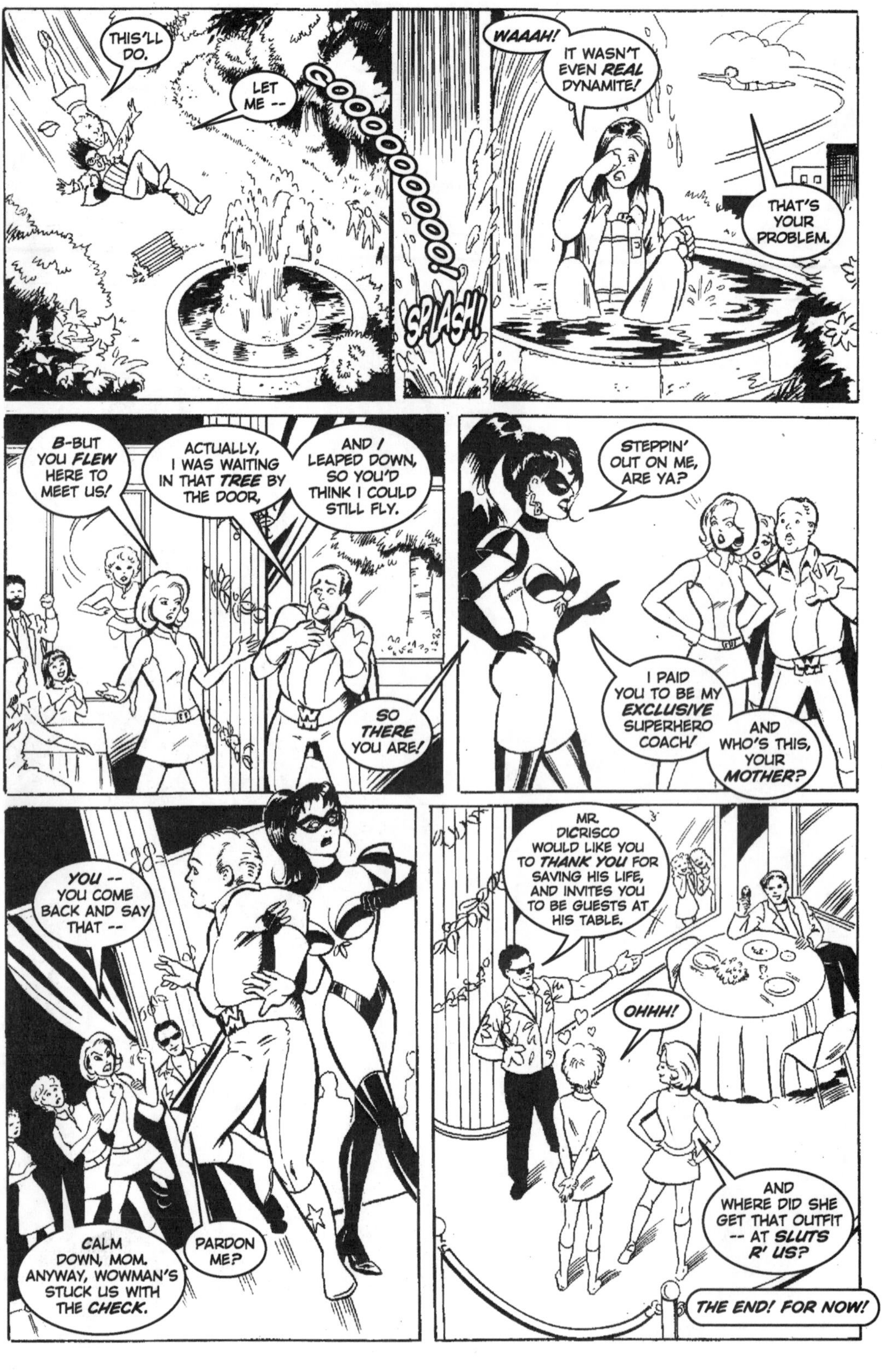

THIS'LL DO.
LET ME --
GOOOOOOOOOO!
SPLASH!
WAAAH!
IT WASN'T EVEN REAL DYNAMITE!
THAT'S YOUR PROBLEM.
B-BUT YOU FLEW HERE TO MEET US!
ACTUALLY, I WAS WAITING IN THAT TREE BY THE DOOR,
AND I LEAPED DOWN, SO YOU'D THINK I COULD STILL FLY.
SO THERE YOU ARE!
STEPPIN' OUT ON ME, ARE YA?
I PAID YOU TO BE MY EXCLUSIVE SUPERHERO COACH!
AND WHO'S THIS, YOUR MOTHER?
YOU -- YOU COME BACK AND SAY THAT --
CALM DOWN, MOM. ANYWAY, WOWMAN'S STUCK US WITH THE CHECK.
PARDON ME?
MR. DICRISCO WOULD LIKE YOU TO THANK YOU FOR SAVING HIS LIFE, AND INVITES YOU TO BE GUESTS AT HIS TABLE.
OHHH!
AND WHERE DID SHE GET THAT OUTFIT -- AT SLUTS R' US?
THE END! FOR NOW!

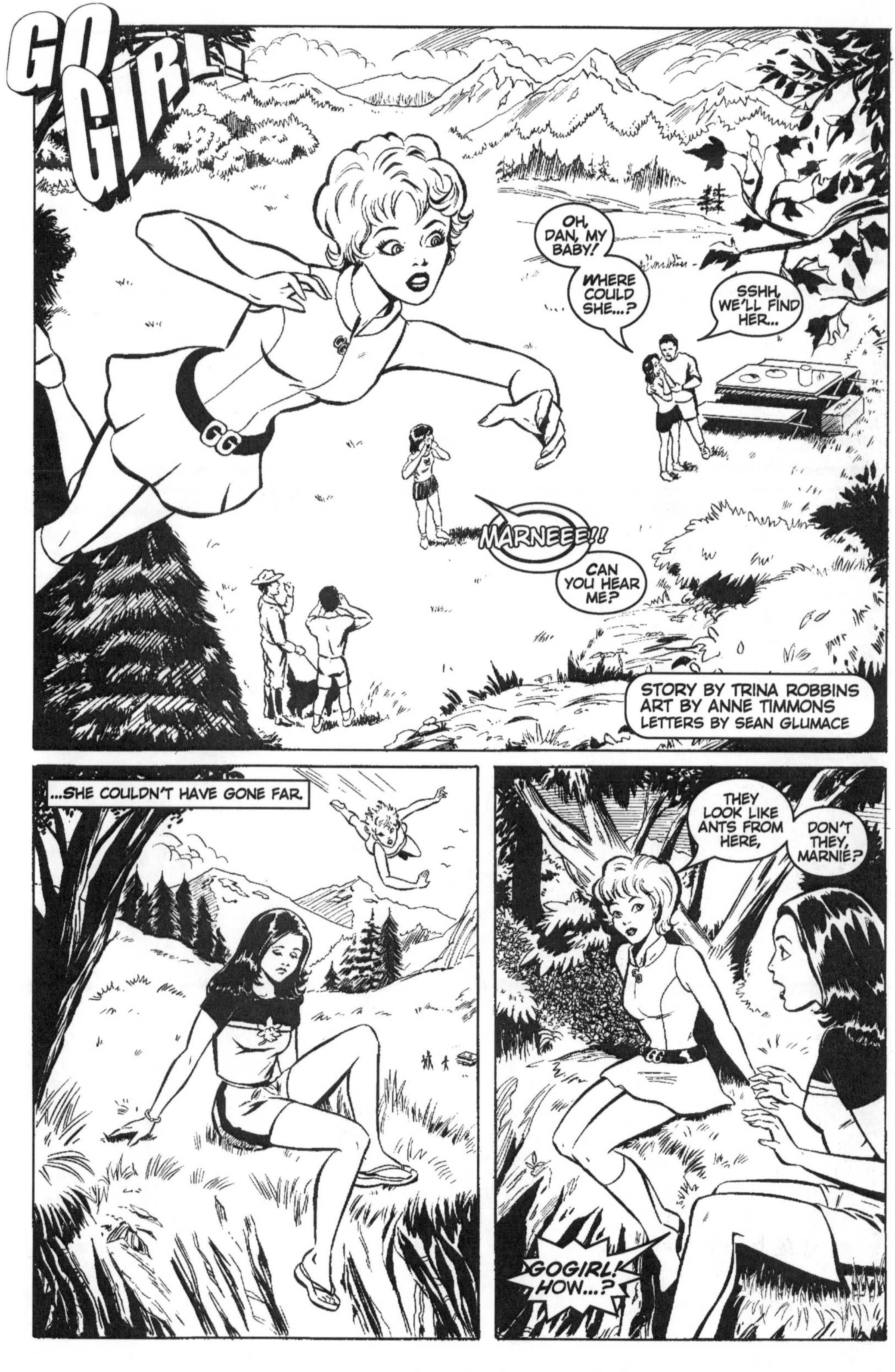
GO GIRL!
OH, DAN, MY BABY!
WHERE COULD SHE...?
SSHH, WE'LL FIND HER...
MARNEEE!!
CAN YOU HEAR ME?
STORY BY TRINA ROBBINS
ART BY ANNE TIMMONS
LETTERS BY SEAN GLUMACE
...SHE COULDN'T HAVE GONE FAR.
THEY LOOK LIKE ANTS FROM HERE,
DON'T THEY, MARNIE?
GOGIRL! HOW...?

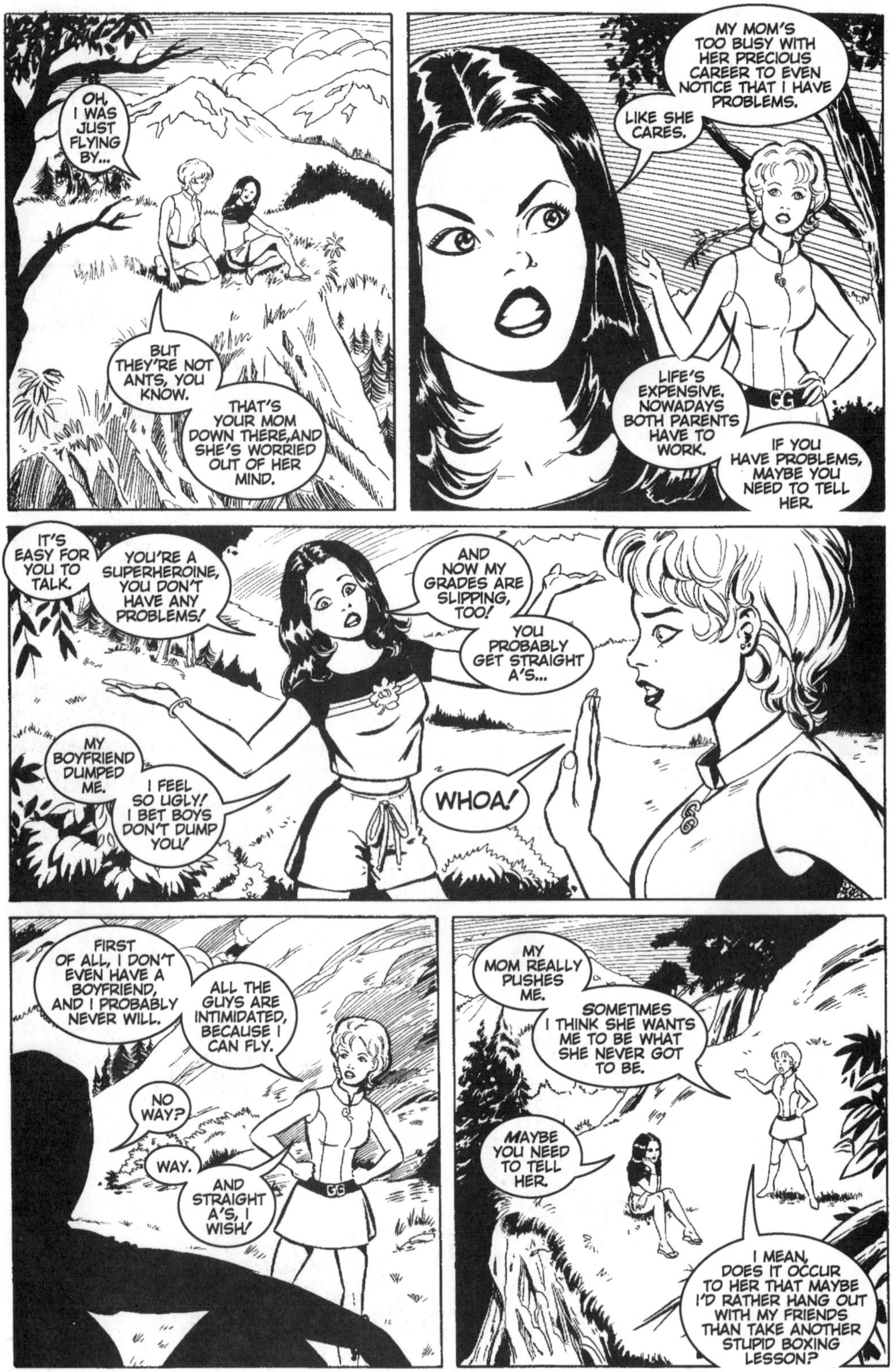
OH, I WAS JUST FLYING BY...
BUT THEY'RE NOT ANTS, YOU KNOW.
THAT'S YOUR MOM DOWN THERE,AND SHE'S WORRIED OUT OF HER MIND.
MY MOM'S TOO BUSY WITH HER PRECIOUS CAREER TO EVEN NOTICE THAT I HAVE PROBLEMS.
LIKE SHE CARES.
LIFE'S EXPENSIVE. NOWADAYS BOTH PARENTS HAVE TO WORK.
IF YOU HAVE PROBLEMS, MAYBE YOU NEED TO TELL HER.
IT'S EASY FOR YOU TO TALK.
YOU'RE A SUPERHEROINE, YOU DON'T HAVE ANY PROBLEMS!
AND NOW MY GRADES ARE SLIPPING, TOO!
YOU PROBABLY GET STRAIGHT A'S...
MY BOYFRIEND DUMPED ME.
I FEEL SO UGLY! I BET BOYS DON'T DUMP YOU!
WHOA!
FIRST OF ALL, I DON'T EVEN HAVE A BOYFRIEND, AND I PROBABLY NEVER WILL.
ALL THE GUYS ARE INTIMIDATED, BECAUSE I CAN FLY.
NO WAY?
WAY.
AND STRAIGHT A'S, I WISH!
MY MOM REALLY PUSHES ME.
SOMETIMES I THINK SHE WANTS ME TO BE WHAT SHE NEVER GOT TO BE.
MAYBE YOU NEED TO TELL HER.
I MEAN, DOES IT OCCUR TO HER THAT MAYBE I'D RATHER HANG OUT WITH MY FRIENDS THAN TAKE ANOTHER STUPID BOXING LESSON?

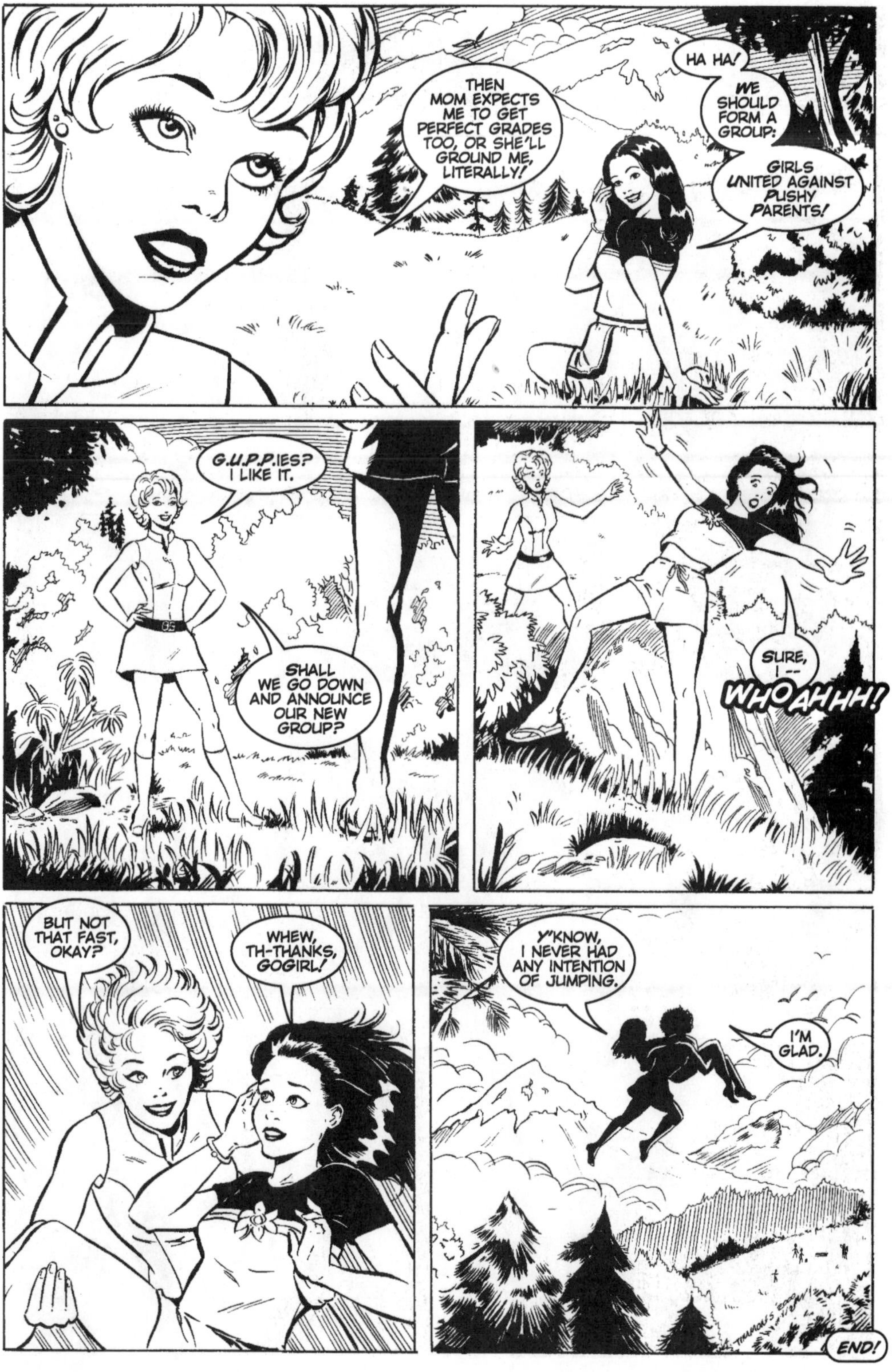
THEN MOM EXPECTS ME TO GET PERFECT GRADES TOO, OR SHE'LL GROUND ME, LITERALLY!
HA HA!
WE SHOULD FORM A GROUP:
GIRLS UNITED AGAINST PUSHY PARENTS!
G.U.P.P.IES? I LIKE IT.
SHALL WE GO DOWN AND ANNOUNCE OUR NEW GROUP?
SURE, I --
WHOAHHH!
BUT NOT THAT FAST, OKAY?
WHEW, TH-THANKS, GOGIRL!
Y'KNOW, I NEVER HAD ANY INTENTION OF JUMPING.
I'M GLAD.
END!

GALLERY

Featuring the original GoGirl! comic-book series cover art by Anne Timmons
and a selection of GoGirl! pinups by guest artists

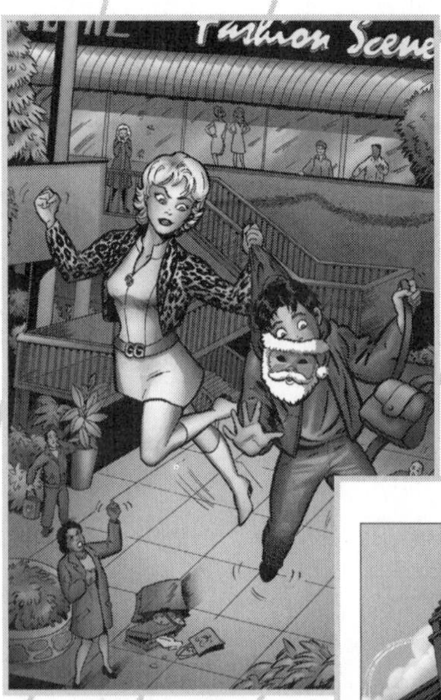
Fashion Scene

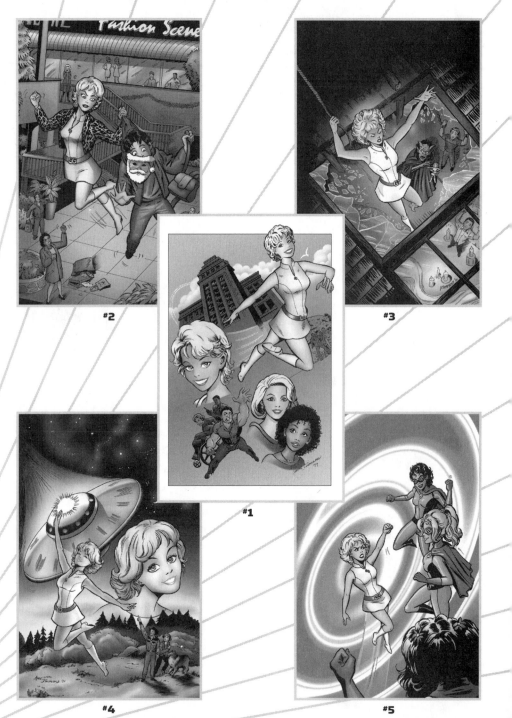

#2

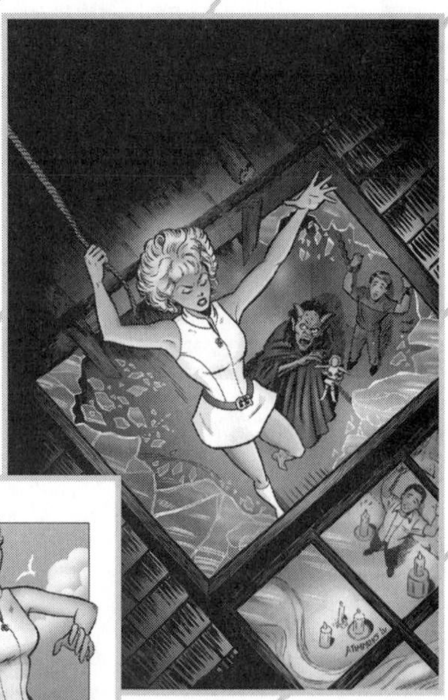

#3

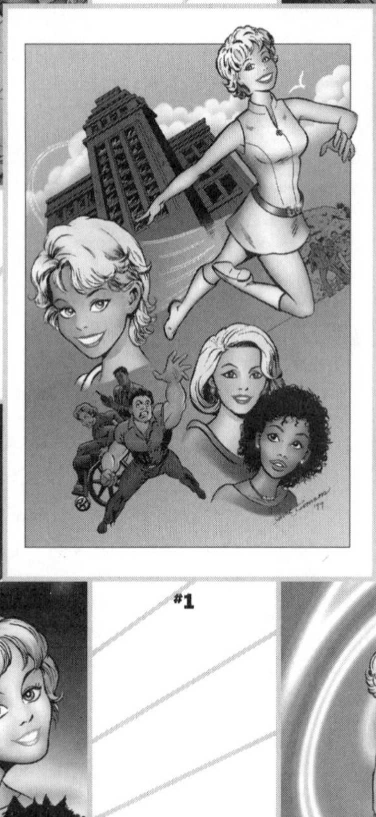

#1

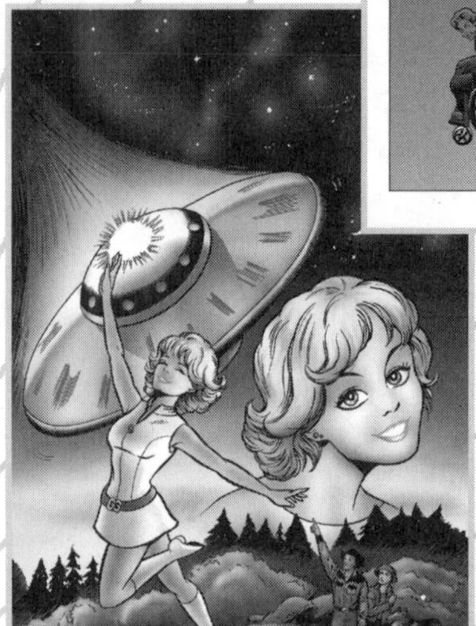

#4

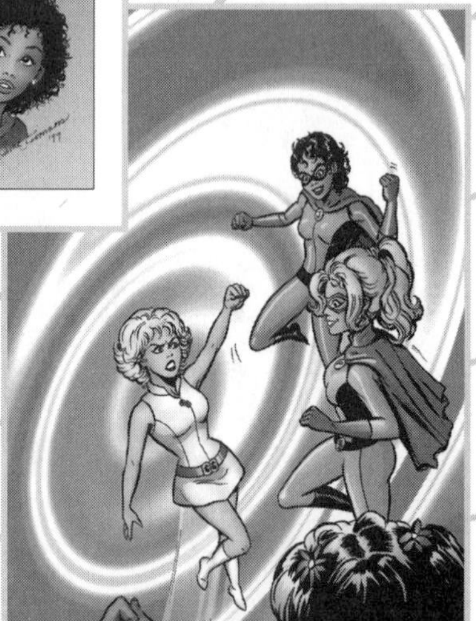

#5

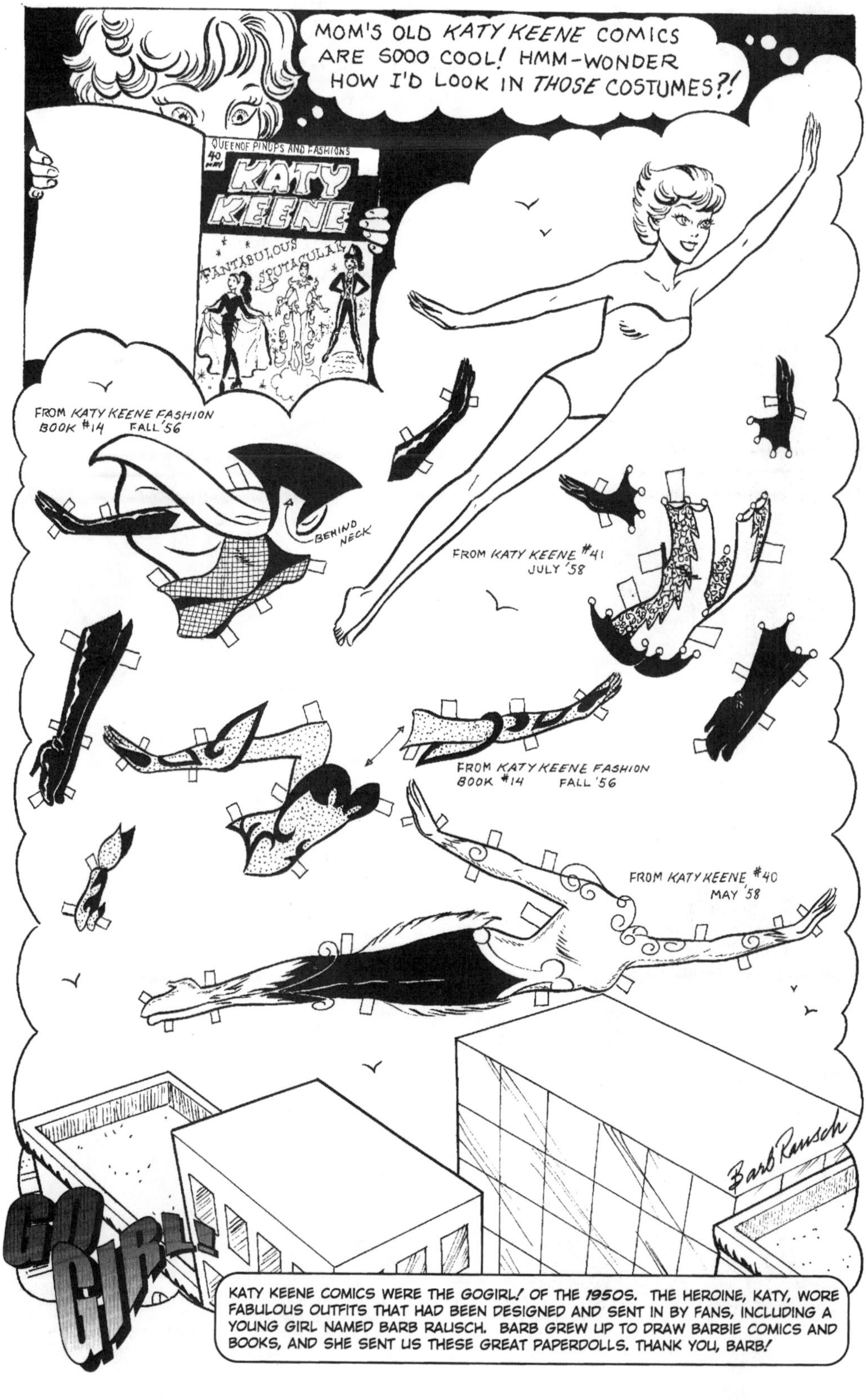
MOM'S OLD KATY KEENE COMICS ARE SOOO COOL! HMM-WONDER HOW I'D LOOK IN THOSE COSTUMES?!
QUEENOF PINUPS AND FASHIONS
KATY KEENE
FANTABULOUS SPUTACULAR
FROM KATY KEENE FASHION BOOK #14 FALL '56
BEHIND NECK
FROM KATY KEENE #41 JULY '58
FROM KATY KEENE FASHION BOOK #14 FALL '56
FROM KATY KEENE #40 MAY '58
Barb Rausch
GO GIRL!
KATY KEENE COMICS WERE THE GOGIRL! OF THE 1950S. THE HEROINE, KATY, WORE FABULOUS OUTFITS THAT HAD BEEN DESIGNED AND SENT IN BY FANS, INCLUDING A YOUNG GIRL NAMED BARB RAUSCH. BARB GREW UP TO DRAW BARBIE COMICS AND BOOKS, AND SHE SENT US THESE GREAT PAPERDOLLS. THANK YOU, BARB!

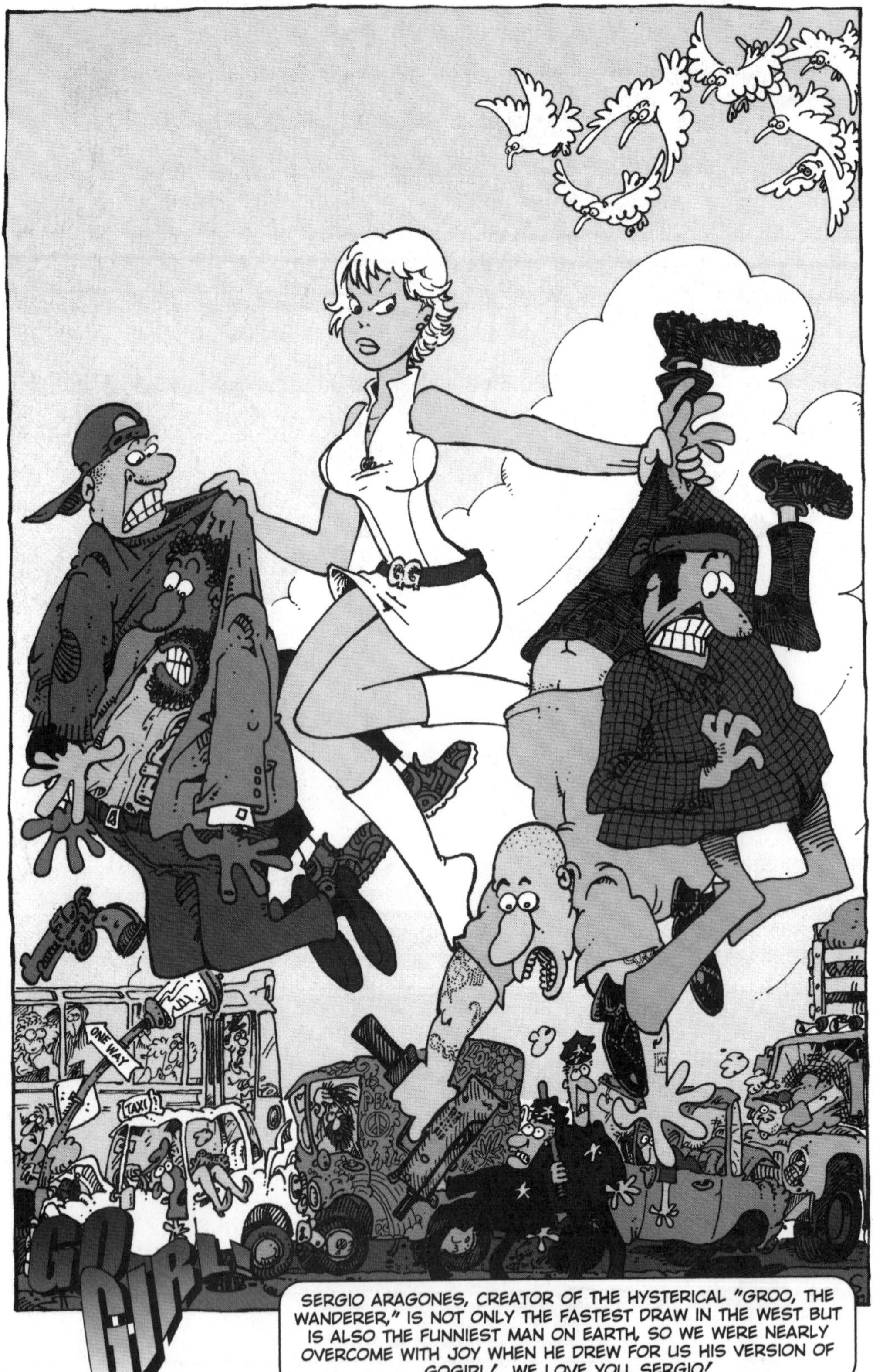
ONE WAY
TAXI
GO GIRL!
SERGIO ARAGONES, CREATOR OF THE HYSTERICAL "GROO, THE WANDERER," IS NOT ONLY THE FASTEST DRAW IN THE WEST BUT IS ALSO THE FUNNIEST MAN ON EARTH, SO WE WERE NEARLY OVERCOME WITH JOY WHEN HE DREW FOR US HIS VERSION OF GOGIRL! WE LOVE YOU, SERGIO!

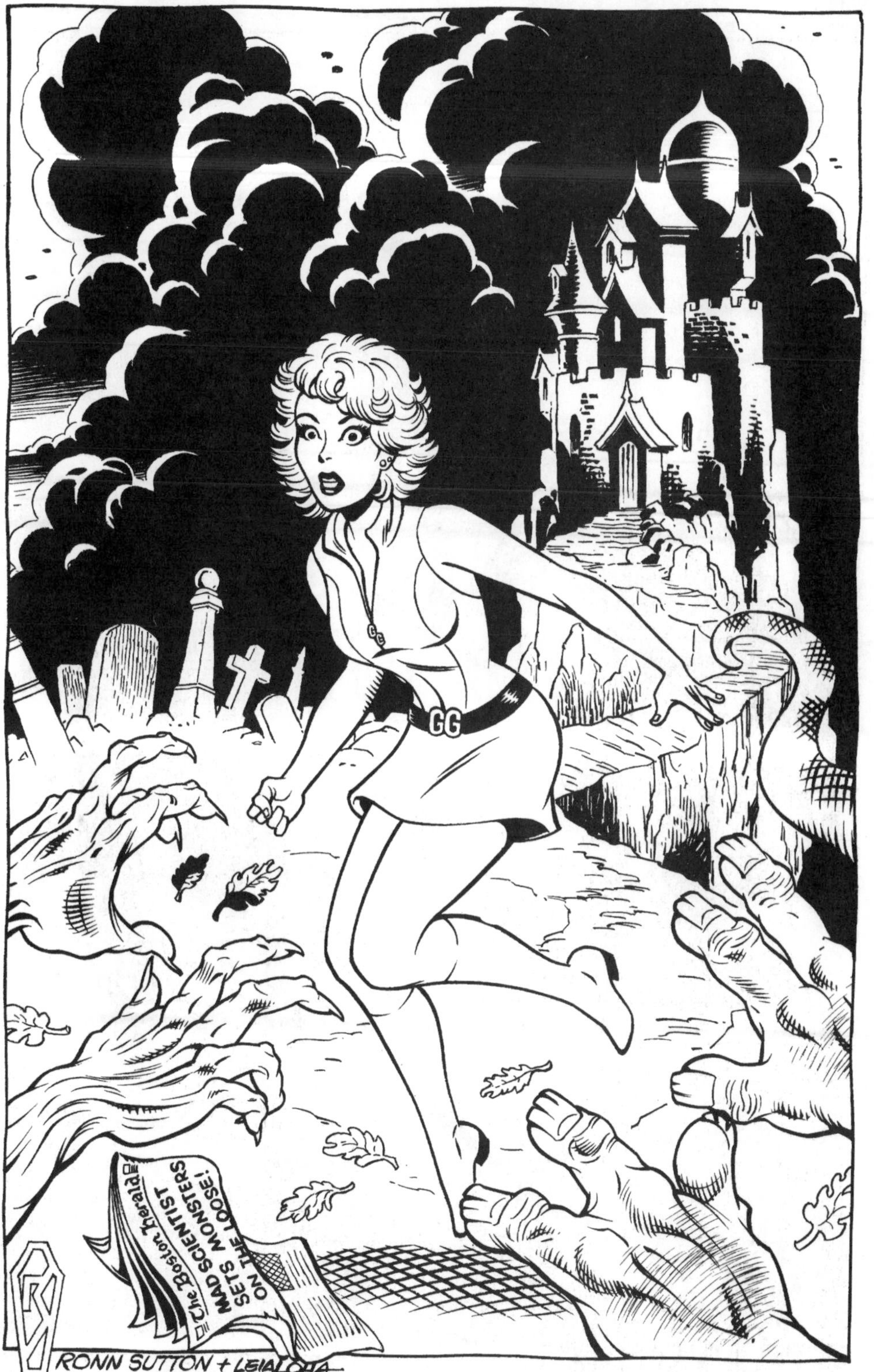
The Boston Herald
MAD SCIENTIST SETS MONSTERS ON THE LOOSE!
RONN SUTTON + LEIALOHA

GoGirl! meets the monsters! Pencils by Ronn Sutton, who draws Elvira, another kind of superheroine, inks by the fabulous Steve Leialoha.

5885

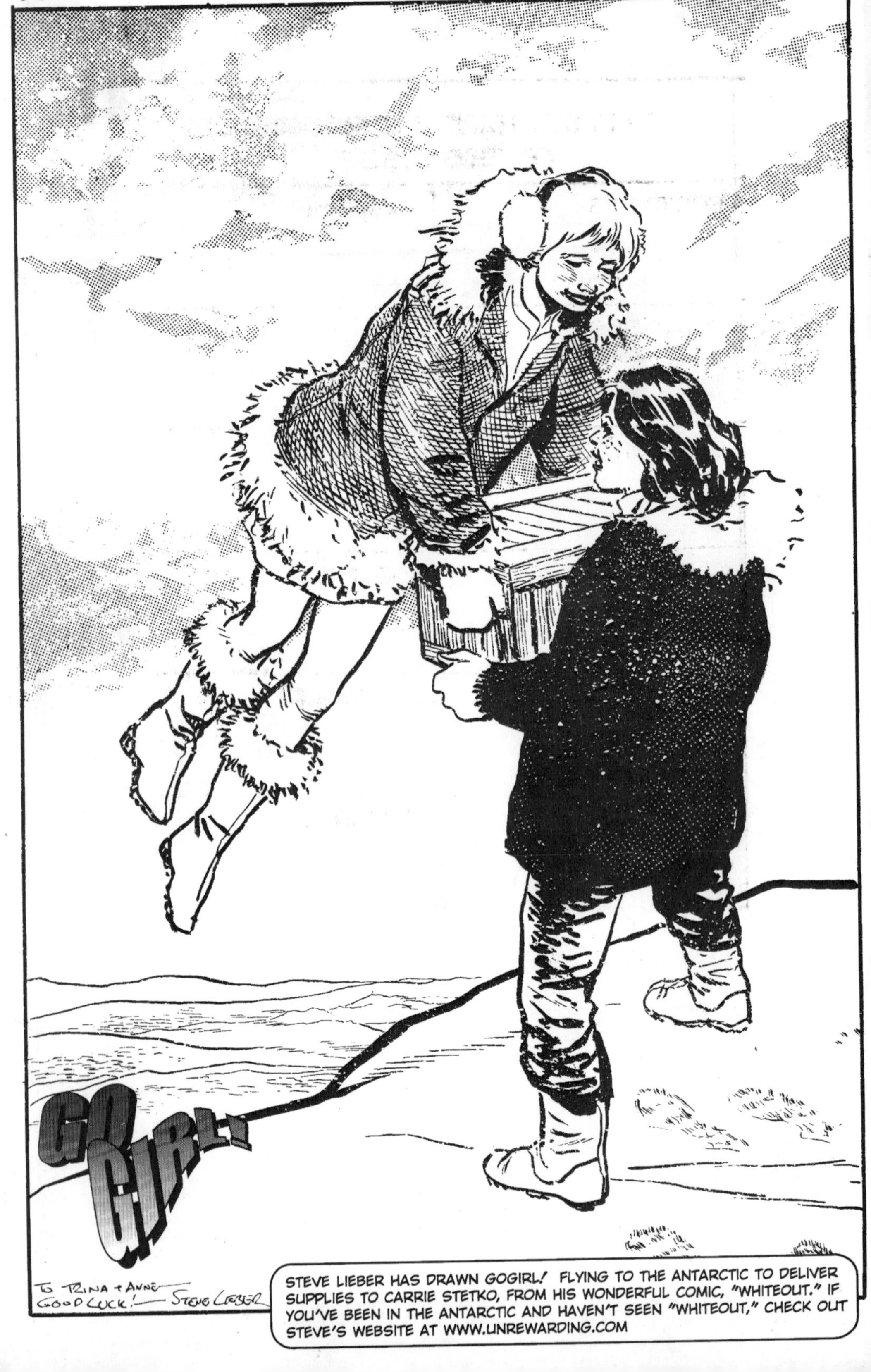
GO GIRL!
TO TRINA + ANNE—
GOOD LUCK! — STEVE LIEBER

STEVE LIEBER HAS DRAWN GOGIRL! FLYING TO THE ANTARCTIC TO DELIVER SUPPLIES TO CARRIE STETKO, FROM HIS WONDERFUL COMIC, "WHITEOUT." IF YOU'VE BEEN IN THE ANTARCTIC AND HAVEN'T SEEN "WHITEOUT," CHECK OUT STEVE'S WEBSITE AT WWW.UNREWARDING.COM